MW00758129

DO OR DIE

DO OR DIE

Léon Bing

HarperCollins*Publishers*

FIRST EDITION

Designed by Cassandra J. Pappas

Library of Congress Cataloging-in-Publication Data

Bing, Léon, 1950
    Do or Die / Léon Bing.
        p.   cm.
    ISBN 0-06-016326-7
    1. Gangs—California—Los Angeles. 2. Juvenile delinquency—
California—Los Angeles.   I. Title.
    HV6439.U7L7   1991
    364.3′6′0979494—dc20   90-55922

91 92 93 94 95 CC/RRD 10 9 8 7

To my mother, Estelle,
and my daughter, Lisa,
with love.

Preface

The county probation office in South Central Los Angeles lies only about twenty-five minutes south of Pasadena if you take the Harbor and Long Beach Freeways. Driving there, with the road unwinding like a grubby bandage under the car, you can almost feel an atmospheric change taking place; you know, somehow, that you are moving into ominous country.

The first time I went to South Central was twenty-six years ago, and I was in a limousine with three other models, a movie star, a photographer, two stylists, and the designer of the clothes that were to be photographed for a layout in *Cosmopolitan*. Somebody—probably a fashion editor in New York—had decided it would be "kicky" if the models and the movie star (James Coburn) could be seen cavorting on and around the Watts Towers, those convoluted, Gaudiesque glass and tile-studded columns that Italian immigrant Simon Rodia painstakingly erected in his back yard over the course of some thirty years. As we drove toward this landmark, past the tiny storefront churches that punctuate each block, past the small, family-owned restaurants and shops, past the cut-rate furniture stores and supermarket chain outlets, I was aware only that this was a predominately black neighborhood. I do not recall any sense of impending danger; the Watts riots were not to erupt until August of the following year. I do remember a half-hearted flirtation with Coburn and a somewhat more serious concern that I would not have to climb too high on the fragile facade of the towers.

The Watts Towers are still standing—you can see their shapes against the cluttered landscape—but it is the writing on the walls, the gang graffiti, that commands the eye today. It covers the sides of every building, every fence and flat surface and it begins as soon as you leave the off-ramp that leads you to the Imperial Highway: sprawling letters shaded and shaped into the numerals and initials of the gangs that have taken custody of these streets. As you drive along, the images that keep coming at you now are of a city in crisis. The small churches, like the Lamb of God Baptist Temple, are still there, but many of the family-run shops are empty, and many of them have "sale" signs taped to display windows. Others have their steel gates pulled across the doorways even though it's the middle of the day. The salespeople look out from behind the gates, suspicious of anyone they see on the other side.

The probation offices are housed in a squat building co-joined by the Department of Public Social Services—the county welfare office. Fronting both bureaus is a vast parking lot. The big double doors of the welfare office stand open to this lot; inside it seethes with people standing in long, alphabetized lines. Little knots of men stand just outside these doors. The men affect relaxed attitudes, they stand easily with hands plunged deep into trouser pockets, and they speak to each other in low tones. Their eyes seek out each new arrival; their faces are neither friendly nor unfriendly. If any expression is displayed at all, it is one of bemused perplexity. Small children run up to one or the other of these groups at intervals, and the men do little more than glance down at them. Every so often a father will speak to his child in whatever degree of loudness he feels is necessary. Then he goes back to the waiting and the watching.

I came here three years ago to interview an eighteen-year-old member of the Grape Street Crips, and as I passed the welfare office on my way to the probation office, I didn't know then that it would be better if I did not make eye contact with any of the people standing there. I didn't know that when I did, I would see so much anger, so much fierceness, so much love and pride dribbling away in the face of poverty and despair.

My first contact with gang members took place in 1986. Many of the youngsters I had interviewed for other articles had mentioned gangs, and I decided to do some research in preparation for a piece I wanted to write for *L.A. Weekly*. At first I simply made inquiries on instinct: one boy, a ticket-taker at a cineplex in my neighborhood, told me where a large body of Bloods congregated every Sunday afternoon. I convinced the photo editor of the *Weekly*, Howard Rosenberg, to go with me the following weekend to a small park in South Pasadena. We walked into a sea of red—the Blood color. Teenaged boys and young men in their early twenties were, as the gang members say, "G'd-up." Shorts, jackets, baseball caps, ninety-dollar running shoes—everything in the same bright, aggressive color. More than a few people sported masses of heavy gold jewelry: rings, big-link chain necklaces called Turkish ropes, bracelets, medallions—most of them paved with diamonds. Porsche sunglasses masked eyes that moved like minesweepers over the streets abutting the park. A teenaged mother and her ten-month-old daughter wore matching ruby and diamond bracelets and earrings.

Howard and I were surrounded as soon as we walked into the park, but I felt no sense of threat. People simply moved in

close in watchful silence. We introduced ourselves, and I explained that I was a journalist, that I was interested in doing
a story on gang life as part of a series of articles on L.A.
teenagers. The initial response was one of polite surprise.
These young people felt—and still feel—virtually no kinship
with any kids who live beyond the streets of the inner cities.
But the fact that I perceived them as part of a larger, more
universal group seemed to lighten the mood. Somebody
laughed and then people on all sides of us were talking. "Yeah,
we bad, we killers!" and "Yo—y'all want me to tell you how I
kill crabs?" ("Crab" is one of the insulting terms employed by
Bloods to describe Crips; Crips, in turn, call Bloods "slobs"
and "snoops.") This chest-thumping went on for several minutes—I was unable to break through the barrage of voices. This
was my first encounter with gang members; I had not expected
them to be so playful. They saw Howard and me as harmless
intruders to be teased but not to be taken very seriously. I
waited for a moment or two, then I asked my first question.
I have forgotten what it was, but I remember that no one
answered. The fooling around continued until I did something
that brought the crowd to an uneasy silence. I got angry.
Turning to Howard I said it looked to me like nobody around
here was interested in anything more than bullshit. I said I
wasn't interested in wasting any more time, and I suggested
that we leave. As we turned to walk away, a youngster I had
noticed standing quietly back in the crowd spoke up.

"I'll talk to you."

Without waiting to see if we were going to follow him, he
walked to a picnic table some feet away and sat down facing the
street. We settled ourselves opposite him and he began to talk.
He told us that his gang name was Silencer, that he was seventeen years old, that he had started in gangbanging at ten.

"When I was younger I was a straight killer. They'd have
me killin'—everythin'. And when you eleven years old and you

get you a gun, you got to be a little shook up. Then you get used to it, no problem. You got to prove a lot when you first start, see. You gotta prove that you down. Then, like I said, you get used to it—it ain't no thing."

As Silencer spoke his eyes—intelligent, full of icy assessment—moved constantly, checking out the street. Another guy, slightly older than Silencer, in his early twenties, maybe, had hunkered down to listen. With him was a bunch of little kids—all boys—who arranged themselves in a tidy row next to him. The guy started to talk about his own exploits, how he was a real O.G.B. (Original Ghetto Blood), how he got sent away to detention camp at thirteen for G.T.A.—Grand Theft Auto. How he was always strapped down with a nine millimeter or a .44 magnum. The little kids listened with rapt, shining-eyed admiration, nodding their heads in tacit approval. Spotting this, Silencer frowned at them.

"Don't get into it—y'all too young to die. You hear me?" Once again the heads nodded in unison.

Yeah, yeah, yeah, I thought. The same way they hear their mothers when they tell them not to eat that chili dog so fast.

As the afternoon wore away, Silencer talked about his doubts and disappointments. He spoke of having been a straight-A student before he took up the gang lifestyle, and of the Cs he had brought home on his report card the past few years. He talked about the questions he asked himself in the rare moments of introspection he indulged in, moments when he looked for reasons behind his decision to live the gang life. Glancing at the President-model Rolex on his left wrist and the massive gold chain around his neck, the answer seemed fairly evident. Silencer caught the look and allowed himself a narrow smile.

"Ye-eeeeeh. Sometimes you can make a little money gangbangin'. But y'all better believe it's a hard way to live. And a fast way to die."

Preface

Four years ago that statement didn't mean much to me. Four years ago I had not seen a twenty-year-old bound to a wheelchair for life, his spine severed by a bullet fired by another youngster standing across a park. I had not felt the bulk and weight of a fully loaded AK-47 assault rifle that had been placed in my arms by a twenty-two-year-old member of the Crips. I had not sat at a dining room table in a small, well-furnished apartment deep in the Blood territory known as the Jungle while six young men played dominoes and a happy, burbling toddler moved unsteadily around our chairs. She was holding a crayon and somebody gave her a piece of cardboard to scribble on. When she was done one of the guys, a seventeen-year-old with bright red rubber bands on his corn-rowed hair, one week out of Juvenile Hall, leaned over to look at what she had drawn. It was only a mass of unconnected green squiggles, but he broke into a big grin and scooped her up, kissing and hugging her.

"Check this out, y'all! She made a *K* and a *C*—she know how to write 'Kill Crips'!"

Four years ago I had not sat in a living room in Watts and leafed through a scrapbook belonging to a nineteen-year-old Crip, at pages and pages of meticulously arranged snapshots of teenaged boys posing in friendly, smiling attitudes. Some of the kids are holding semiautomatic weapons—Uzis and AK-47s—others cradle shotguns and heavy-caliber pistols. More than a few of the boys are wearing serious bandages; one kid has both eyes swathed in white gauze. Memorial programs from the funerals of homeboys are scattered throughout the scrapbook. These programs invariably include yearbook photographs of the dead person, engraved quotations from the Bible, gang logos, and, often, a picture of the open coffin surrounded by the boy's closest friends, all of them flashing the set's hand signs, some of them brandishing weapons.

Four years ago I had not shared a burger and coke in a

coffee shop in South Central with a sixteen-year-old homegirl whose denim school notebook was covered with gang slogans. She was soft-spoken and unfailingly polite. She giggled often and she had already been arrested twice for beating up other girls who had pledged allegiance to rival sets.

Four years ago I had not sat in the employees' locker room of a midtown hospital and talked to a thirty-six-year-old woman whose son had been assassinated on the front porch of her mother's house. Gloria was both angry and frustrated. She was filled with guilt even though she knew that she loved her son and cared for him as deeply as any other mother. Barely speaking above a whisper she talked about a boy who had skipped two grades in school, whose ambition it was to be a doctor and who played in the Little League. She took a snapshot from her wallet and handed it to me: a pair of twelve-year-old boys in freshly washed blue-and-white baseball uniforms stand grinning into the camera. Behind them, across a patch of grass, the brick wall of a school building is splashed with gang graffiti. Gloria pointed to her son, a chunky, dimpled kid. The boy standing next to him was his best friend, she told me. That boy went into the Crips; Gloria's son became a Blood. Both boys were dead before they made sixteen.

And somehow she kept blaming herself: for not making enough money to move out of the neighborhood; for not having been home when her job at the hospital kept her there late; for not having been able to stay married to her son's father; for not having taken a stronger stand. Her voice dropped even lower when she talked about having argued with her son to stay out of the gang. She tried to reason with him, telling him that he was likely to get killed out there on the streets, that his dreams of becoming a doctor were fading away. He told her to mind her own business, and when she continued to plead her case he looked at her and said, "Don't make me hurt you."

Gloria did not blame the Bloods for what happened to her son. She did blame an indifferent system and the environment at the bottom of the present-day American economic barrel. She knew that falling in with a gang came as naturally to her boy as hanging out at malls comes to suburban kids.

Los Angeles is a city of gangs. There are Chinese gangs and Central American gangs, Vietnamese and Cambodian gangs, Philippino, Korean, and Samoan gangs. There are white gangs. The oldest street gang in L.A., dating back to the thirties, is Mexican-American. The Hispanic gangs got their start in the steamy barrios of East L.A. where they fought each other for dominion over schoolyards and street corners. They now extend all over Southern California. It was the *cholo* home-boy who first walked the walk and talked the talk. It was the Mexican-American *pachuco* who initiated the emblematic tattoos, the signing with hands, the writing of legends on walls.

But the white hot glare of public interest focused sharply on gangs only a little more than two and a half years ago. And then it centered on the ghetto gangs, the Bloods and the Crips.

It began outside a theater in Westwood, two blocks from the UCLA campus, when members of opposing sets faced off and a young woman waiting in line to see a movie took a bullet to the head. Her death snapped people into a new and horrified awareness: the beast had slithered out of its cage to prowl streets where insularity is the rule and privilege the norm. Suddenly the specter of South Central Los Angeles—a nightmare landscape where shadowy figures of young men stalk the streets and cars burn unattended in alleyways, where there is a nightly roar of wind from the rotors of the police helicopters that hover overhead at tightly spaced intervals, where everything is illuminated by the surreal beams of their searchlights— descended like nuclear ash over a city that had not been more than marginally aware of its existence.

Suddenly the lead stories on local newscasts were about

the latest gang-related shootings. Terms like "payback killing" and "drive-by shooting" entered the public lexicon. Items that had been buried in the back pages of the *Los Angeles Times* began to make it to lead features. And a new set of figures was implanted in the consciousness of a city already obsessed with the numbers of weekend box office tallies, television ratings, audience shares, and albums shipped. The new demographics had to do with the number of gang homicides committed. L.A. was getting the stats on what was initially perceived as murder-for-empire. The name of the empire was drugs, the name of the drug was crack, and suddenly people who had *maybe* tried a couple of toots in the executive rest room, or even those people who boasted about killer coke habits they had had all through the seventies, habits they kicked right after—or just before—John Belushi's death (depending on whether the boast included the flourish of mega-lines snorted with the actor himself), were hearing about a new, deadly high that was being sold in the inner city by kids coded by color and armed like terrorists.

This new stuff, they learned, was nothing like the soft white powder that had been the calling card of hipness a few years ago. This was a much cheaper product, available to any-body with five bucks to spend for a small yellowish rock. Crack was "the drug that would love to kill you" and there was nothing glamorous about it. It wasn't the mound of glistening crystals that you laid out on a mirror in the back of a limo on the way to the Academy Awards; it was the new six-pack of the guy who washed your car. The image of the new Big Dealer bore not even the slightest resemblance to the good-natured, street-smart guy who used to drop by the house with the week-end supply of Bolivian flake. Whatever aroma of benevolent menace there was about that guy, you always knew it was never going to wash over you. It was the stuff of delicious, shivery imaginings.

The new dealer is a young black entrepeneur, and he is called either a high roller or a baller, depending on his gang allegiance. He is a gangbanger who has made it big, even if he is not at the pinnacle of the distribution pyramid. He drives a BMW, a cherried-out El Camino, a Ford Bronco loaded with extras, a Land Rover. He wears flashy jewelry and a beeper on his belt—or he has a closetful of Ralph Laurens and Georgio Armanis tailored so the beeper doesn't bulge. He takes very good care of his entire family, extending the benefits to include all his relatives. He is often painfully aware that his money comes from a business that is creating a climate of genocide among his own people—but it is his way of buying a ticket out of the ghetto and into the mainstream of life in Los Angeles.

To the people who live here, Los Angeles is the elephant in the legend, and they are the blind men describing it. It is "fifty small towns in search of a community"; it is "two-, three- and four-story buildings littered across an endless landscape bordered by downtown highrises that might as well be the ramparts of a foreign country"; it is "the world's most urban resort"; it is "a blank wall—you just project your fantasy on it and that's what it is, like a Rorschach test"; it is "a city without character or personality—you can never fall in love with L.A. the way you fall in love with Paris or New York. You can't get close enough"; it is "a place where nothing is given to you except the weather and the ease with which things can be done. But you just cannot like the place—you can only like your life in it"; and, finally, it is "a black hole—the people here just get swallowed up by it."

The last statement was made by a nineteen-year-old gang member, and this book is about those people who inhabit the city he describes.

Acknowledgments

I am more than grateful to those people who supported me, not only in spirit but in actuality, during some hard times. I thank them and I salute them. They are Rod Amateau, Asa Baber, Barbara Flood, Estelle Lang, Dr. Oreste Pucciani, Victory Rain, Dan Robbins, Howard Rosenberg, and Thomas Lee Wright.

I thank Paul Slansky for his eagle eye and intractable good taste. My thanks to Sierra Pecheur and Larry DuBois for similar reasons, and then some.

Thanks to Eric Mankin for giving me my first shot at journalism.

Thanks to Margo Kaufman for being there, always.

I am grateful to Mike Duran and Jim Galipeau of the Los Angeles County Probation Department for their generosity of time and experience. I also thank A. C. Jones, Nancy Block, and other staff members of juvenile camps Miller, Kilpatrick, and Gonzalez.

I owe a great debt to my editor, Craig Nelson, and my

agent, Eric Ashworth. They have become more than business associates to me. They are valued friends.

For their constant attention and unconditional love I thank Dexter and Woofie Bing, the best cat, the best dog in the world.

And, finally, I thank the homeboys, both Bloods and Crips, who opened their hearts and their lives to me. Not all of them have been included in this book but, in a broader sense, each of them lives on these pages.

The individuals who are portrayed in this book are actual people. However, in order to protect the privacy of certain individuals (including all the underaged children) mentioned here, most of the names have been changed, and in some instances composite characters have been created.

1 Camp Kilpatrick

As you travel the northbound 101 out of Los Angeles heading toward Malibu, you leave a vista of faded bungalows and crumbling apartment houses. You drive past Koreatown, Sunset Boulevard, and the Hollywood Bowl, past Studio City, Encino, and Topanga Canyon. Past Hidden Hills where newly erected office complexes, designed in the style of the Greek Revival, and vaguely Tudoresque condominium townhomes—mustard stucco and pressboard crossbeams—loom fortresslike over the freeway. The foothills are covered by a scrubby pelt of sunscorched brush and they bristle with new enterprises: Porsche bodyshops and three-storied Nissan and Acura showrooms; real estate offices disguised as Hopi villages; one-hundred-room, twenty-seven-dollar-a-night motels.

If you are a thirteen-, fourteen-year-old kid from South Central Los Angeles, from Compton or Watts or Inglewood, maybe, if you are a hardcore—or just a wannabe—gang member and you are sitting in the back of an L.A. County Probation Department van, the odds are that you are seeing this panorama for the first time. You're straight out of Juvenile Hall, and the judge has just sentenced you to one of the county juvenile detention camps situated in this area—Miller or Kilpatrick; Gonzalez if you're a hard case—for at least four months, maybe longer, and this is probably the first time you have ever been out of your neighborhood.

There are eleven people inside the van: two deputy probation officers, nine kids. The van itself, a late-model Ford, has barred windows and the Juvenile Hall logo stenciled on both sides. One of the D.P.O.'s (deputy probation officers) does the driving; the other keeps an eye on whatever is going on in the back seats during the trip. Not much, actually; not much more than goes on inside a school bus. The kids who are friends engage in a little light bullshitting, the kids who are enemies ignore each other. Some of the relationships are automatic, based on association; some have developed in the two or three weeks spent in the confinement of the Hall. Every kid in this van knows everything he needs to know about every other kid who's in here with him: who's a straight killer, who's a buster (a coward), who can't open his mouth to speak without lying.

If you're that thirteen- or fourteen-year-old kid you're probably sitting quietly, trying to wind your thoughts into as tight a package as you can. You probably go back over what got you a ticket for this ride in the first place. Maybe you got picked up just for being out on the streets too late and the cops found a concealed weapon on you. Maybe you stole a fancy car so that you could strip all the parts off it. Maybe you got pulled over with a bunch of your homeboys after some of your enemies got shot up in a drive-by. Maybe you got arrested with a stack of twenty-dollar bills in your pocket and a litter of bagged-up dope thrown down on the pavement too near your feet to be coincidence. You think about your hands cuffed behind your back and the way one of the cops covered the top of your head with his hand to keep it ducked down as you got into the back of

4

the black and white. You think about the property search they did on you, and the fingerprinting, and the way the cop read you your rights, explaining to you how you had all the same rights as an adult, excepting bail. No bail for minors. You think about how they separated you from whoever it was you got picked up with, and how you sat in a holding cell for three or four hours before they loaded you back in the cop car and rode you over to Juvenile Hall. You got a pat-down search there, they looked for hidden weapons—unless you were in on a drug beef, then you got a full strip-search—and a shower and a change of clothes. But before that some nurse took a needleful of blood from your arm and gave you a plastic cup to pee in. Then you waited, sitting on a long bench with a bunch of other kids, and a guy read you more of your rights and laid down some rules. The rights were all about phone calls and three meals a day and going to the bathroom and having a lawyer. The rules told you how you weren't allowed to curse or talk back to the officers or ask another kid where he was from. You weren't allowed to throw your gang sign[1] and you weren't allowed to look at anybody in "a challenging manner." You hid your smile when the guy said that—why the hell didn't he just say not to mad-dog somebody? All the rules were going to get broken anyway, you could tell that by the way some of the kids were sitting there on the bench like fucked if this place was going to break them down, and fucked if they were going to look at an enemy with anything but death in their eyes. All of you knew one thing though, and that was that however you acted in here, it was going to get back out to the homies. And it would be part of your reputation forever.

[1]Gang members identify themselves by signing with their hands in gestures similar to the alphabet for the deaf. For example, extending the index finger of one hand to approach the extended index and second fingers of the other hand is the sign that you are affiliated with the Eight Tray Gangster Crips. Index and little finger extended, second and third fingers folded in is the sign of a Blood from the Brim set.

Your homeboys, the ones who had already been away, told you about that early on, along with the advice that once you got sent up the only way to get along was to do your own time and try not to act like a fool. If you had to stand up for yourself and your neighborhood, you knew that you'd handle it, but you wouldn't go looking. And you wouldn't back down. Play the coward once, drop your eyes and take a step away just once and you never really lose the mark. You wondered, sitting on the bench, listening to this guy talk at you, how many of the kids on either side of you were going to hang themselves out in the name of reputation. After the guy finished with the rules, he filled you in on visits, told you how your family could come to see you on Sundays. You remember that first Sunday when your mom came in, how she cried when she saw you and how you did too, a little. She cried again when you stood in front of the judge and he sentenced you to camp. You didn't cry that time, but that's when you felt the lowest, when your mom cried in front of that judge. That's when you felt like a loser.

As the van rumbles through Hidden Hills, heading toward Calabasas, it moves past billboards that announce the care with which families are handled at Royal Oaks Estates, or at Mira Monte, or at Colonnade, an environment so hospitable that it also offers sailing. There are icon-like photographic renderings of these invited families smiling out from the billboards. They gaze securely at passersby, wrapped in their blondness.

Kanan Road leads you up into the mountains and it is here that you leave the freeway. Less than a half mile in you pass one of these residential developments. A clutch of newly constructed houses crowd the lip of a hill—sprawling tile-roofed villas of the Mediterranean persuasion, Norman monstrosities, neo-Victorian conceits, all cupolas and turrets. The van begins to move up, passing richly-stocked horse farms and fancifully named ranches. It shotguns through one of a pair of side-by-side tunnels and just before the darkness surrounds you, you catch a glimpse of spraypainted slogans; someone has written, in letters that curve above the mouths, "Debbie, I loved you" and "In gold we trust."

You climb higher, moving past huge, oddly balanced rock formations that seem somehow otherworldly, like the landscape of a different planet. Hawks circle high overhead and a dead snake lies at the side of the road, its belly gleaming whitely in the sun. An early morning mist is just beginning to burn off; later it will get hot and every car that passes will kick up a powdery dust that leaves a salty film on your skin. The salt taste reminds you that the ocean is close enough, a mountaintop away.

Juvenile Probation Camps Miller and Kilpatrick are located at the end of the same road in the Malibu Hills. The main buildings of both camps are vaguely hacienda-like; there are terra cotta tiles on the roofs, bougainvillaea vines climb near the doorways. You might think that these are private homes until you notice the locked steel-mesh fence that surrounds Camp Kilpatrick. Miller is an open camp, one of the last in existence; it has no walls, no lockup (solitary confinement) area. The inmates—they are called wards—sleep in a single, unlocked dormitory. There are usually about 115 boys in residence at Camp Miller; first-timers might be sent here but it is not the rule. The general population count is about the same at Kilpatrick, but because it is a security camp the staff numbers are larger: about twelve to five. There are three dormitories here, all locked, and twenty-five lockup rooms. Within the dorm setup boys are assigned—as they are at the other camps—to different units named for birds and animals. Ten or so kids to a group—Falcons, Mustangs, Tigers, and so forth. And in most cases a sense of loyalty to the group develops, in sports, in general conduct, in school. It is perhaps not quite the sublimation of a gang mindset; more likely it is something even more generic: these are kids, and certain formulas tend to work.

When you arrive at camp you trade whatever you have on for the clothes that you will wear during your time here: white T-shirt, baggy blue pants, black high-tops. If you have been wearing your hair in one of the prescribed g-ster[2] do's—rows of skinny French braids secured with red (or blue) barrettes, it is cropped close to the scalp.

Then, when you are dressed, you go for your talk with the camp director. He's not ready to see you yet so you wait, sitting on a wooden bench with another new kid, in the hall outside his office. If you look to your right, into the big room that's mostly an enclosed bullpen, you see a couple of guys answering phones while they keep an eye on the window that covers one whole side of the room. If you stretch your neck a little, you can see what they see—the main camp grounds: basketball courts and open grassy stretches bordered by walkways that open into classrooms. To your left are the swinging doors that lead to the outside. You know that these doors are unlocked because they brought you in this way; the driver of the van just pushed them open. You wonder how many kids have bailed from this bench, and how far they got up that road before they got caught. You wonder how many times a kid can try that before he gets sent to C.Y.A. (California Youth Authority; not a camp, but a juvenile prison with a school attached). The kid sitting next to you nudges you with his elbow then indicates, with a gesture of his head, a galaxy of framed photographs and citations on the wall opposite the bench you're sitting on. The photographs are of different teams—football, basketball, baseball, track—and individual players. The players are all kids; you figure the older guys standing next to them have got to be staff

---

[2]the short version of "gangster"

members. Everybody is wearing Camp Kilpatrick shirts and caps.

When you are called in for your meeting with the camp director, Mr. Turner,[3] you can tell that behind the handshake and the smile he's sizing you up, just like you're doing with him. He tells you to sit down on the chair across from him and then, as if he were dealing cards, he begins to lay out facts. You will have a meeting with the camp psychiatrist the next time he comes up here. (Psychiatrists are provided by the county; they visit the camps on a biweekly basis, evaluating incoming kids, having short sessions with other boys on an "as needed" schedule.) You will be going to classes mornings and after-noons—real school with teachers from the L.A. school system. You will be expected to keep your area of the dorm clean and tidy. You may have visitors on Saturdays, Sundays, and holi-days. You are welcome to enter any of the camp's sports pro-grams. Next he goes over the point system. Every boy assigned to a juvenile camp is given, by the judge who hears his case, a number of points that he must earn before he can be released. A kid can need as many as nine thousand or as few as four thousand, and he must earn them day by day by following the rules and keeping a good attitude. A spin on attitude can lose you points as quickly as not doing a homework assignment or mouthing off to a staff member. Getting into it with one of the other kids is, of course, the big point grabber. This guy Turner lays it out for you at the end of your time with him: "You're here to get along. Nobody's interested in the gang missions you went out on or who you're enemies with. The gangs don't count here. This is our ride you're on. And there are a couple of ways you can go: you can take the freeway out of here by sticking with the rules. Or you can do it your way and take the scenic route. Do whatever you're told and do it like you love

---

[3]Chuck Turner has since been assigned to head up another camp.

it, whether it's making your bed or doing your homework. The staff is here to help you, not guard you. Someone on staff will always be around, and not just to mark your names down in a notebook. You don't have to be friends, but sometimes it helps to talk. You might be surprised."

A. C. Jones is considered to be one of the heaviest hitters on staff at Camp Kilpatrick. Whatever the kids who are sent here need in order to meet the future, it is located at the juncture of this barrel-chested man who moves with the grace of a good welterweight and their own intentions. If they are the enforcers of an unquestioned code, then Jones is the vigilante of rational choice. An ex-gang member, he looks to be in his late twenties, maybe, but then you learn that he saw action in Vietnam and you look a little closer and see on his face the heavy parenthetical lines of resistance to attack. He works full-time at Kilpatrick and is a year away from earning his master's degree in criminal justice at Cal State in San Bernardino. He is the person that Chuck Turner suggested I talk to before I interview any of the boys.

We meet in a small office overlooking the main campgrounds; this is where I will be talking to the kids. The lobby is close enough so that the voices of staff members and the sound of ringing telephones filter through. It is morning and classes have begun, so the grounds outside are quiet. The room that we are in seems uncluttered by human occupancy; there are no plants, no family snapshots, no calendars on the wall; the battered desk is bare of files and stacks of paperwork. Three wooden chairs have been placed haphazardly near the door. A pair of metal filing cabinets are too dusty to be in use.

Jones has a question before we begin our conversation. He wants to know why I have chosen this subject to write about. I tell him that I have been writing about teenagers—runaways living in abandoned buildings, kids placed in psychiatric hospitals by their parents—and that gang members, Crips and Bloods in particular, seemed the next logical choice of subject to me, as equally disenfranchised American kids. Jones shakes his head. "It goes further than these kids simply being perceived as American kids. These are African-American kids and they're dealing with the added aspect of disenfranchisement that goes along with that. These kids are black in America. Every time a seventeen-year-old black male walks into a mall, or a liquor store, or a market, every time he buys a ticket to an Eddie Murphy movie, he knows that every person who sees him is viewing him as a menace." He leans forward, tapping the desk for emphasis. "I'll tell you something—I grew up here, I was a Marine, I have an education and a nice family, I'm a peace officer . . . but every time I walk through the parking lot of a shopping center I see older white women clutch their purses closer to their sides. I hear the click of car door locks as I move past. And that's a haunting thing. Now, you start feeling that when you're nine, ten years old, then by the time you're fourteen or fifteen you've got to figure that you're unwanted. That nobody likes you. Even though you're hearing in history class that everybody loves you, that you *can* be all that you can be." Jones smiles and shakes his head again. "Well, it sounds pretty but it's just not true."

He talks briefly about time spent in the Marine Corps brig for refusing to put on his dress blues for a Fourth of July celebration. "I told the adjutant that American Independence Day wasn't important to me because my particular forefathers were still slaves two hundred years after that. I didn't—and don't—feel a freedom based on that event. Kids today can't articulate why they're feeling what they feel, but those same kind of rebellious emotions are getting them in trouble because they have no way to vent the pressure. So they end up hating those things that have put them in that position, and if what has put you there is the fact that you're black, you end up hating that. You don't kill yourself but you kill others who are like you."

There is the sound of kids' voices from outside; a couple of classes are having recess and some of the boys are tossing baskets. Jones suggests a walk around the grounds.

There is bright sun outside, the air is simply air. This is raw country up here; it is a pleasure to breathe. We stand watching the kids play. One of the boys glides around the court with the graceful, thrifty moves of the natural. When he throws the ball his hands curve inward and the two index fingers remain pointing at the rim of the basket until the ball swishes through the net.

When Jones speaks it sounds almost as if he is talking to himself. "What do you think happened when that kid there first began to seek out his masculinity? What happened when he first tried to assert himself? If he lived in any other community but Watts there would be legitimate ways to express those feelings. Little League. Pop Warner. But if you're a black kid living in Watts those options have been removed. You're not going to go play Pop Warner. Not in Watts. Maybe if you live in Bellflower, maybe if you live in Agoura, but not in Watts— its just not there, there's no funding for it. But you're at that prepubescent age, and you have all those aggressive tendencies and no legitimate way to get rid of them. And that's when the gang comes along, and the gang offers everything those legitimate organizations do. The gang serves emotional needs. You feel wanted. You feel welcome. You feel important. And there is discipline and there are rules."

He is interrupted as the staff member who has been monitoring the basketball court walks over to where we are standing. He appears to be in his early thirties, chunky with heavily muscled arms. He is wearing a T-shirt with the printed legend "Los Angeles County Probation Department." After introductions are made he nods his head in Jones's direction. "You sure picked the right one to talk to about gangs. This guy's an expert." Jones shakes his head in that slow gesture that is becoming familiar.

We head toward the dormitories located on the other side of the playing field. As we walk Jones picks up the thread of conversation. "I'll tell you one thing I'm real sure about and that's the commonalities between gangs and cops." Seeing my look of disbelief he grins briefly and then his face sobers again. "Look, take away the moral imperative and the legal aspect of who has the right to kill and who does not, and what you have left is the very same organization."

Now it's my turn to shake my head; I don't see it. Jones begins to tick off similarities. "There are so many parallels—the jumping-in process of a gang member is similar to the training process of a police cadet; they're both run through the same kind of gauntlet. Even the recruiting process. With the police you get a picture on a billboard—here we are, driving around in a nice, shiny car, got a badge, we're *somebody*. You be somebody, too. Well, that's almost the same thing Crips and Bloods are telling nine- and ten-year-old kids. Be all that you can be. Even the retirement plan—with gang kids it's going legit."

We turn to our right at the end of the playing field and walk along a covered walkway that opens into some of the classrooms. As we pass windows kids look up and wave at us.

Jones continues. "Gang members will associate with non-gang members but they don't consider them important. They might get to be friends but they'll never be close. Police officers might get tight with people—friends—who aren't cops, but everybody will fall in place behind their police buddies. Police officers will often slight their families in favor of their partners. Gang members do the same thing—the homeboys come first. And if a police officer is killed in the line of duty, there's only one thing that will stop his partner from taking it out on the next person—and that's the law. But if he could get away with it . . ." He shrugs. "Gang kids don't have that governor on their accelerators. If their homeboy gets killed, they'll go ahead and do what the police officer wants to do if his partner gets done."

Jones opens the dormitory door and we step into a large, barnlike space. There is a raised platform with a desk and chair on it situated in the middle of the room; this is where the D.P.O. on duty sits. There are about forty beds, single-size iron cots, each of them neatly made up with its flat pillow, cotton sheets, and tan blanket. There is a metal locker next to each bed. A low partition separates one side of the room from the other. No pictures of family and friends. No posters. It is simply a place for sleeping, clean and impersonal.

We walk back across the camp grounds toward the small office where the interviews will take place. Jones has suggested that I talk to two kids at once; he feels that they will be more comfortable talking about themselves together, and that two at a time will help to keep them honest. The basketball game has broken up now, the kids are heading back toward the classrooms. They're walking single file, no talking, and I notice that every boy has his hands tucked all the way down in his back pockets. Jones explains that this is a safeguard against anyone throwing his gang sign. He stands still for a moment, watching the line as it moves along the walkway: An expression compounding anger and remorse travels briefly across his face.

"The very fact that a kid is in a gang means that something is missing. So many of them are functioning illiterates. So many of them come from abusing backgrounds. The hardest cases were probably sexually molested or they were routinely beaten—probably both. Depends on what kind of father influence was around the house. If any. You find a gang member who comes from a complete nuclear family, a kid who has never been exposed to any kind of abuse, I'd like to meet him. Not a wannabe who's a Crip or a Blood because that's the thing to be in 1990, I mean a *real* gangbanger who comes from a happy, balanced home, who's got a good opinion of himself. I don't think that kid exists."

There are two boys waiting for me outside the small office; I can see them from the lobby. As I shake hands with Jones one of the other D.P.O.'s behind the counter of the bullpen says something complimentary about Jones's expertise with gang members. Jones grins and makes a short gesture of dismissal. Then he looks at me again and the smile fades away.

"People say that enough, you might start to believe it, so I'll tell you one more thing: there are no 'gang experts.'" He looks down the hallway at the two kids waiting for me.

"There are your experts."

■   ■   ■

Each boy takes a chair on either side of me. They barely glance at each other. I have just enough information about them to know that they are sworn enemies, these two, that even though they are barely acquainted, there is a river of blood between them. They are both members of different Crip sets that have been warring with each other for a longer time than either youngster can possibly remember.

The taller of the two kids looks as if he is taking an easy step into manhood. He is as lean and dark as a Doberman pinscher and although he is not particularly big, he can't seem to help giving the impression of power. Maybe it's his eyes. Guarded and icy, they don't miss a trick. I ask him to tell me his gang nickname.

"Gangster Roc. G-Roc is what they usually call me." His voice has already reached the timbre of adulthood. I have been told that he has been placed here for participating in a drive-by shooting.

"How old are you?"

"Fifteen last month." When G-Roc speaks it is with a calm, rather frightening authority. The other kid is watching him with big eyes.

"How about you?" The boy turns his head quickly, to look at me; he seems startled by my question. "What do they call you?"

"Me? Tiny Vamp."

"Well, tell her how old you are." G-Roc's voice is harsh, impatient.

"Fourteen and a half." He is still very much a child, all puppy fat and awkward angles. G-Roc is making him nervous; it's clear that he wants to make a good impression on the older boy.

"Why are you here?" I know why he's here, but I want to hear him say it.

"Rape." His head is down as he says the single word. His voice is soft, muffled. It is very quiet in the small room. "It was just that my homeboys had a . . ." He clears his throat, begins again. This time his voice is stronger and there is a hint of bravado right around the edges. "Everybody just wanted to get theirs on, so we just went at it. There was about ninety of us homies and this one girl. She was eighteen and she was . . . like a hooker. I didn't get her or nothin', but my homeboys knew her already and took her to our treehouse, our kickback place."

"What's a kickback place?"

"Just a old shack back of a vacant lot in our 'hood."

"Your neighborhood?"

"Yeah." He mentions a vague address in South Central Los Angeles. His eyes move, again and again, to the boy sitting across from him. G-Roc is looking at him with what appears to be cold, pure contempt. Tiny Vamp's voice falters, and when he speaks again, it goes up a couple of notches and he begins to talk faster. "She wanted to come with us—she liked it." He pauses, regrouping. "I don't remember too good, I was

16

drunk." Now he is speaking only to G-Roc and I can see how important it is to him that he say the right thing to this silent, watchful youngster.

Tiny Vamp makes a stab at a grin. "But she like it, that's real. She didn't do no fightin' back." He nods his head for emphasis, an abrupt up and down gesture. "That's real, too."

G-Roc maintains an even, steady gaze, holding it, not blinking until the younger boy drops his eyes. From outside some kid yells a word, it sounds like "faggot," and only then does G-Roc glance away, breathing out a long hiss of contempt. The silence in here lasts for another couple of seconds as G-Roc shakes his head in a deliberate back and forth motion. Then he begins to talk, aiming his words directly at me. "That is scandalous. Scandalous! They did it, and that's on them, you know? All right? That's on them. But ninety niggers? That's fucked up."

Tiny Vamp sits up straight in his chair. "Well, she liked it!" He actually sounds indignant.

"Oh, yeah? Did she?" G-Roc's lip curls into a sneer. "The way I heard it—oh, yeah, I heard about it, too . . ." Now his eyes are lasering into the kid's face, "and it wasn't *nothin'* like that shit you talkin'. I heard the girl was *twelve*, and there wasn't no ninety niggers, there was eight or nine niggers and one little twelve-year-old girl that y'all grabbed off the street." He jerks his thumb at Tiny Vamp. "His homeboy, Capone, was in the Hall with me, and he was tellin' me about that shit with the little girl, and it was"—he makes that explosive hissing sound again—"scandalous. If it was me, if I was that little girl, I probably woulda killed some of 'em. 'Cause I heard she *was* like fightin' back, cryin' and kickin' out and like that. If she had liked it how *they* gonna get locked up for it?" He is talking only to me now; his body leans forward in the chair, all of his energy aimed directly at me; both elbows rest easily on his outstretched knees. "I ain't blaming this dude here personally but,

17

you know, I don't understand how no girl is gonna lay there and accept ninety—or nine, or ten, or whatever—niggers on top of her. And *like* it?! And eighteen at that?! A eighteen-year-old is gonna have more sense than just open her legs for a whole buncha niggers, you know? 'Cause she say, 'yes,' then that be like girlfriend and boyfriend." He turns his attention to Tiny Vamp again and I sit quietly. Whatever emotions G-Roc feels about the rape of a child—outrage, contempt, anger, whatever—compassion is not among them.

"Y'all got arrested for *rape!* A rape is . . ."

"They droppin' that, maybe . . ." Tiny Vamp's voice is only marginally louder than a whisper.

G-Roc continues as if the kid had not spoken. "A rape is takin' from her unwillingly. Like she didn't really want to give it up to y'all. Y'all just forced, you know what I'm sayin'? *That's* what *rape* is. You understand what I'm sayin'?"

"Yeah . . ." This time it is a whisper. The kid's head droops; he sits gazing at his hands which are now folded meekly in his lap. Those hands, smooth-skinned and stubby fingered, the cuticles savaged by constant nibbling and tearing, are the hands of a ten-year-old. It is nearly impossible to imagine those hands reaching out to commit an act of sexual assault.

G-Roc stares at Tiny Vamp for another few seconds then he gets to his feet, moves to the window, and stands looking out at the camp grounds. The only sound in the room is the soft pat of his fingertips as he beats out an intricate rhythm on the sill. When he speaks again he doesn't turn around right away. "I mean, my homeboys be doin' rapes, but I'm like, 'Man, y'all go on with that ol' type shit, man—I ain't doin' no rape.' They, you know, they'll just rape a girl, any girl, if she look good and she don't wanna kick in." Now he turns to face me again. "Hey, if they want it bad enough, they gonna take it. All of them together. And beat on her, too, if she try to hold back. That's why I don't do all that, you know, because I wouldn't want nobody raping *my* girl, or *my* mama, you know? Man, I'd fuck around and be on Death Row if somebody did me like that. You know, on the outs[4] this pig was sayin', 'You shouldn't steal because then somebody steal from you.' And I agree with that, but the kinda stealin' I'm sayin', well . . ." He begins to stammer in his earnestness to get his thought across. His voice doesn't sound so much like a man's now, it is merely the husky rasp of a teenager. "It's like, like . . . I steal, but I don't jack.[5] Like, people jack, like . . ." He begins to act it out now, his voice plummeting into his chest, " 'Get out yo' car!' " His voice returns to normal. "You know? I jack that way but I don't jack like"—back to the low scary tones again—" 'Give up yo' wallet!' and all like that, 'cause I got money. I don't have to pull a gun on nobody for they money." Tiny Vamp nods vigorously, sensing a way back into G-Roc's better graces. "And jewelry." He pronounces it like the word "jury." "I won't jack nobody for no jewelry—or drugs—or money. Car. I'll jack for a car."

"Ye-eeeeeh." G-Roc draws the word out of his mouth as if it were a long strand of bubble gum. "I'll jack for a car. I *got* a car, though—big old Monte Carlo. Had an Essay[6] fix it up for me, all white with blue pearl and chrome-base gold leaf. Look *good*. So if I jack for a car it's only for somethin' we can use for like shootings, or g-rides, you know? But, like I said, I wouldn't jack nobody for they money. All that ain't called for. I *got* money"—he hisses loudly again—"I sell dope for *my* money." He is sitting down again, relaxing in his chair, one leg crossed rather elegantly over the other.

Tiny Vamp leans forward eagerly. "If I was livin' on the streets like some bum or somethin', just livin' in some alley I'd

[4]out of prison or detention; free
[5]commit a holdup
[6]anyone of Hispanic origin, usually a gang member

jack for money. But I ain't that bad off." G-Roc nods absent-mindedly; the kid presses this minor advantage and asks a question. "How long you been from your 'hood?" He is asking G-Roc how many years he has been active in his gang.

"Been in since I was eight. I was just like born into it, you know? I got two O.G.[7] cousins and one cousin about to be O.G. My oldest cousin, he up in Soledad for attempted murder, he twenty-four; the twenty-two-year-old just got outta Folsom. When I was born it was like, 'he gonna be from my 'hood,' and when I got eight they put me on the baby homies and that was just it. At that time I didn't even know what was goin' on, I just like got beat up. Just fought back. My cousins took me up to the park one day, see, and we got drunk and I got hit and I fought back. That's how I got jumped in—the old-fashioned way. And then I was from my 'hood."

"Do your mama get on you about 'bangin'?"[8]

"Well, she don't like it but she can't tell me how to run my life, you know, because any normal child our age, you know, they'll love their parents . . . I mean, my stepfather, he like a father to me, but still, you can't . . . you know . . . you still gonna have to say something back. Like, 'You can't tell me what to do, woo-woo-woo' . . . you know?"

Tiny Vamp nods his head knowingly. He's trying very hard to be cool but I can see that he's thrilled to be included as an equal in G-Roc's general observation.

G-Roc goes on. "My mama work hard, she got a job in a bank, and she don't want me doin' it, you know, but I'm my own person. If I want to mess up my life, she gonna love me anyway. She know my cousins and stuff was in it, she know all I'm tryin' to do is make a name for myself. I tryin' to have a

[7]Original Gangster, a respectful term meaning someone who has earned his gang stripes
[8]gangbanging—being in a gang

20

bad rep—I got a little reputation, but it ain't nearly where I want it to be. I want to fulfill my name. Be a straight criminal, be devious, do anything, be bad to the fullest. You know what I'm talkin' about? Anybody want to fight, we can fight. Anybody want to shoot, we can shoot. Want to kill, we can kill. *Whatever.* You know what I'm sayin'? *Whatever.*" This last declaration has been aimed directly at me; the words have been spoken in the calmest, coldest voice imaginable.

Tiny Vamp chimes in: "I feel the same thing he's sayin'. Just the same way." He turns to G-Roc. "You still a li'l homie, or what?"

G-Roc nods his head solemnly. "Li'l homie. I ain't probably gonna reach O.G. stage for a while yet. I got outta baby homie when I was like thirteen and a half. How 'bout you?"

"I'm still a Tiny. In my set[9] you get a rep by straight killin'. I been on drive-bys and I been stabbed. That feel bad—whew—that hurt." He winces a little, remembering. "But if I stab an enemy of mine, I don't feel sorry." He looks at G-Roc for a long moment; there is no expression on his face as he gazes at the older, tougher kid. "I guess I could hurt you if I had to, you're my enemy." He is simply giving information, there is no emotion in his voice. G-Roc returns the look; his expression is equally blank. Tiny Vamp turns toward me. "He could hurt me, too."

G-Roc's lips curve into a smile that, somehow, never makes it to his eyes. "Yeah, I could hurt him. I could *hurt* him. Just depend on who get to each other first. Just 'cause we in this place together, ain't no truce between us. He just don't say nothin' to me, 'cause I got two other homies here at camp and there's only one of him, he ain't got no backup. So, I'll leave it like, he don't want no 'plato'—that's the way the Essays say it: he don't want no beef, no problem. So he just keep to hisself

[9]any particular gang clique, e.g., Grape Street Watts Crips, Mad Swan Bloods

21

if he want to keep it neutral. 'Cause I ain't gonna get really crazy unless somebody just get right up in my face, 'woo-woo-woo!' And then we can have at it. It might not be on like we tryin' to kill each other, but we *will* fight. Only *I* probably won't, 'cause if I fight, I'm gone. I'll probably get sent to Y.A. But my homeboys is gonna get him. Understand, it don't make no difference to me, but I ain't in no rush to get sent to Y.A. 'cause I only got two or three more months 'til I can go home. I'm lookin' forward to gettin' up outta here, I been here four months."

G-Roc smiles again, and this time it is warm, almost child-like. His whole face softens, you can see how very young he really is. He talks for a moment about the long bath he's going to take when he gets home, how he's going to relax with his family and go to visit his cousin in prison, the one who's locked up for attempted murder. "That charge is bogus—the dude just like walked up on my cousin, put the gun in his mouth. He was a youngster, he was only like seventeen, and he thought my cousin was gonna run. My cousin just looked at him, like, 'do or die,' and he was like, 'What's that suppose to mean?' and I splashed on him. I shot him in the stomach. He didn't die, though, but he was out. He wearin' a bag for the rest of his . . ."

Tiny Vamp cuts in, "One of them bags you pee and stuff in?"

G-Roc nods. "He got shot twice."

Tiny Vamp's voice quivers with excitement. "Take his guts out, put that thing, that bag on. My homie had that after he done got shot up."

I ask both kids if they can tell me why so many of the Crip sets are at war with each other, why there are so many deadly enemies within their own organization.

G-Roc picks up a pen that's lying on the desk and asks if he can have a piece of paper from my notebook. "People think

Crips only fight Crips but we fight Bloods more than we fight each other." He has been drawing quickly as he talks, a rough map of Los Angeles. Now he uses the pen as a pointer. "See, Crips is like here—here—here—here—but there's Bloods all in between us."

Tiny Vamp has gotten out of his chair to look. "See, all the Bloods get along together and they think that we all fightin' *us* instead of them. 'Cause they all get along."

G-Roc slams down the pen. "Shit, man, all Bloods do *not* get along, what's wrong with you? Some of them Blood sets don't get along for shit." He mentions two Blood factions that are supposedly warring with each other.

Tiny Vamp defends his position. "Well, that's what people say. They say they don't even kill each other."

"Yes they do!" G-Roc is really annoyed now. "Them two sets I just named are killin' each other off, they sprayin' each other with AKs and Uzis! They's a couple of 'em from one of them sets in here and one of the dudes is a buster. He a real coward."

Tiny Vamp nods his head and makes a face, as if he and G-Roc were in on the same secret. "He an Essay, too."

"Yeah. He say somethin' like, 'C.K.'[10] to me and I'm like, 'What, nigger? *Fuck* slobs!'[11] and he like put his head down. He's a bust; he ain't down [12] for his 'hood. He just want people to think he is. But he ain't down to do anything."

Tiny Vamp nods solemnly. "Do or die."

G-Roc nods his head, just once. It is a hard won, almost benevolent gesture of near-approval for this younger kid who, although he is an enemy, is also, indisputably, a Crip. "You got to be ready to do anything if somebody dis'[13] your 'hood. You

[10]Crip Killer, as in "I kill Crips"
[11]insulting term for Bloods
[12]tough, loyal to the set, ready to fight or shoot
[13]disrespect

going to have to represent. If you don't, you a buster—you shouldn't even 'bang. If you scared, forget it. It's like when I got jumped in [14]—all my homeboys and my cousins told me, 'You in now, man. You know what you got into before you got into it. It's Do or die, Crip or cry.' You know? Either you be down for it or"—he delivers that disdainful hiss again—"get out now. 'Cause you *know* you gonna have to go to jail; you *know* you might end up gettin' killed, gettin' stabbed, gettin' shot. You know all this. My homeboy, Li'l Lazy, just got killed and he only sixteen. Hell, I know it ain't like no Roadrunner cartoon—get smashed flat, get up again."

It is 11:30—time for lunch. G-Roc and Tiny Vamp join their dorm groups and fall into line. No talking, no looking around, hands tucked safely out of sight in back pockets. The boys wait at the entrance of the cafeteria and are allowed to move inside, single file, in their dorm groups of ten or twelve. The food is dished up on metal trays, cafeteria style, by trustees wearing plastic shower caps and disposable sterile gloves. Today's luncheon menu consists of spaghetti with meat sauce, mixed fresh fruit and tossed salad, homemade chocolate cake. Cartons of low-fat milk have been placed at each table. The kids sit at round tables for four, and the rule of silence applies in here as it does in lineup. D.P.O.'s patrol the room, clipboards and pencils at the ready. A boy can lose precious merit points at mealtime not only for talking but for any discernible "attitude," such as looking at another kid in a manner that might be construed as challenging. "It's all about pencil power in here," as one member of the staff puts it. And it seems to work. The only sounds you hear in the cafeteria, other than the random comment from a staff member, are the chitter of cutlery against metal, the squeak of rubber soles on linoleum.

After lunch, as we walk back to the main building, Tiny

---

[14]joined up, initiated (by being beaten up by other gang members)

Vamp claims that somebody, he won't say who, "looked at him crazy" in line outside the cafeteria. "It's like I got all enemies in here. There's only a couple people I can count on here, they from a friendly set. So if anybody try to head up[15] with me, I got 'em."

G-Roc actually laughs in the younger boy's face. "Don't bet on it. If me and my homeboys jumped you, they wouldn't do shit about it, 'cause we got no beef with them. But we don't got the same enemies, either, so even though they Crips, too, we don't really trust 'em. They'll turn on you in a minute."

We are passing a row of picnic tables that extends along the side of the main building. This is where kids sit with their visitors on the weekends. The weather has turned hot, but there's a breeze and nobody's that eager to go back inside the small, stuffy office. We take seats at one of the benches, and Tiny Vamp picks up the conversation.

"That's why the O.G.'s will tell you, like, what's happening, see? They will tell you who your enemies are, who you can trust."

This time G-Roc doesn't laugh; this time he looks at Tiny Vamp as if he were nuts. "What's wrong with you? Can't trust nobody. *Nobody!* Not even your homeboys. They'll snitch on you too, you know?"

Nobody says a word. Tiny Vamp just sits and stares. G-Roc's eyes travel back and forth from my face to the kid's face "Well . . . like . . ." He is having trouble with this. He has said it, it's out there on the table, but this is very hard for him. "You know which of your homies you can trust, and which ones of 'em that you . . ." He clamps his lips together, pulls in a deep breath through his nostrils, lets it out slowly. "You will . . . trust . . . , all of them, right? But if you do a murder you will start having suspicions, like . . ." You can see this kid gathering

---

[15]start a fight

strength for what he is about to say. "All right: if somebody snitch, you gonna know who did it. You can't trust 'em, you know that, but you got love for 'em, anyway. You know . . ." He pauses for a moment; Tiny Vamp is watching him carefully, expressionlessly. "Ain't nobody forced to snitch."

Now Tiny Vamp slides in quickly. *"I* can't be forced to snitch."

G-Roc plows on. "They can threaten you with time, they can threaten you with the death penalty, they . . ."

"Like they did me. That's why I'm in here doin' time right now. For not talkin'. If I said somethin', I'd probably be gone a long time ago." Tiny Vamp states this proudly and receives, in reward, another slight nod from G-Roc.

"Well, nigger, if you don't snitch, your rep go up just that much."

"Ye-eeeeeeh." If a single syllable can sound like a swagger, this is the one.

G-Roc makes a graceful gesture with one hand. "If you don't snitch, all your homeboys be, like, *'Damn!'* Like my homie, Stagalee? He on Death Row for somethin' he didn't do. He didn't do *nothin'.* He was there when they hit an army base for some guns and stuff. Like, he was there, but some of the other homeboys killed like three M.P.'s and then when they left, on the way back, they shot up a gang of our enemy 'hoods, killed a gang of people. The pigs caught 'em, went in everybody's houses and got 'em, but Stagalee's the only one doin' time for it. He doin' time for the whole *everybody* 'cause he won't . . ." He shuts his eyes for an instant, squeezing the lids together. "He more than doin' time. He on Death Row." G-Roc shakes his head, thinking about it, outraged by what he perceives as a gross injustice. Then, astonishingly, he smiles a thin twitch of a smile. "You know, all the time people be askin' why *we* don't join up in the army."

Tiny Vamp smiles too. "Naw. Like to have them guns, though. Sure like to have them guns."

G-Roc reaches down in a sudden, fluid movement and scoops up a small rock from the ground near his feet. He juggles it lightly in his palm, then he sends it spinning to hit the trunk of a nearby oak tree. "Man, this country don't do nothin' for me. Why should I fight for this country?"

The younger kid nods his head. "That's what everybody says."

"I love America, but I ain't gonna fight nobody over no country I can't call no shots for. Like . . ." He pulls in air. "Okay, I can't go to the White House and just walk in and sit down like this and say how I feel about things. I can't say, 'Well, we gonna do *this* this year—instead of havin' tax evasion, we ain't gonna have it.' I can't call shots like that. So why should I help them fight people and kill Russians for somethin' I don't even know what's goin' on about? They don't tell you what's really goin' on in this country in the news."

Finally, the moment feels right and I bring up the subject of drive-by shootings. Tiny Vamp looks immediately at G-Roc, ready to take his cue from the older boy. G-Roc plants both elbows firmly on the picnic table.

"I don't really like to do drive-bys, because innocent people might get hit, you know? My homeboy shot a baby in the head. He felt bad about it, you know, but he was like, 'That's how it happen sometimes.' He felt bad but wasn't nothin' he could do about it. Me, personally, I don't feel nothin', 'cause I didn't do it, but if that *had* been me, I'd been hurtin', like—'*damn!* A baby, and one of my own people, too.' See, me, I'm like this: if I want somebody, if I want one person—or if I want more than one person—I park in front of they house, camp out all night, drink a little, smoke some weed and just wait for 'em. Soon as they come out they house, I get 'em and I leave. I ain't gonna drive by and . . . br-r-r-r-r-r-r-t . . . get

27

off on *anybody*. Shit . . ." He leans back with a dismissive little wave accompanying it with the familiar, sizzling sound of disgust.

You can see it in your mind: the car, stolen for this occasion, headlights doused a block or two away, gliding up to park a couple of houses away from the target area. You can see the shapes of people, one behind the wheel, one in the passenger seat or in the back, maybe. The glowing tip of a joint as it is passed back and forth. Maybe you catch a random strain of music from a tape deck as the hours pass.

Tiny Vamp, eager as ever to make points, pipes up: "I do it. I do a drive-by. I may worry about hittin', like a baby, but, like—I do it. I do like the homeboy here say . . . just camp out."

G-Roc leans forward and levels a stiffened forefinger at Tiny Vamp's forehead. When he speaks his voice is nearly a caress. "Don't be callin' me your homeboy, nigger. I *ain't* your homeboy." The younger kid wilts in his chair. G-Roc turns to look at me now, jerking his thumb at Tiny Vamp. "Like to hear hisself talk. He ain't never camped out to get no enemy in his life, probably. Ain't put that much work in, he still a Tiny." Tiny Vamp opens his mouth to say something but whatever it was, he thinks better of it and remains silent, squirming a little on the wooden bench.

G-Roc continues: "Now, me—I do a drive-by, I do it. But you know, it ain't my style. I don't like to do it all constantly. If I want somebody, I want *them*. I want to have the joy in my heart of just to, like, get out the car and, like, 'Remember me?' and then just shoot him. I don't want to be just shootin' up his house and *hopin'* I get him, and might get his mama. Or his father. I want *him*. I want that person. I don't want to be like that nigger who blasted the wrong family. That's a stupid nigger, and what he did is scandalous."

G-Roc is talking about the infamous case that sent Teiquon Cox, a member of one of the largest and most notorious Crip sets, to Death Row at San Quentin. Cox was condemned to the gas chamber for the 1984 murders of the mother and three other relatives (two of them children) of former football star Kermit Alexander of the San Francisco Forty-Niners. According to trial testimony, Cox and another gang member entered the front door of Mrs. Alexander's house in South Central Los Angeles with a .30 caliber M-1 carbine. When they came out again three minutes later, everybody in the house was dead, their heads reduced to pulp by a barrage of gunfire. Mrs. Alexander had been in the kitchen preparing Sunday morning breakfast before the family went to church. Her youngest daughter and two grandsons were killed in their beds. What emerged at the trial was that Cox had meant to murder the people who lived in a house two doors away from the Alexander family; he had misread the address.

G-Roc has a strong sense of family, and he claims a strong bond with his stepfather. On a later visit to the camp, on a weekend when I would travel up there to see another boy, I saw G-Roc's parents: youngish, good-looking people, conservatively dressed, eager to make contact with their son. They would sit across from him, both of them leaning in close as they struggled to build a conversation with the unsmiling boy.

He has some potent feelings about his real father, too. You can hear it in his voice; the passion roils there just beneath the surface. "If I could, I'd go see him. 'Cause he's my real father. I wouldn't go now, not right now, 'cause I got hostility towards him. He just left, he left my mama for nothin'. I don't know why. Just fuckin' left her. She went to the store and when she come back, he gone. Just like that. I remember that day, I was with my mama and she like to die, cryin'. All us kids, except for my little baby sister, is his kids. If I could change things, I'd make him not leave. But if I see him now, boy"—he puffs out that stream of air—"I'd probably try to kill him or something. I probably would. My brother be always sayin', 'If I ever see him again, he gonna die.' "

There is a long beat of silence, then Tiny Vamp begins to speak. His voice is muted, and for the first time he is not trying to make points. He is simply sharing something with G-Roc.

"I ain't seen my pa since I was about seven years old. My real pa . . . my father. He up at Folsom. He did somethin' to a sheriff. He had already did time, and then he got out and done a robbery, and that other, to the sheriff. They come back to our house and found a gun and all kinda suits and stuff, and he doin' eleven years now. I write to him sometimes, you know, but I never see him." Tiny Vamp looks down at his hands and maybe he's crying a little, maybe not, it's impossible to tell. After a moment he looks up again. "I wouldn't change nothin' about my life, though."

G-Roc nods his head. "Me too." The camp dog, an ancient and immensely fat black Labrador, has ambled up to the table and he is petting her, smoothing her fur and scratching behind her ears. Her tongue lolls with pleasure. "I wouldn't want to be no one else, I'm just glad I'm me. Like, look at Mike Tyson—or Michael Jackson—they got all that little money but look what it's doin': Mike Tyson gettin' sued every other week over that girl. Michael Jackson's face fallin' off—he ain't happy, you know, he can't go nowhere without people jumpin' all over him. I don't wanna be like that."

But wait a minute, isn't it just like that for gang members? Don't they run the risk of getting shot every time they go outside? G-Roc thinks about that one, then he delivers a short, mirthless laugh. "That's true, too. That's a gamble, all right— this 'bangin's a gamble. But it's like I said before—'do or die.' "

It is at times difficult to remember that G-Roc is only a year and a half older than Tiny Vamp; by comparison he seems like a man. I ask if he goes to school.

"Hell, yes, I go to school. I don't go to classes all the time.

Most of the time I just go up there and see what, you know, mess with some little females or somethin'. I got a couple girls at school, but my girl*friend,* she livin' with me. And I tell you somethin' . . ." He leans forward and drops his voice to a lower pitch, as if what he is about to say is too intimate to be spoken in normal tones. "As far as gangbangin' goes, I'd mop her up if she come to me with some dis' and like that."

I ask him what he would consider disrespect from a girlfriend. From the way Tiny Vamp is leaning in, it looks like he'd like to know, too.

"Well, she don't even dare say 'Cuz,'[16] you know? I mean, she know all my homeboys, and she say, like, 'What's up?'— you know, everybody say that—but I don't even let her call my homeboys by they gang names. At one time when my homies come over, she was like, 'What's up, G-Man?' and I like say, 'No, his *name* is *Darryl.*' You know? 'Cause if she get too carried away with all that then they probably gonna have her doin' somethin' that gonna, you know, get her in trouble. I keep her protected. Like when my house got shot up? And we was there together? I push her down on the floor and throw my body on top of her. Some of my homeboys just scatter. Like my homeboy, Frog? That nigger"—G-Roc hisses—"He was walkin' down the street with his girlfriend, see, and somebody shot at him, and he twisted her around in front of him. The bullets hit her. That nigger got his own girlfriend killed. Scandalous. When they shot up my house, we was in front of the window, big old window like this"—his arms form a sweeping arc—"and I bend right on over her. I ain't gonna let my girl get hit for somethin' *I* did. I ain't gonna let her get killed or shot up for my doin's. I'll *take* whatever's comin' to me because of what I did, but . . . you know . . ." His voice trails away, he shrugs.

[16]alternate generic name for Crip

The afternoon is closing in now. School will be letting out soon, and then the football team will suit up for practice. G-Roc plays first-string fullback, and you can tell that he's anxious for this interview to be finished; he wants to get out on the playing field. A game is coming up in a couple of weeks—the camp will be playing a prep school located a few miles up the coast.

But first he is willing to talk about the way he makes his money on the streets.

"I mostly sell crack cocaine. You can make some good money that way—it all depends on where you go. Some places pop more than others, you know? Like when I first got started—me and my homeboy, Abdul?—we had our own dope house. We made money, shit, we made money. Made like eight, nine hundred in about . . . well, from about eight in the morning to about one, one-thirty in the afternoon."

Every day? What does a fifteen-year-old do with that kind of money?

"Spend it. And stack[17] it. Buy clothes, get some food . . ."

Tiny Vamp cuts in, "Hang with yo' girl a little bit."

G-Roc doesn't seem to mind the interruption; the kid must not be as much of an annoyance to him now. "Spend about five hundred bucks and stack like three, four hundred. That's how you keep your money."

Tiny Vamp asks the obvious question: "You give your mama some money?"

If G-Roc is offended he doesn't let on. But it takes a long, long beat before the answer comes. "Naw." Another long beat. "Naw. She don't want it. I don't even stay with my mama when I'm doin' that . . . when I'm sellin'. I go to my mama's house like Friday through Sunday, and I bone out. Rest of the week

[17]put it away; save it

I like stay at my grandmama's, and sometimes I just stay at my dope house. But I don't do that too often, 'cause I don't feel like gettin' ran up on."[18] He takes another beat. "I work for my own. I ain't no high roller,[19] but I make money for myself. Why should I let someone else run up on me for it?"

Tiny Vamp shakes his head. It is a slow and thoughtful gesture, filled with empathy. "I make money, but I don't hardly sell that much dope no more. I do jewelry licks. I go in jewelry stores, jack 'em up, go sell the jewelry. I can make about three thousand a day, sometimes. Just sell to . . . anybody. Gypsies, anybody who wanna buy. Just walk in a store . . ."

". . . hold 'em up." G-Roc finishes the kid's sentence for him. But Tiny Vamp shakes his head; this time G-Roc is wrong.

"Naw. I just go in a store like . . . use a knife or somethin' to break in."

G-Roc nods approvingly. "You can do it that way, too. You can hit a store and"—he snaps his fingers—"get money just like that. One time we hit a store when it was closing. They was takin' all the money out to go put it in the bank, you know? So when they was comin' out the doors, we just kicked in." He grins at Tiny Vamp. "They ain't gonna fight, all they gonna do is just drop . . . if you catch 'em by surprise, the gun up in they face, they . . ."

". . . they gonna tell everybody to . . ."

". . . just drop the money." Their words are colliding in the air now, as if they were Monday morning quarterbacking a great game. "They gonna drop that bag and you just pick it up. If they try to duke it out all somebody is gonna do is shoot 'em. Hell, you don't even have to shoot 'em, just shoot up in

[18]robbed in a sneak attack
[19]Crip slang for a big dealer. Bloods call them "ballers."

the air and they gonna run. They'll back off. If you say, 'your money or your life,' people gonna give up the money. But lemme tell you somethin' . . ." G-Roc is speaking only to Tiny Vamp now; I have been forgotten in this discussion of financial options. "We talkin' about makin' some money, but really, the people who *really* makin' it is the people we buy the dope from. Like my homeboy, Wack, he an O.G., he got hooked up with Cambodians. He go out of town, fly dope in, big keys. He give them a coupla hundred thousand and he get us a gang of dope. But they the ones makin' the money."

Tiny Vamp isn't so sure about that. "Yeah, but my big homie, Ghost, he go to Arkansas and he just rotate dope. See, he take dope to Arkansas, back and forth, back and forth. He do about ten keys that way, make a nice profit off it."

G-Roc dismisses the statement with a languid gesture. "Whatever it is, it probably ain't enough. He probably gettin' cheated." Now he turns to look at me. "Sounds like a fucked-up world, don't it? But, see, if you made everything good, everybody happy, everything perfect, then the world would be too hard. 'Cause then you wouldn't know what it feels like to have downs, to be at the bottom. If you always at the top, if everything always goin' your way, then if somethin' happen that's gonna hurt you, you wouldn't know how to take it. Lemme say it like this: the world is like it *should* be. If this country got bad times, everybody around the world would have bad times, but things don't get too bad unless we have a war and a nuclear bomb happen. Then we'll have drought and starvation for a coupla years. Maybe more than a couple. But pretty soon things gonna be like the Watts riots when every-thing burn down. It all got built back up. Now you see Watts, it's not all clean, not all good, but it's better than it was before it got burnt down."

There is a brief discussion about Martin Luther King. Both kids agree that he was "cool," but beyond that impression

34

they do not seem to have any knowledge of the man or of his accomplishments. G-Roc does say, however, that there's a picture of him in the dining room of his parents' house. I ask them about Malcolm X, have they heard of him? Tiny Vamp shakes his head. G-Roc admits, "I don't even know who that is." He *has* heard something about the Black Panthers, though. "Wasn't that in Detroit or something? Wasn't they all about beatin' people up to get some action? I'm down for that."

But both boys know about Raymond Washington. Washington—dead for almost ten years, the victim of a shotgun blast—was one of the cofounders of the Crips. These two kids revere his memory because, as G-Roc states, "He really knew what it meant, Crippin'. It ain't like it was, though, and I doubt if it ever comes back. See, at first, when the gangs first come out, there was only Crips, wasn't no Bloods yet, not really. And we was at a party and it was everybody . . . Hoovers, Sixties, everybody. Wasn't no beefs yet. Well, like I said, we had a party, and everybody was playin' that song, 'Knee Deep'? and my homeboy, Joker—he in the pen now for killin' a Sixty—he hollered out our 'hood, and they hollered out they 'hood. Everybody was drunk, so he hollered out our 'hood again, and somebody dis'ed. And, you know, he went like, *'What?!'* And they say it again, and everybody start in fightin'. This was a *while* back, when they first come out, when gangs first started havin' beefs."

Tiny Vamp has been listening with avid interest. "Was you there?"

G-Roc looks at him with undisguised contempt. "Hell, no, I wasn't there. What I look like? That's how my big homeboys was tellin' me about it." He turns to look at me. "It's like when you get in a gang they gotta let you know everything, get you all filled in." His attention refocuses on Tiny Vamp. "You know what I wish, man? I wish . . . I feel *all* the Crips oughta have a big, humongous meeting. Every Crip in the world. Just a bigass meeting and say, 'You know, man—we gotta stop trippin' on each other.' "

"Ye-eeeeeeh. Then we could probably be more powerful."

"Probably?!" The hiss explodes out of his mouth. "We be *way* more powerful." He shakes his head in slow motion; it is an awe-filled gesture. "Crips, man—*deep!* [20] There's a gang of Crips. There's Crips I ain't even heard of. There's Crips that not even black! There was one in here—he was a Samoan Crip!"

"And there's that kid over at Miller."

"Ye-eeeeeeh. Shit, he a *white* Crip. He cool, too; he down. And he a little, biddy dude. There's some oriental Crips in here, too. One of 'em just left here—they down, too." He pulls in a deep breath then sighs it out slowly, puffing out both cheeks.

"You know, I trust all Crips. Until they trip." [21]

[20] high in membership numbers
[21] get out of line, make mistakes

2 | South Central

He is seventeen years old, and he is homeless. I met him through one of his homeboys on whose couch he has been sleeping for the past week. This is how he lives, from couch to couch, or in a sleeping bag, or in the back seat of a parked car. A couple of days in one place, maybe two weeks in another. He does not remember the last time he went to school, and he does not know how to read or write. He is as close to invisibility as it is possible to be.

The reason he's talking is because his friend has vouched for me. We are in my car because I have to run some errands, and I want to save time, so I have decided to take this kid— Faro—along. He sits next to me, looking out the window. His mouth is slightly open, and I can see that his teeth are small and straight. The tip of his tongue is almost, but not quite, the exact shade of raspberry sherbet. His hair has been sectioned into a myriad of tiny braids, each with a blue rubber band at the tip. He is wearing shabby sweats and busted-down Nike high-tops. He is very thin; the bones of his wrists stick knobbily out of the elastic cuffs of his hooded jacket, which is at least two sizes too small for him.

We ride in silence for a while, and then I ask him about his family. It takes him a long time to answer, and when he does, his voice is soft, controlled.

"My mother, she died from a drug overdose. I got a grandmother, but she gonna go the same way—she just wanderin' the streets day and night, lookin' for handouts so she can fix herself a pipe. My brother got killed in a holdup three years ago."

I ask which end of the gun his brother was at, and Faro looks at me in surprise. It is the first time we have made any kind of eye contact. He has sixty-year-old eyes set down in that seventeen-year-old face. Graveyard eyes.

"Most people think he was holdin' the gun." He almost smiles; it is a pained expression. "He wasn't but eight years old. He was lookin' at comic books in a 7-Eleven and some dude come in to rob the place." He turns away to look out the window. "The homies give him a nice funeral. I used to have a picture of him, laid out, in my scrapbook. It got lost."

He continues to look out the window. We are moving through an intersection where the streets are torn and gaping with road work. A pneumatic drill is blasting, and Faro winces a little at the sound. As we come to a stoplight a Mustang convertible pulls up on Faro's side of the car. The driver and the guy in the passenger seat are both young, both black. Their haircuts, called "fades," are highly styled, carefully constructed flattops with geometric designs etched into the closely shaven sides.

"See them two dudes?" Faro's voice, unaccountably, has dropped to a whisper. I nod my head.

"I'm gonna look crazy at 'em. You watch what they do." He turns away from me, and I lean forward over the wheel so that I can watch the faces on the two guys. The driver, sensing that someone is looking at him, glances over at my car. His eyes connect with Faro's, widen for an instant. Then he breaks the contact, looks down, looks away. And there is no mistaking what I saw there in his eyes: it was fear. Whatever he saw in Faro's face, he wasn't about to mess with it.

Faro giggles and turns back toward me. He looks the same as he did before to me: a skinny, slightly goofy-looking kid. The light changes and the Mustang speeds away, turning right at the next corner. I ask Faro to "look crazy" for me. He simply narrows his eyes. That's all. He narrows his eyes, and he looks straight at me and everything about his face shifts and changes, as if by some trick of time-lapse photography. It becomes a nightmare face, and it is a scary thing to see. It tells you that if you return his stare, if you challenge this kid, you'd better be ready to stand your ground. His look tells you that he doesn't care about anything, not your life and not his.

I ask Faro what would have happened if the guy had looked crazy back.

"Then we woulda got into it."

"With me sitting here next to you? Are you kidding?" I can hear an edge of shrillness in my voice.

He laughs softly. "Never woulda happened. That was just some damn preppy out on his lunch hour."

But if he *had* returned the challenge. What then?

"Then I woulda killed him."

My eyes slide over his skinny silhouette. No way can he be hiding a weapon under that sweatsuit. He smiles slyly and pats the top of his right shoe. I peer down and there, unbelievably, is the glint of metal. I look up at Faro's face, and without knowing why, I'm shocked. I feel as if he has betrayed me, and it makes me angry.

"What you expect? This ain't no game." He is disgusted.

"You played a game with that guy, though, didn't you? That whole thing was a game."

"And what kinda game *you* playin', lady? You come on down here, and you ask a whole lotta questions, and then when it get too real fo' you, you start in hollerin' like somebody dis'ed you." Cold, icy anger in his voice. His eyes are narrowed again; this time it's for real. I want to meet the challenge, I want to defend myself, but what he's saying is true. I got mad when it got too real.

"You're right, you know."

"Ye-eeeeh."

"I get scared. And then I guess I get mad."

"Be like that with me sometime, too." We are both beginning to relax again.

"So I can ask questions again."

"Ye-eeeeh."

We pass a group of little kids, five- and six-year-olds, walking in line behind their teacher. As they get to the corner, the teacher raises both arms in readiness to cross the street, signaling for the children to do the same. All of them lift their arms high over their heads, like holdup victims, following the teacher to the other side.

"I watch out for the little kids in my neighborhood. So gangs who we don't get along with"—he names several sets, both Bloods and Crips—"don't come in and shoot 'em up. All them I just named, they come in and shoot us up, then we catch one of 'em slippin'[1] and it's all over for them."

He is looking at the children as he talks. His voice is soft, but somehow it is not calm.

"Like there was this fool, this enemy nigger from our worst enemy set, and he was with his wife and his baby. They was walkin' down there near Vermont, where he had no business bein'. He was slippin' bad and we caught him. We was in a car, all homies, and I was like, 'Let's pop this dumb nigger,

[1] being careless; not watching your back

42

let's empty the whole clip in him.' " Faro turns to look at me, as if he wants to make sure I understand what he is saying. "We had an AK—two-barrel banana clips, two sides—and I just . . ." He hesitates only for an instant. "I just wanted to make him pay."

Careful to keep my voice as soft as his, I ask him what it was he wanted the guy to pay for.

"For all our dead homeboys. For bein' our enemy. For slippin' so bad." He is warming to his subject, his voice is coming alive now. "You gotta understand—enemy got to pay just for bein' alive." He is quiet for a moment, then he gives a little hitch of his shoulders, like a prizefighter, and he goes on. He is animated now, reliving the event for me. "I was like 'fuck it, Cuz—I'm gonna strap this shit to the seat and I'm just gonna *work* it.' " He twists around to face the passenger door and mimes the action of holding and aiming an AK-47 rifle. "So I strapped it to the seat, like this, and we circled around and pulled up on this nigger from two blocks away, crept up on him slow like, and I just gave it to him." Faro begins to jerk and buck there in his seat as the imaginary weapon in his hands fires automatically. *"Pah-pah-pah-pah-pah-pah-pah!* You know, just let him have it. Just emptied the whole . . ." He is wholly caught up in his recollection, inflamed with it, drunk with it. "I lit his ass *up!* I killed him—shot his baby in the leg—crippled his wife!" He is facing me again, his eyes fixed on some point just to the left of mine. "She in a wheelchair now, I heard, wearin' a voicebox, 'cause one of the bullets caught her in the throat." Then, in afterthought, "The baby okay."

We are silent for a moment; when Faro speaks again his voice is a fusion of bad feelings: despair, remorse, a deep, biting resentment. "I just lit his whole family up and . . ." He sucks in air, holds it a couple of seconds, puffs it out. "It was like, damn, Cuz—I killed him, that was my mission, but still—his whole family." He shakes his head several times, as if he cannot will himself to believe his own story. Then he places the tip of one index finger on the glass next to him and taps it in a nervous, rhythmic beat. "That's a crazy world out there, and we livin' in it."

"Dying in it, too."

The finger stops tapping.

"If you die, you die. Most gangbangers don't have nothin' to live for no more, anyway. That why some of 'em be gangbangin'."

He seems to sense what it is that I'm thinking.

"I ain't just talkin' 'bout myself, either. I'm talkin' for a lotta gangbangers. They mothers smokin' dope. Or somebody shot somebody else's mother, and that person figure if they gangbang they got a chance to get 'em back." He is silent again for a beat or two. Then, "People don't have nothin' to live for if they mother dead, they brother dead, they sister dead. What else they got to live for? If people in yo' family is just dyin', if the person you love the most, the person who love *you* the most be dead, then what else *do* you got to live for?"

"Yourself."

It's as if I hadn't spoken; he doesn't even hear me.

"I tell you this—you see enough dyin', then you be ready to die yourself, just so you don't have to see no more of death."

3 Camp Kilpatrick

The two boys are happy to get out of attending classes this morning. They are not at all sure what this visit with me is about, but anything beats going to school.

Bopete is a fourteen-year-old Blood from the Jungle, in Baldwin Hills. He was sent to camp a few months ago for a strong-arm robbery he committed at thirteen when he held up a jewelry store with a Mac 11 automatic pistol. He has been active in his set for four years.

Sidewinder is also fourteen, a member of one of the largest Crip sets. He is here for participating in a drive-by shooting in which another Crip was killed. Some of Sidewinder's homeboys were also convicted of the shooting, but he is the only one who was placed in this camp; the others were sent to different detention facilities. Sidewinder's weapons in the crime were "a 'gauge and a deuce-five automatic." He claims to have been jumped into his set at the age of eight.

Before we begin to talk, Sidewinder has a question for me: "Are you gonna take us outta here and drive us to our worst enemies' 'hood and drop us off there?" I assure him that we're not going anywhere, that we are only going to talk. I tell both boys that nothing said in this room will go on their records and that their real names will not be used.

They drop into chairs facing me. Sidewinder is a nice enough looking kid, slender with smooth, lightly muscled arms and deep dimples on either side of his mouth. But there is a feel of starved intensity about him; he looks as if he might grind his teeth in his sleep. Bopete has a round, open face, and he is shorter than Sidewinder, and more compact. He is like a small, strong pony. These two met here at camp and have become guarded friends in spite of the deadly rivalry between the Crips and the Bloods. Sidewinder figures this is "because we don't fight too much in here. We talk more in here, like we be brothers. Try to make good outta bad. See, we sit around, crack jokes with each other in here, but on the outs, I ain't gonna fuck with him. Like, see him walkin' down the street—" he makes a gesture as if he were waving someone away, "—go on with his business." Sidewinder's voice is immature but, somehow, not young.

Bopete nods his head. "Ye-eeeeeh. It's like, if I meet a Crip in jail, and we get along, that's cool. Then, if I run into him on the outs, I'm lookin' forward to him not messin' with me. So, if I happen to be in his 'hood, visitin', say, my gramma, and he standin' there with his homies—well, they probably say, 'Get him,' but if we got respect goin' back and forth, then I think we can still be cool when we get out."

Sidewinder nods his head slowly. Bopete echoes the gesture, then he speaks again. "Sometimes I think about not goin' back to bangin' when I get outta here. I play in sports a lot here, and I . . .."

Sidewinder's laugh interrupts. "Sound like a regular ol' teenager, don't he? I sound like that, too, after the drive-by. I got shot twice in the leg, 'cause they was shootin' at the car, and when that happen I didn't want to 'bang no more, either.

48

Makin' promises to God, all like that. But when it heal up . . ."
He shrugs, then he grins at Bopete. "You gonna feel the same,
once you get back on the outs." He is silent for a moment;
maybe he's thinking about a freedom he won't taste for a while.
Then, "I tell you somethin'—I don't feel connected to any
other kids in this city or in this country or in this world. I only
feel comfortable in my 'hood. That's the only thing I'm connected to, that's my family. One big family—that's about
it."

"In my 'hood, in the Jungle, it ain't like a gang. It's more
like a nation, everybody all together as one. Other kids, as long
as they ain't my enemies, I can be cool with 'em." Bopete lapses
into silence. "I'll tell you, though—if I didn't have no worst
enemy to fight with, I'd probably find somebody."

"Ye-eeeeeeh." Sidewinder picks it up. "*I'd* find somebody. 'Cause if they ain't nobody to fight, it ain't no gangs. It
ain't no life. I don't know . . . it ain't no . . ."

"It ain't no fun."

"Yeah! Ain't no fun just sittin' there. Anybody can just sit
around, just drink, smoke a little Thai. But that ain't fun like
shootin' guns and stabbin' people. *That's* fun. Like, see . . .
people you kill . . ." He stops, starts again. "Okay, look, I'm
so high"—Sidewinder holds up his hand to indicate his height
when he is standing—"and killin' somebody, that make me
higher. 'Cause you got enough heart to kill somebody, then,
like you got the heart to destroy. Make you tall."

"Kinda pumps you up."

Sidewinder likes that image. "Yeah. Pump, like. You gets
fired up, like you can beat anybody up then."

"Even somebody stronger than you, or with a bigger gun
or a sharper knife. You just try your hardest to bring 'em
down."

Suddenly Sidewinder is quite serious. "Sometimes you get
beat up in your own 'hood. 'Cause the O.G.'s, they get drunk

and they look at you and, like, 'Let's see if this little nigger down,' and bam!! You have to head up with 'em. That happen to me all the time, 'cause I hang around with my O.G. homies at night. And that's when they be drinkin'. And you can't cry or nothin', 'cause then you busted, then they dis' you—say, 'Go on, coward, get the fuck outta here.'"

Bopete looks at him, and what might be a trace of sympathy appears in his eyes. Sidewinder sees it, too, so he manages a weak laugh, and after a beat or two Bopete joins in, and now both kids are laughing at the very notion of being made to cry because your O.G. homies beat you up for simply being there.

Sidewinder sees himself as an O.G. "in five or ten years." Bopete's dream—for the moment—is "to grow up and play football, have a nice car, a nice lady, and a baby."

Sidewinder shakes his head. "I want a lady and a car. I'd like to go places, like different states and visit, like . . . waterfalls, see somethin', meet people. I don't want no baby, though. If I had a kid, years from now, I would kill him myself before I'd let another gang kill him. I'd kill him before I'd let him suffer so much, bein' shot by another gang. I'd kill him because I love him so much."

If Bopete is surprised by this sentiment, it doesn't show. "I followed in my father's footsteps—except he was a Crip. I forget where. He twenty-nine now, been in jail for about ten years."

"My father at home—he a cop." Now Bopete is surprised. Sidewinder's features arrange themselves into a pattern of disdain. "I don't talk about stuff with him, though. I don't talk to him, period. And I sure don't want to be like him when I grow up. I wanna be like Bruce Lee—get to be a master in karate, learn how to control my temper. Bruce Lee had a lotta control, lotta power. I'm tryin' to meditate so I can control my temper. If you can't do that, you got no power at all."

Bopete nods solemnly. "When I'm with my homeboys I

feel powerful. It's like I can do anything because they got my back. I'm covered, no matter what. That make *me* feel powerful. Even though I might get mad at 'em sometimes, even if they get rank with me. I can take what they say 'cause I know they care about me. Even when they get drunk and act like fools, even when they fool around with aiming their guns at you and stuff."

"Yeah. Like they play Russian roulette. Last time I tried to do it, my homeboy, Sniper, he was drunk and he went like this—" Sidewinder points his index finger at his temple and clicks his tongue to make the sound of a hammer hitting an empty chamber. "He was serious. But it didn't do nothin', so then he handed the gun to me and I went like this"—he points at his temple again but then the finger moves upward, aiming at the ceiling—"and it went *pow!!* It was a .38 revolver. If I had did it I'd been dead!" His voice is filled with wonder. "I thought about doin' it, you know, but then at the last second, just before I pulled the trigger, I thought, 'Hell, fuck it.' "

There is a sound of furious barking from across the camp grounds. Bopete grips the arms of his chair, pushing himself up so that he can peer out of the window. He stays like that for a moment, then lowers himself back to a sitting position. "It's nothin', just the dog barkin' at somethin'—coyote, maybe." Then he goes back to the subject. "This one time, my homeboy, Klipper, he made me mad. He was seventeen, I was thirteen and he was drunk, right? And he kept playin' me—you know, teasin' me. I had a gun in the bushes, so I said, 'Maybe you stop playin' me if I shoot you.' He said, 'I don't think you will do that.' And he kept on playin' me, so I got the gun, right? And I clicked it back and he kept closin' in on me and *bam!!* I shot it off right next to his ear, and he was like all . . ." Bopete sticks out his tongue, rolls his eyes, shudders with exaggerated jerks. Then he laughs. "It was funny, him

51

actin' like that, 'cause I put in work[1] with him, and when he out there—whew—he fearless."

"Yeah, but when you out there and if you buzzed,[2] then you feel like you cannot die."

"Yeah, like when somethin' happen and an enemy roll by, you don't think about dyin'—or gettin' killed through it . . ."

"All you be thinkin' is kill the motherfucker!" In their eagerness to talk both boys seem to have lost sight of the fact that out on the streets they are each other's prey.

"It's like you both sayin', 'Kill me! Kill me! I don't care!' And the next day, you try to tell your homies what happened, and *damn!*" Bopete laughs. It's a high, childish sound and it reminds me how young he is.

"But then, once you shoot 'em, and once the police come, you think about it and you be, like, all nervous and everything. After you done did it, you like, 'ooooooh, man!,' shakin' and all paranoid and nervous, you know? But *while* you doin' it . . . it's like"—he giggles and shrugs—"it ain't no thing. Don't make a difference even if it's a kid like you. While you shootin' 'em, it don't make no difference." Sidewinder is silent for a beat or two. The light inside the small room has suddenly gone quite dark; a soft rumble of thunder sounds from the distance. "I did feel a little bad when I did that drive-by. 'Cause I mighta hit somebody's mama, or somethin'." His voice has gone pious; it is the first noticeably untrue statement that he has made.

"Mighta hit the whole family." Now it is Bopete's turn to take a moment to think. "Like, here at camp, if I steal from somebody—like they skin lotion or hair grease, or whatever they got for personals—then somebody steal from me. Like . . .

[1]rob, shoot, kill, any activity that is dangerous. Also called "getting busy."
[2]high, or drunk

52

what go around, come around. And some stuff come around faster than others."

Sidewinder shakes his head. He doesn't believe that at all.

Bopete goes on. "I seen that stuff happen lots. I watched people take somebody off they job and then they get *their* job taken away from them. I seen people hurt somebody bad and then they get hurt—or worse. I'm just young but I be sittin' there watchin' everything, and I say, one day everything catch up to you. Just watch. But then I say, 'Who cares?' But the truth is, I ain't prepared for it. I ain't prepared to die."

Sidewinder is busy with his thumbnail, worrying the skin around the cuticle. His legs are wrapped around the legs of the chair so that his knees are nearly touching; his toes point inward toward each other, and his feet are jiggling nervously. His voice, when he speaks, is a murmur, as if the words were shameful. "I think about that a lot. 'Cause I think to myself, 'When I die, I ain't gonna see nobody no more.' Make me scared."

It's as though Sidewinder hasn't spoken at all; Bopete simply continues his thought. "But when I'm with my home-boys, I don't think about dyin', never at all. Only when I get alone."

And Sidewinder is talking to himself, too. "You only got one life to live, I know that. Ain't like a cat, got nine lives, or whatever."

Now both boys are quiet. They look at each other for a long, long moment, and private images of death tangle in the air between them.

It has begun to rain now, big drops plopping on the roof. The light outside is nearly purple. Bopete breaks the silence. "When you alone by yourself, say, after y'all get to doin' some-thin', that's when you start . . ." He looks at me, squinching up his face as he searches for the right example. "Say, like he"—indicating Sidewinder with a sideways nod of his head—

"just shot somebody, and the next day y'all by yourself, walkin' down the street and you go, like, 'I wonder if they gonna get *me* now.' " He grins to himself. "And you become scared when you the one *doin'* the shootin', too, 'cause then you go outside that night and . . ." He catches Sidewinder's eye and both of them collapse into giggles, caught up in the delight of complete mutual understanding. Bopete stops laughing first. "It's pretty scary, all right. You jump guys, they jump you back. Pull the earrings out yo' ear, beat on you—anything. And you do it back."

"We do it just for the hell of it."

"Take-back stuff. You know, like, 'Let's go on a mission tonight, let's do somethin', anything.' So you walk down the street . . ."

". . . and just hit 'em, *bam!* From out the pocket,[3] from anything." Sidewinder pauses; he wants to be clearly understood. "Not women, so much—unless they be cluckheads."[4] He purses his lips and shakes his head vehemently. "Cluckheads just be wanderin' around, looking for more dope to smoke, anyway. Ain't hardly human no more." Now his thought changes and he grins, ruefully. "You be walkin' down the street and, like, one outta ten—depend on how many you hangin' with—one of 'em got to fuck up, huh? One of 'em got to talk shit to somebody. And it always"—he points at Bopete and himself in a fast, circular motion—"be the little motherfuckers like us. Always be the little dudes. Like tryin' to throw bottles at cars and stuff. And then you runnin' through the 'hood with some guy chasin' you, yellin', 'What you do to my motherfuckin' car?!' And then the O.G.'s get mad at *him* and jump on him, beat him up, jack him and *we* just up there

[3] with a gun
[4] crack addicts

kickin'."[5] He shakes his head at the wonder of it all.

Bopete smiles thinly. "Our *own* O.G. homeboys can beat up on us, see, but if *another* O.G. from some other set come around, and *he* beat on you, they like, 'Hey, man, you about twenty-six, and this little motherfucker only about thirteen, fourteen—beat up on somebody your own size.' If somebody big be beatin' on you, they *will* jump in."

Sidewinder's eyes focus on something on the other side of the room. "Or they'll sit there and watch."

Bopete looks at him, and there is the sense of a missed beat before he speaks again. "You know what makes me feel sad?" He doesn't wait for answer. "To see people jacked up in they car. It's *their* car, they bought it with they own money. I don't see why they need to get jacked. 'Specially if it's a old lady."

Sidewinder is back with us now. "I hear that. If I'm with a bunch of T.G.'s[6] and they want to jack some old lady, I say, 'Fuck that, man—go for somebody else, like a man or somethin'.'" He is warming to his subject, improvising. "I say, 'It probably be hard for her to feed herself right now, and we got parents and they can feed us. We just *tryin'* to be greedy when we jack people and that's all they have.'" This has been mostly for my benefit; now he turns his attention back to Bopete. "Like a bum we jacked? Took everything he had. Took everything out of his pockets, took his marketbasket with all his stuff in it. Jacked him up with a knife and took all he *had*, man. Shit . . ." Sidewinder slumps in his chair and for that instant he appears to have wizened, to have somehow shrunk, until I can see in him, briefly, an old man. "I went back over there later, gave him some of the money I done stacked up. Dope money." He is silent for a couple of

[5]relaxing, "chillin'"
[6]Tiny Gangsters: younger gang members

55

seconds. "He was a brother, too. I remember, he said, 'Thanks, son.'"

"In the Jungle when some little fools be actin' stupid, bustin' out windows and jackin' people, our O.G.'s face 'em off and take the money back." Bopete stops talking for a moment, like someone who has forgotten what he was going to say next. "Well, like *I* was doin' the same thing, stealin' cars—or *anything*, and they'd sock me in the chest, tell me, 'Don't mess around—we don't need the police howlin' as it is.'"

Sidewinder leans back in his chair. He's frowning a little, the way a parent might when he's talking about the problems he suffers with an unruly child. "Little motherfuckers make the police hot over where I stay, too. Little kids, about that big"— he holds his hand out to approximate the height of a six- or seven-year-old—"be makin' the police *hot!* Throwin' rocks at cars, hasslin' people, stuff like that—and these kids ain't been courted in yet, even, but they claim the 'hood. And they nothin' but *little* people."

The rain has stopped, and we go outside for some air. The aroma of fresh, wet earth is wonderful. As we walk toward the row of picnic tables, the conversation turns to the subject of anger. Both boys seem to want to talk about that, and Sidewinder goes first, but his response comes a little too quickly, as if these are words that he has spoken before, for effect.

"When I get mad I take it out on other people. I kill 'em."

Bopete starts to say something, changes his mind, and the three of us walk along quietly until we reach the tables and benches. The two boys sit down next to each other; I take a seat opposite them. I notice that Sidewinder is squinting his eyes as he peers at something across the grounds and it occurs to me that he probably needs glasses. His attention is brought back as Bopete begins to talk. "When I get really angry it's like I don't care about nobody. I just want to get my anger *out.* Fight somebody, do something to get it off my mind. Here,

I just sock the wall—can't hit nobody here 'cause you get in trouble, go in the box, lose your go-home date. At home—on the outs—when I get mad I leave the house, and I don't come back for a while. I go somewhere and get in some trouble. Like, the first thing I look for is my gun. Then I go out and just hold it in my hand—I don't pull it out of my pocket or nothin', I just hold it—"

"Shoot it, man," Sidewinder whispers. Bopete doesn't even notice.

"—and I walk up and down the street. Maybe I go and jack somebody or somethin'. Might just see somebody in an alley and go, 'bah-bah-bah-bah-bah' "—he makes the sound of a gun firing. "I might not shoot *at* 'em. Maybe I just aim their way. But when I'm mad I'm liable to shoot at anybody." He laughs softly. "Just for the fun of it."

"I hear that. But here, if *I* gets mad, it seem like I'm happy. I get hyper, and I start baggin'—talkin' about somebody, everybody."

Bopete nods vigorously, grinning broadly. "Like, 'you so ugly!' or 'you think *I'm* ugly?' This and that."

"Just act stupid. But it make me feel good. *Very* good. On the outs—I don't know." He thinks about it for a few seconds. "I get mad if somebody try to steal my customers. Like—you can't sell dope around O.G.'s 'cause they try to take all the customers. I started off workin' for an O.G., but then I branched off on my own. See, at first, when I was workin' for a roller, I thought a hundred dollars was a lot of money, but then I came up and came up and came up. Kept buyin' more dope, like—if you get twenty rocks of crack, see, you sell that, go get a forty. Or you can sell weed cookies. Or popcorn with dope in it—mixed in with the butter. People love to get high off stuff they can eat. Like a *big* cookie can have a gang of weed in it—like a kilo of weed."

I ask how this can be possible. That would have to be a

tremendously big cookie. Bopete backs up Sidewinder's statement. "He tellin' the truth. We call them big cookies Boodas—you mix it up, put it in the oven and cook it. Get you *high!*"

Sidewinder snaps an impatient glance at Bopete; he is eager to get back to the story of his rise as a dope dealer. "Anyway, like I was sayin', you get you a twenty, right? You go sell that, then go get a twenty double-up—that's forty pieces. And that's how you come up." He nods smugly. "But I don't smoke it."

Bopete looks to his right, looks to his left, then he looks past Sidewinder's head, as if there were other people sitting there with us. "I don't even come *close* to smokin' *co* caine. I just sell it." He looks at Sidewinder. "Who you sell to?"

"Sell it to anybody who ask, to tell the truth. *Anybody.* I look at the eyes first, before I sell to them—you can tell if it's a cop or not from the eyes. If they be smokin', they eyes get all red, like Rudolph Red, and I say, 'What you need?' If his eyes are white, he's a cop."

Bopete gives a small shrug; he doesn't agree or disagree with Sidewinder's theory. "This is how *I* do it: say if a lady come walkin' up to me, ask what I got, I say, 'I got *everything* you need.' But I don't say nothin' else to her—I watch her around, keep my eye on her, see who she is and how she is before I sell her anything."

"In my 'hood when a car go by, you go like this," Sidewinder holds up one hand, like a student with the right answer. "They go, 'Yo! Yo!' and they stop. And you only stay *by* the car, you don't go in *front* of the car, and you for sure don't go *in* the . . ."

"Yeah!"

". . . car, 'cause they might blow your head off, man. Somebody could yell, 'Yo! Yo!' and it could be your worst enemy—you go in the car and *boom!* You dead right then. You gotta stand back and, like, 'Where y'all from?' He lowers his voice so that he will sound older, say eighteen. " 'We ain't from nowhere, man, we just want a little Yay-o.' " Back to his own voice: " 'How much y'all need?' 'We got a twenty here.' 'Okay, throw it.' And they drop the money down in the street—just drop it down and it's time to go 'round the corner. Dope be right there, hid. Maybe a hundred rocks. And when I get finished sellin' those I go in the house, get some more. I used to sell in Bakersfield—two O.G. homeboys and a couple of us T.G.'s would go up there, get us a motel room that was right by a trailer park. We give some people who was livin' there in the park ten bucks each for a five-hour watch, lookin' out for the police for us. Then, afterward, we give 'em some smoke. That's all they was workin' for anyway, them little biddy rocks we give 'em." He makes a contemptuous sound, reminiscent of G-Roc's hiss. "Cluckheads." He turns his whole body to look seriously at the kid sitting next to him. "How would you feel if a member or your family was doin' that shit?"

Bopete narrows his eyes and shakes his head. "Tell the truth, if my family was on drugs, it'd be just like they was deceased. And I wouldn't care if I lived or died, either. I wouldn't care about nothin'. Might even kill 'em myself, put 'em out of they misery."

"Yeah, that's what I'd do, I think. It'd be hard to kill somebody you love, though." Sidewinder looks hard at me. "See, when you shoot someone—like with a .45 automatic, one that goes, pow-pow-pow, that like hits someone ten times in the same place? Like that—br-r-r-r-r-t—in the same place? Make a big hole."

"It look nasty, too. Look real nasty."

"Yeah. You wouldn't want to kill somebody you knew like that. Take they brain right out."

"Afterward, you might feel like you want to throw up.

Like . . . 'Hey, *I* did this?' " Bopete delivers a half-baked little snort of a laugh. He may be only half-kidding, both of them may only be trying to get a rise, a shudder, a scream from me, but I am sure about one thing—there is a kernel of terrible truth in this.

"Just sittin' there, watchin' somebody's brains come out. If you shoot 'em in the head, 'specially with a 'gauge, whole halftheheadcomesoff.Iseenthat.Ididn't*do* it, it was . . . like I was over there when . . ." Tiny Web's voice trails away.

Sidewinder picks up the slack. "Like a hollow point. They blow up *in* your head."

"Yeah." Bopete is suddenly subdued.

"And then comin' out, it make a big hole, like that"— Sidewinder holds up both hands, thumbs and forefingers placed tip to tip to show the size of an exit wound—"and the brains just come out like water. I didn't do it—I saw it. Looked like oatmeal."

"Hollow point, they got a little plastic thing on the end, filled up with beebees. You get 'em at any sportin' goods store."

Sidewinder explains further: "They against the law, and they real expensive. But if you got the money . . ." He shrugs eloquently.

"They shoot you like this—blow up in yo' head, *boom!*"

Sidewinder reaches over and pokes Bopete in the shoulder. "Hey, remember that movie we saw on TV? Where the guy shot the lamppost and made a big ole hole? Well, I wanna get me one of them."

"I don't remember what kinda bullets they was. The long kind."

"Yeah, and fat."

Bopete snaps his fingers, grinning hard all over his face. "Oh, wait! I got it—thirty-thirty! Went *boom!* Man, them booms made you happy. *Boom! Boom!*" He laughs softly, thinking about it, then his face goes serious. "It's funny, you never think about anything like that happenin' to you, though. Like gettin' *your* head shot off."

"Never think about a lotta things 'til they happen. Like one day this Crip I didn't know was talkin' to my sister and I asked him (the way Sidewinder pronounces it, it sounds like 'axed'), 'Where y'all from?' And when he tell me what set he in, I realize that he's one of my worst enemies. But all I said was, 'Righteous, righteous.' Then I went behind my fence and I ran all along the Boulevard to get three of my homeboys. And we went back over there and caught him. And when we beatin' him up, one of my homies say, 'I gotta idea, Cuz,' and I say, 'What's that, loc?'[7] and he say, 'Drag him with a rope.' So we put him in the car and went over to a field and put a rope over that thing you hook a trailer on with. Then we tied 'Homes'[8] on it and drag him in the field. He got skinned up all bad, tore his scalp half off. Got all dirt and like gravel and stuff stuck in the blood. Then we put him back in the car and drove him over to where one of the homies had two pit bulls in the back yard, and we threw him in there with them. Man, they chewed him up—big ole chunks of meat comin' off his arms and legs, blood pourin' out, and Homes just screamin' and cryin' for us to take him on outta there. At first, you know, when we grabbed him, he tried to act tough, but when it started to hurt—whew—he hollered loud. After we let him out the yard we made him kneel down and say stuff like, 'I'll suck your dicks,' and 'fuck my dead homeboys,' stuff like that. Man, we almost killed him. Then we just dropped him in the riverbed, until somebody find him or he climb out. Whatever." Bopete has been sitting quietly, not saying anything, not giving much of anything away. He has simply listened politely, with an expression of disbelief building on his face. But now he has to talk. "Man, that's

---

[7]generic gang term, short for "loco." Bloods spell it with a *"K"*: lok.
[8]variation of "homeboy"

61

crazy. I tell you true, we never did *nothin'* like that. That's—whew—that be crazy."

Sidewinder looks at Bopete for a moment, and there is a little glint of anger just behind his eyes. Then, surprisingly, he smiles slyly. "What about puttin' a gun, like a 'gauge, in they mouth? I *know* y'all did that. Put a 'gauge in somebody's mouth and *boom!*"

Bopete shakes his head vigorously. "I never did nothin' like that, though. I mean, I was right there when somebody did that, but I wasn't close to 'em . . ." He is looking at me now. "That shit crazy. I didn't *do* it, I saw it happen. His head just come out his neck—boom! Then throw the body in the riverbed." There's no swaggering talk of high-caliber bullets now; he's no longer boasting. He's just a little kid who is afraid that he has gone too far.

Sidewinder's voice is quieter, too. "See, the missions I'm talkin' about, we just grab 'em, throw 'em in the trunk of the car and take 'em out and torture 'em. They always say what we want 'em to in the long run. They *will* even say 'Fuck my dead homeboys' if we hurt 'em enough. But then, when we tired of lookin' at 'em, we let 'em go. Nobody got killed yet. Almost dead, but we let 'em go before they dead." He is quiet for a beat, thinking, then he adds one last thought to the subject. "And that enemy Crip? The one we dragged under the car? Well, his homeboy killed my homeboy—he was probably there when that happened. He *deserved* what he got."

■　　■　　■

"I moved into the neighborhood and started to hang around black people every day. And then one day I went to take out the trash, and they put me on the 'hood. Three guys jumped me in—I was about twelve and a half years old. I told my mama she just had to accept it."

The boy speaking, in a voice that is just beginning to change, is red-haired and freckled, with that kind of skin you often see on redheads: so pale as to be almost luminous. He looks like a kid on a cereal box; his accent and speech patterns are, however, pure South Central. He speaks African-American gangbanger and he belongs to the Crips. "I'm here at camp 'cause they think I did a burg'—a robbery. I didn't do it; they set it up on me. Some white boys I used to hang 'round with a long time ago, before I moved to my 'hood. They got caught for a burg' they did, and they said I come back and pulled it. That was *bull*shit. I ain't jacked nobody unless they come in my 'hood—that's real. I sell Yay-o, Cavvy—caviar crack—fo' my money, and on a good day I can make like, six, seven hundred dollars. So why I got to pull some burg' in another 'hood?" He gestures with both hands, index fingers jabbing down, thumbs cocked up, like the other kids, the black kids. "Had me a nice little gun—deuce-five—but I threw it away when the pigs come up on me. When I first got put on my 'hood I was puttin' in work every day. I'd go blastin' slobs."

There are four of us sitting at a picnic table under a small covey of shade trees on the Camp Miller side of the grounds. There's this white kid, Diamond, there's a Hispanic kid from an eastside Mexican-American gang. Li'l Bandit, and there's a thirteen-year-old Crip called Baby Sin. Baby Sin is something of a legend here at camp; he has made himself a name for being tough, for being fearless, and for being scrupulously fair. He and Li'l Bandit giggle as Diamond talks about "killing slobs." Another, older boy walks by the table on his way to the dorms and he cracks up the kids even more by calling out, "Tell the truth, now. Don't be lyin', now." That makes Diamond laugh too, but Baby Sin gets serious fast.

"This dude, Diamond, is okay, he down. 'Cause I seen a lotta Bloods in here tryin' to, you know, talk all little shit towards him. But he tell 'em, you know, 'What's up?,'[9] and they won't say nothin' to him after that. They just back off. He down."

Diamond actually blushes at this endorsement. "My homies told me they'd kill me if I wasn't down for my 'hood. They said they'd shoot me."

Does that get said to the black kids?

Baby Sin is quick to answer. "Well, it don't get said to me, 'cause I been in it too long. I didn't really get put on my 'hood—I been in it six, seven years now. I started kickin' with my homies when I was about six years old."

Diamond wants to further explain his position; clearly it is important to him that he make himself understood. "My homies didn't really tell me they was gonna kill me, you know, but I know they'd beat me up bad if I wasn't down for my 'hood. If I punked out, you know, act like a coward and let somebody dis' my 'hood."

Baby Sin breaks up again. "It do kinda make me laugh to hear this dude talkin' like us. 'Cause he ain't from my 'hood, you know? But I got a Mexican (he pronounces it 'Mescan') from my 'hood, look just like him"—he points his thumb at Li'l Bandit—"I don't laugh when he say it, the way *he* [indicating Diamond] say it. We got some Mexicans in our set, we treat 'em just like blacks. And I think positive of him." He points at Diamond again, smiling this time. "Ask him what he wants to do when he get older."

Diamond's features slide into a grin. "Kill off-brands."

Baby Sin and Li'l Bandit giggle softly. Then with the rather solemn air of a teacher of foreign languages, Baby Sin explains things to me "Off-brands, that's slobs—Bloods. They's

---

[9] a generic gang password used as a greeting and/or a challenge

some Crip sets off-brands, too, even though they Crips. They gotta go, too."

Now two other kids join the group at the table. The smaller of the pair seems different than any other boy I have seen today. He is soft where they are hard, timid where they are swaggering. His hands are busy with a small eraser that he keeps turning over and over with his fingertips. The older boy, as if embarrassed to be caught in his company, introduces him as a "wannabe."

The youngster flinches. "I ain't no wannabe! If I'm a wannabe, you one, too!"

The older boy laughs. "Then throw up yo' sign."

The younger kid mutters something under his breath. Everybody's looking at him now and, with a rather surprising show of spirit, he holds his own. "I don't gotta do that." He is close to tears, and it is Baby Sin who steps into the breach. He leans over the table and looks hard at the new arrival.

"You right. You don't gotta do that. You don't wanna 'bang, you shouldn't 'bang, man. You don't have to claim[10] —just, like, be yo'self."

The little kid looks up at him, and I can see that he has no idea how close in age he is to Baby Sin. I can see the desperation in his eyes, and I can hear it in his voice. "That's how it is on my street—ain't nothin' but gangbangin', you can't get out of it. They gonna want you to claim, and they gonna beat you up if you don't."

Baby Sin asks him what set controls his neighborhood. The kid mentions a name, the same Crip set that G-Roc belongs to. Baby Sin nods his head slowly.

"It ain't like that in my 'hood. Nobody can force you to 'bang and it don't make you a punk if you don't. That's how it is where I stay at. *Nobody* can force you to 'bang; that's what

[10]announce your gang affiliation

65

time that is." He turns to the others. "He don't have to feel like less of a man 'cause he don't wanna 'bang."

Now Baby Sin asks the kid—whose name is Jeffy—why he's here at camp. Truancy, the kid tells him. How old is he? Thirteen last month; he knows he's the youngest kid in camp and maybe that's why . . .

The older boy, the kid who walked over with him, rides past his words. "Listen, I see him here tryin' to hang out with G-Roc and them dudes. He tryin' to claim, all right."

Baby Sin answers him. "Then that's just how he'll get in—he don't have to claim." He turns back to look sternly at Jeffy again; the difference between these two boys is startling. "Just keep stayin' with 'em, kickin' with 'em. Keep right on hangin' 'round 'em. You'll be in quick. You don't want that, just keep to yourself."

"I try not to, but every time I turn around, there's Crips. Just like at home; everybody in my apartment house is a 'banger." He's whining now.

Li'l Bandit makes a dismissive gesture. "Some gangs just put anybody on they 'hood, you know. Just to say they deep."

"Maybe I just oughtta move." He is a breath away from crying.

Baby Sin shakes his head impatiently. "Don't be all worryin' about movin'. Just try to get along here." He offers a thin slice of smile to Jeffy. "You okay by me, anyway." He turns toward me again. "Some people be messin' with him here, call him a faggot, call him a crybaby. But like I say, he okay by me, long as he be himself."

At that moment there is the sound of loud voices down by the schoolrooms, and a couple of camp deputies race past the table. Everybody turns to look—Tiny Vamp has gotten into it with another kid, probably the same one he thought "looked crazy" at him in the lunch line. The fight is over almost as soon as it has begun, and even though there is a small crowd

66

of boys pressing in to watch, everyone is looking on in silence. You know that sides have been taken, you know that emotions are running high, but not one of the onlookers is about to get his name on any list. Not one of the kids is ready to pit his loyalties against the power of the deputies' pencils. To do so would mean a trip to "the box" along with the two kids who got in the beef and points lost toward freedom. The box is camp slang for the area that houses the isolation cells. These are a dozen or so single rooms, each with a cot and basin, that face a raised platform where a deputy sits at a desk. The doors to each of these cells are made of reinforced steel with a thick safety-glass window set in at eye-level. School books are allowed in the box, and notebooks and pencils. Meals are brought in from the camp kitchen. Visitors are not allowed. A kid might be sentenced to only a few hours in the box, or he might get as long as three weeks. Tiny Vamp and the boy he got into it with will probably be kept in isolation for a couple of days. As the two youngsters are hustled up the rise of ground toward the isolation block, Tiny Vamp glances over at the table where we are seated. From here it looks as if he is crying. Without bothering to hide the disapproval that clouds his face, Baby Sin ignores him.

"That dude been lookin' to go to the box ever since he done got here—thinks it gonna make him look down." He shakes his head slowly. "Now he cryin' about it where everybody can see. Should've tried to get alone before he cry." He thinks about what it is he just said, and then he laughs, softly and without humor.

"Hell, that's what goin' to the box is all about, ain't it?"

4 South Central

The first time I saw Bianca she was wearing a solid gold revolver around her neck. The gun was about three inches long, perfectly detailed, and it was hanging from a thick golden chain—a Turkish rope. Bianca was fifteen at the time, an accepted homegirl in one of the largest Crip sets. Her gang moniker is Cricket, a nickname given her by her older brother (an O.G. of serious reputation) when she was a baby.

Several months have elapsed by the next time we meet and Bianca's personal style has undergone some changes: she is no longer a painted cat; the golden gun is gone, as are the heavy makeup and talon-like fingernails embellished with diamond chips. Without these distractions it is possible to see what this girl really looks like. She's pretty, with her smooth, dark skin and finely chiseled features. We have arranged to meet at the house where she lives with her mother, her grandmother, and her brother, who has been in County Jail for the past month or so, charged with aggravated assault.

The house is located on a residential block in South L.A.

and it is neatly kept and heavily barred. There are even bars covering the front door. The adjacent house, the one directly next door, looks as if a bomb was exploded in the living room: windows are blown out and heavy streaks of soot cover the exterior walls. (Later, when I ask Bianca about it, she shrugs and says that the people who live there had some trouble with the law.) In the driveway between the two houses the hulk of a car rests on four flat tires. This used to be Bianca's brother's greatest source of pride—a fully restored Chevy Impala, what the homies call a bomber. Now it is covered with a thick layer of grime and a great gash on one side has rusted over.

When I ring the doorbell it is answered almost immediately by Bianca's grandmother, who steps out onto the porch, closing the door firmly behind her. She is a tiny, sweet-looking woman with silver hair skewered into a knot at the nape of her neck. She has been expecting me, she says; Bianca went up to the corner to meet a friend and will be back in a few minutes. She stands on the corner with me, her eyes sweeping up and down the block. When I ask her how Bianca's doing, she presses her lips together tightly, buttonholes them, and shakes her head back and forth.

"She just messin' up with the gangs. Won't go to school at all anymore." We stand quietly for a moment, then she points to a three- or four-unit apartment house on the opposite corner. "See that building? Well, the young man who lived in that lower apartment got shot three nights ago. Nicest, quietest youngster you ever saw, and two boys just went on in there and shot him."

I ask her if the boys were gang members, or, for that matter, if the young man had been in a gang. She shakes her head again. "I just don't know. He was such a nice young man." She stands gazing at the windows of the shooting victim's apartment. "These is terrible times we livin' in. You don't know who comin' in your house to harm you, and you don't know what whoever livin' there with you is goin' to do."

She squints her eyes, peering at two figures walking toward us. "Here come Bianca now." She turns to go back into the house, turns back to smile at me. "It was nice meetin' you." She looks at me for another few seconds. "You be careful, hear?"

There is another kid with Bianca, whom I recognize from the first time I met her; she referred to him then as her brother even though they are not actually related. His name is Baby Track and now, seeing him again, I remember hearing that he had gotten shot a few months ago. He is holding something in both hands, and as they get closer, I see that it's a puppy. He lifts it up to show me.

"I just paid eighty dollars for her, she was the biggest one in the litter. Gonna be a killer dog." This tiny bundle of soft, warm flesh and snuffling, whimpering sounds is a pit bull. Bianca takes it from him, holding it by the nape of the neck; the puppy dangles bonelessly until it is dropped into my arms. Then it snuggles and burrows, searching for the comfort of its mother. Bianca reaches out, plucks a flea from the folds of fur at the puppy's neck, and holds it out to show Baby Track.

"We better get this dog to the doctor, see if it need any kind of medicine. You got some money left to pay him?"

Baby Track pulls some crumpled bills from his pocket. "Ye-eeeeh. Got some left."

They get into my car; Baby Track sits in back with the puppy, crooning softly to it as Bianca directs me to the veterinarian's office. The doctor examines the puppy, prescribes worm medicine and flea powder. Baby Track listens carefully to the instructions and pays out forty dollars for the medication and the first of a series of injections. He's not happy about parting with the money, but he seems intent on doing the best he can for his dog. When the doctor takes a thermometer out of a container of alcohol, Bianca quickly leaves the examination room.

"I ain't watchin' while somebody sticks somethin' up her little booty."

After the doctor has given the puppy her shot, we drive to Baby Track's house. I ask him if his mother knows that he's bringing home a dog. He shakes his head slowly; Bianca laughs. "She gonna wear you out when she finds out you got a present that *she* gonna have to take care of."

"Nuh-*unh!*" Baby Track doesn't agree.

"Uh-*huh!*" Bianca knows better.

Mrs. Macon is not pleased. She is off work today—she has a job in a health food store—so that she can study for her real estate license; there are papers spread out all over the dining room table. A warm, vibrant woman in her late thirties, she acts as unofficial counselor for many of the neighborhood kids. They call her "Mom," as does Bianca, who moves in close to hug her.

"Don't be tryin' to get 'round me with hugs and kisses." She is frowning, but her hand pats the space between Bianca's shoulders with great affection.

"I'm gonna take care of her, Mama." Baby Track holds the puppy up for inspection, the way he did for me. "Look how cute she is. She was the best one of all of 'em. Guy I bought her from said—"

"I ain't interested in what he said. What I'm interested in is who's gonna be the one cleanin' up after this dog." She takes a closer look at the wriggling puppy. "Lord, that's one of them bull dogs. That's a vicious animal, kill you when it grows up."

She turns to look at me. "Did you buy that dog for him?"

I assure her that I had nothing to do with it. She turns her attention back to her son. "That dog stays in *your* room, Christopher. And if it starts in yelpin' and cryin' for you when you out with your friends, I promise you I'm goin' to take it to the shelter." She looks hard at him. "Bringin' a dog into my house without my permission. I don't know who you think you are."

"Aw, Mama . . ." He places the puppy in her arms. "Just hold her for a minute. She sweet."

Mrs. Macon pets the dog's head then hands it back to Baby Track. "Just remember what I told you. Now go find you a box to put it in and some papers to spread out on the floor of your room." He hurries off. "And a bowl of water!"

Bianca holds up the bag of puppy chow the vet gave Baby Track. "This her food."

Mrs. Macon takes the food; she seems resigned to defeat on this issue, and it occurs to me that she came too close to losing this child when he was shot to deny him much now.

As we leave the house she asks Baby Track what he plans on calling the dog.

"I'm gonna call her Cuppy."

"Huh. What kind name is that?"

"Just a name. I like the way it sounds—suits her."

"Well, whatever you gonna call her, just make sure you the one pickin' up after her. And she better not try to bite me, or it's the shelter for sure." She is reading the directions on the puppy chow as she walks back into the house and shuts the door.

We drive over a couple of blocks to see if we can meet up with a friend of Baby Track's, Quacker. I ask how Quacker earned his nickname.

" 'Cause his lips look like a duck's."

As we round a corner four or five blocks away from Baby Track's house, we see a small crowd of people standing around a car that has stopped in the middle of the street. Baby Track leans forward from the back seat.

"Pull over here." And to Bianca, "That's J-Dog's car, ain't it?" She nods her head.

"Somethin's wrong." Baby Track gets out and walks quickly to the other car. He leans in the driver's window, talking to whoever is behind the wheel, presumably J-Dog. Bianca gets out too, and goes up to a group of three or four guys standing at the curb. I hesitate for a moment, and then I follow her. She introduces me as a friend of Li'l Monster and his older brother, Monster Kody, mentioning in passing that I am a writer. These are older guys, early to mid-twenties, and even though they are willing to shake my hand, their expressions, if not exactly hostile, are something less than welcoming.

"How you know Monster Kody?" The guy asking the question is perhaps the oldest in the group. He is short, compactly put together and there are two teardrops tattooed just under the outer corner of his left eye. Looking at him I think about the legends I have heard: each teardrop stands for a year spent in prison or, in some instances, for a person you have killed. I explain that I have visited Monster Kody at Soledad prison, that we have been writing to each other for months. I tell them that he has been transferred to the maximum security unit of Pelican Bay State Prison in Crescent City, near the Oregon border.

Brief glances are exchanged, and then the guy with the teardrops nods his head in a terse gesture. I have delivered an acceptable answer to his query, and now I am perhaps marginally secure. Enough to look over at J-Dog's car and ask what happened. I can see someone in the passenger seat; he seems to be slumped to one side.

"One of the homies got stabbed. J-Dog's fixin' to take him to the hospital."

This information is relayed to me in the calmest voice imaginable. The man speaking is big, rough-looking. He is wearing an earring in the shape of the Cadillac emblem, inlaid with blue and yellow stones. I ask him how the stabbing occurred.

"He went up to Carl's Junior for a burger, and some slob just crept up on him and stabbed him in the back. Got him good." I ask how they can be so sure that the attacker was a member of the Bloods. He simply looks at me with eyes as cold and flat as a snake's.

"Baby Track callin' you." Another member of the group is pointing at J-Dog's car. I glance over and Baby Track is gesturing to me. I walk up on the driver's side; I am hesitant about leaning in on somebody who has just been stabbed and I am not at all sure that I am ready to see a knife wound.

The guy behind the wheel, J-Dog, has something he wants to say to me.

"Listen, when y'all write about this, tell it true. This"—he indicates the wounded man—"is a workin' man. He got a job and a family, he ain't out there hangin', 'bangin' and slangin'. [1] All he did was go up to that place on his lunch hour, and that slob come at him with a knife."

J-Dog looks older than the guys standing together on the sidewalk. He looks closer to thirty. He has very dark skin and a picket-fence lineup of teeth that probably makes him look friendly any time he grins. His hair has been carefully arranged into a longish mane of jheri curls.

The wounded man is about twenty-four, twenty-five. He is almost skeletal in his thinness, and this is emphasized now by the bluish, ashy cast his skin has assumed. His eyes are closed and the eyelids themselves are fluttering a little. His forehead and upper lip are dotted with a mist of sweat. An unbuttoned dark blue shirt covers his upper torso, and he has his right arm wrapped protectively around himself. The skin on his right

---

[1] hanging out; gangbanging; selling dope

wrist has been scraped off and the flesh underneath is a bright, raw red.

"Look what that fuckin' slob done to him." J-Dog has reached down to the floor mat, and now he is holding a white T-shirt up for me to see. One side of the shirt is sodden with blood. I ask him if it might not be a good idea to get his friend to the hospital immediately.

"We goin' right away." He stretches out his right hand to graze the back of the injured man's hand. His touch is delicate, caring.

"You holdin' on, Cuz?" He receives a brief nod in reply. Now Bianca has walked up to the passenger window, and she leans in to take a look.

"How you doin', Wimpy?" Her voice is almost motherly.

"Feel a little bit cold, that's all. I be okay soon as I get stitched up." He sounds as if somebody punched the air out of him.

J-Dog eases into gear, and we step away from the car. As it heads up the street toward the intersection, I look over at the group on the sidewalk. A middle-aged woman has approached and is standing nervously a few feet away from the men. She stands there waiting until one of the guys glances at her, and then she takes a couple of hesitant steps toward him. He moves back to talk to her, and she whispers a few urgent sentences, reaching into her purse for something that she does not bring out. He nods his head, reaches into his pocket and they exchange whatever it is they are now holding in their hands. Then he turns back to the group, and she melts away back down the street. The entire transaction takes maybe one minute.

"C'mon, let's go find Quacker and get somethin' to eat." Baby Track is clearly agitated. He signals Bianca, and the three of us go back to my car. He sits quietly in the back seat as we drive up and down the blocks; then I ask him to tell me what it is that's bothering him.

"What you think botherin' me? My homie got shanked, that's what's botherin' me."

I ask him if there will be a payback.

"You damn right there will be. They gonna pay with lives for what they did to Wimpy." I look over at Bianca; she nods her head in affirmation. Now Baby Track leans forward so that his head is between Bianca and me. "There's Quacker—pull over."

I steer over to the curb and Baby Track sticks his head out the back window, calling Quacker's name at a group of kids—girls and boys—standing in the middle of the block. The tallest of them turns around to peer in our direction; he looks about the same age as Baby Track. Spotting Baby Track and Bianca he ambles over to the car and leans in with both arms on the roof to support his weight. His eyes flick quickly over my face. Baby Track introduces me as "the lady who writin' a book about us" and then tells Quacker about Wimpy's stabbing.

"No foolin'? Somebody shanked Wimpy? That's heavy, man." Up close I can see why he got his nickname: his lips are full and well-shaped and the underside of the upper lip curves out a little.

Baby Track twitches with irritation. "Not *somebody*, fool. A damn Blood got him."

Now one of the little kids has come up to stand beside Quacker. She is about seven or eight years old, and she is almost extravagantly pretty. Her hair has been arranged in a sideswept fall of tiny, precisely parted braids. She waves languidly at Bianca, and Baby Track, looks curiously at me.

"Where y'all goin'?"

"Gonna take your brother to go eat so this lady can interview us." Baby Track likes to keep things straight.

"Can I come along?" She dimples at me as she speaks.

Now it's Quacker who is annoyed. He mimics her voice, "No, you can't come along." Then, in his own voice, "Y'all gotta be gettin' home soon, anyway."

"When *you* comin' home?" You can tell, watching her interact with her brother, that by the time this little girl is his age she will be using her looks to get her way just as he uses a pistol.

Quacker's not going for it. "When I gets there. Now goodbye." He swings into the back seat and settles himself next to Baby Track. Bianca suggests that we go to a restaurant in another part of the city; Wimpy's stabbing has spooked her. She suggests a Mexican restaurant near Hollywood, and although the two boys are unsure about whether they will like "that kinda foreign food," I head out in that direction.

As we drive up one of the residential streets, heading toward Western Avenue, we pass a bunch of kids on bicycles. Bianca sits up straight in her seat, staring at each kid in turn as he or she rides past. Each of them looks away quickly. When the last of them has passed the car, Bianca turns to face the back seat.

"You hear what that one girl said? She told the rest of 'em not to look at us, that we was 'bangers." She huffs out a small sound of contempt. "What the hell them niggers think we was gonna do? Smoke 'em?"[2]

I can see the little group in the rearview mirror. They have come to a stop and are standing at the curb, legs straddling their bikes, staring after the car.

Western Avenue is clogged with traffic. It's as good a time as any to ask Baby Track about his own shooting. Quacker chortles and nudges him a couple of times.

"Give it up, loc."

Baby Track nods his head solemnly. "I was over at one of

[2] kill them

my cousin's house and . . ." He hesitates for an instant. "He was stayin' in the wrong neighborhood, I guess."

Bianca laughs derisively. "Yeah, I guess."

Baby Track leans forward and pushes the back of her head in a light, teasing move.

"Shut up." He relaxes against the backrest again. "Anyway, there was a girl I was talkin' to over at my cousin's—just a girl—and she asked me to take her over to her grandmother's house. So I drove her over there, and there was a gang of dudes standin' out there in the street. About five of 'em walked up to the car, and they like leaned in the windows and asked me did the hat[3] I had on stand for"—he names a particular Crip set. "So then another dude walks up to the car and he leans in real close to my face. Then he said the name of *his* set—and that's all he said, just the name—real cold like, and he looked at me crazy, give me a real mad-dog look, so I looked crazy back at him, and I said, "Eff[4] yo' set and eff yo' dead homeboys.'" Baby Track pauses dramatically. Bianca and Quacker have probably heard this story a few times by now, but they are as caught up in it as if it were the first telling.

"After I said that he walked back to where the other dudes was, the whole pack, and I leaned out and said, 'You comin' back?'" Baby Track pauses and, once again, Quacker nudges him.

"Give it *up*, Cuz."

"Okay. So after I said that, the dude come runnin' back to the car, and he said, 'Fuck yo' set *and* fuck all yo' dead homeboys.'" In the excitement of the retelling of the story,

---

[3]The members of different sets (both Crips and Bloods) wear baseball hats with sports logos or plain initials on them. In each case all or one of the initials are the same as those of the names of the sets. A blue cap with the initials *KC* embroidered on it in white, for example, would indicate that the wearer is a member of the Kitchen Crips. A hat with a red *P* identifies a member of the Piru Bloods. Some members of the Bloods also wear caps with the letter *B* or the embroidered image of a red bird.

[4]"F" for "fuck"

Baby Track has forgotten to replace the word *fuck* with "eff" as he had earlier. "Then he brung out a gun and shot it off three times. *Boom! Boom! Boom!*" His voice sounds loud inside the car, but in fact he is speaking in little more than a conversational tone. "I swear, if I hadn't heard that click, and if I didn't reach up and slap that gun the second I saw him bring it up in my face, I woulda been dead. He woulda shot me in the face. As it was, he only got me once, in the chest. See?" We are at a stoplight; I turn around to look as he lifts his T-shirt to show me the scars. There, on one side of his chest, is an ugly, nickel-sized indentation surrounded by other, slightly oblong scars. He looks down at them as he speaks.

"That big hole is where the bullet went in, and them little holes is where they stuck the tubes in to keep drainin' the wound. I only got one lung now." He touches the scars delicately, as if they were on somebody else's body, as if he were seeing them for the first time. His voice is so young, the tone of it is so cavalier that he might as easily be talking about a high school football injury. And even though I know he is not, all I can keep thinking is that this kid has got to be crazy to be so casual.

I ask if the pain was terrible when it happened.

"I didn't feel nothin' 'til I got to the hospital. I drove myself, even, 'cause the girl didn't know how to drive, plus she was like all cryin' and shook up."

Bianca makes a small sound of contempt for the unknown girl's state of panic and inability to take over in an emergency.

"Anyway," Baby Track goes on, "that first hospital said they couldn't take me in 'cause they wasn't no emergency room, or somethin'—I'm gonna show you which one, it's right here on Western . . ." He cranes his neck, peering out the window. "It's right around here someplace."

Bianca looks, too. "I know which one you talkin' about."

"So they got an ambulance, I guess, and sent me over to

that other big hospital across town—I forget the name right now, and then I remember I was sittin' up on like this table with all these doctors around me, and they got to cuttin' me open and pullin' out the bullet. They showed me the bullet." He stops talking, lost in the remembered nightmare of that moment. "Damn. It was crazy. *Damn.* The only thing I really remember, though, is that nigger, that dude who shot me—him sayin' 'Fuck yo' set."

I ask how old the kid who shot him was. About his own age, Baby Track tells me—sixteen, seventeen. I ask if he thinks he got shot because he was the first one to mouth off, when the guy asked him about his hat. Baby Track shrugs.

"What was I supposed to do? Can't be no buster."

Quacker jumps in on this one. "Besides, the dude prob'ly wanted to get his name up so he could add to his rep."

Baby Track nods solemnly. "Yep, that's just what it was. But they caught that nigger and give him nineteen years. He got tried as an adult—I don't know where he is now."

I ask if Baby Track feels now that justice has been done. Nineteen years, after all, add up to a very long time.

"I'll say it like this: the only thing I kept on sayin' in the hospital was, 'I'm gonna get him one day.' And I will. Some day. Some place. In jail, if I happen to go there—somewhere. I *am* gonna get that nigger."

I ask the other two kids if they agree with Baby Track. Bianca speaks up first: "Get him. Shit. *Get* him."

Then Quacker. "Ye-eeeeh. That dude'll get got. No doubt." He glances at Baby Track then reaches over and pats his arm. "Hell, see my friend, my homie sittin' up there in the hospital for weeks with tubes and stuff all in him? And now he only got one lung? Shit."

Baby Track looks down at his hands rather shyly. "When they took the bullet out they wanted to put me to sleep, but I wouldn't let 'em. I was afraid if I let 'em put me to sleep, I wasn't gonna wake back up." He makes a little face and chuckles softly as if he were laughing at some childish foolishness that happened years ago. "They said, 'This is gonna hurt you bad, and if you gotta scream, scream as loud as you want to, but we gotta get this out.' They was pullin' on my chest—whew—doctor's hand was all the way up to here"—he clasps the wrist of his right hand with the fingers and thumb of his left hand—"in my chest. I couldn't scream, though, 'cause there was just too much pain, you know what I mean? I just went, '*Arrrrgggh.*'" He makes a long, gasping rasp of a sound, then he laughs again, that little self-effacing laugh. Quacker shakes his head in a slow gesture of awe and admiration.

Baby Track continues in his soft voice. There is not a trace of swagger about his attitude as he describes the shooting; he is not showing off for me or for his friends, he is simply telling it the way it happened.

"Then they took the bullet out—big ol' bullet, nine millimeter, all ate up from goin' through my body. Just all ate up. They showed it to me later."

"Man, it was crazy." Quacker sighs this out; he isn't talking to anyone in particular.

"That's the worst pain I ever felt." Baby Track takes a deep breath, as if he might be remembering how hard it was to breathe and how bad that pain really was. He shakes his head in the wonderment of it. "Now I'm like shell-shocked."

We ride along in silence for a moment; everyone in the car is caught up in private thoughts. Next to me, Bianca opens her purse and begins to forage through it. She comes up with a tube of lip gloss, pulls off the cap, applies the gloss to her lips without bothering to look in a mirror. In the back Baby Track and Quacker are both looking out their respective windows. I ask Bianca and Quacker how long it took for them to hear about the shooting. Quacker answers first.

"I was in jail—I heard it there."

Bianca nods her head. "Yeah, he was in jail when it happened. Baby Track's brother came 'round to my house that same"—she turns her head toward the back seat—"When you get shot, night?"

"Yep."

She turns back to look at me. "Then it was the next mornin' his brother came 'round to my house in the car he got shot up in. I didn't believe it at first until he took me outside and showed me all that blood all over the seat and stuff." She shakes her head, "Man, front of that car was a *mess.*"

"I didn't even know I was shot at first. You know how you wet yo'self and yo' shirt get to stickin' to you? That's what I was doin, I was like, *'Dang,* what's this?' Thought I was sweatin', and it was just blood all over me. It wasn't 'til I went down to that first hospital—the one that couldn't help me—and I sat down . . ." He actually shudders, sitting there in the back seat of my car. "When I tried to get back up, I couldn't see no more. Everythin' was just little black and white dots swarmin' around. I couldn't even see the lady I was tryin' to talk to. Thought I was gonna die then for sure. I kept sayin', 'Am I gonna die here? Am I gonna die?' "

I ask him if he was afraid at that moment. Bianca speaks in a soft voice—she says that she would have been very afraid. But Baby Track just shakes his head.

"Nunh-unh. I was just like in shock." He is quiet for a beat or two. "The doctor who operated on me told me the average person woulda died real soon after they got shot like that. 'Cause the bullet was real near my heart. The doctor told me I was strong. And lucky. Told my mother the same thing."

Suddenly Baby Track sits up very straight in his seat. "There it is! Comin' up now!" He is jabbing his index finger at the window, reaching across Quacker to do so. He is pointing at a drab brick and stucco building fronted by a long flight of stairs.

"See them stairs? I bled all the way up them stairs. Big ol' drops fallin' down all over them stairs. Right there!" He continues to point, his finger waggling from one spot to another.

Bianca laughs humorlessly. "Los Angeles hospitals." The words slide slowly out of her mouth, each one freighted with her contempt.

"Ye-eeeeeh. They said they couldn't do nothin' for me. They tripped. I leave a damn trail of blood all the way into that place, and they tell me to have a seat? Man, they tripped bad."

Bianca, ever reasonable, has a question. "But they did finally call the ambulance for you, right?"

"Yeah." It is a reluctant admission.

"Well, they got that right, anyway." Now Bianca leans forward, pointing at the restaurant. "There it is—we can park in the lot across the street."

There is a security guard on duty in the parking lot. Young, in his late twenties maybe, with a sulky, boy's face. Looking at him, you imagine that for whatever reasons they might not have let him join the police, he probably shouldn't be wearing this uniform either. His eyes narrow in a mean little squint as he watches the three kids making their way across the lot. They're wise to his attitude, and they ignore him; there is real hatred glittering there behind the yellow glasses in the aviator frames.

We are shown to a table along the wall and given menus by a young Hispanic woman. She smiles easily at all of us, asks if we would like something to drink. The kids begin to clamor for Margaritas; she shakes her head no. Not without the proper identification. Quacker suggests, with a show of great innocence, that I get a pitcherful for myself. And four glasses, I ask? I order Cokes all around.

Bianca laughs deep in her throat. "I sure wouldn't have minded a nice, cold Margarita."

Halfway through the meal I bring the subject back to Baby

Track's shooting. I ask how he felt when he came to after surgery.

"Mostly I kept thinkin' about that fool who shot me. I kept thinkin' that him and them other niggers were gonna come up there and get me, finish me off."

I ask if, during the worst of the pain, he ever had the thought that gangbanging just might not be worth it. He shakes his head vehemently.

"I never did think about that."

Bianca interrupts. "He thought about it. He even said it for a minute. 'Cause he was like all shot up, and they didn't go out and retaliate for him." She looks at Baby Track. "Right?"

"Yep." He begins to cough; it has a deep, racking sound. It's a cough that belongs on an old man.

Bianca reaches out and places her hand on top of his. "You all right?" Baby Track nods, still coughing. She looks at me again. "And, see, he felt like, 'Shit, what am I gangbangin' for?' You know, when they suppose to be his homies and go out and do somethin' for him. And they wasn't doin' nothin'."

Baby Track moves uncomfortably in his chair, muttering. "Shit. Just get out and do it myself."

I ask him why he thinks there was no payback. He shrugs. "I don't know."

I look at Quacker. He shrugs too.

Bianca isn't content to simply let it go at that. "We gotta be fair about it, you know what I'm sayin'? I can't be a hundred percent sure why they didn't do nothin', but the truth is everybody didn't know the whole story, see? 'Cause the guy said he was from one neighborhood, but he was really from another. So our homies didn't know *who* to go on. And that's probably why nothin' got done."

Baby Track polishes off the last shrimp on his plate and drops his napkin on the table. Then he tilts back his chair so that it is balanced on the two back legs and looks at Quacker.

"Y'all wanna go outside and grab a cigarette?"

Bianca watches them as they swagger through the restaurant heading toward the front doors. We look at each other and smile; it is tacitly understood that the two boys will be ducking around the corner to share a couple hits of pot.

She takes a sip of her Coke. "You know, I been around this gangbangin' for a long time now, ever since I was a baby walkin' around, and it's somethin' else now." She pokes through her salad searching for morsels of chicken. "My big brother has always been with the neighborhood, and he took me everywhere with him, so all the big homies know me. Little homies know me, too. But things sure have changed." She smiles again; her teeth are slightly irregular, very white. "Now everyone's just sellin' dope. Before it was just gangbangers against gangbangers, Crips against Bloods, like that. Now it's just all kinda gangs—little gangs—preppy stuff, all like that. You see dudes dressed all trendy, got them square hairdos and funny-lookin' clothes, go out dancin' all the time, and then they turn around and act like real gangbangers do, fightin' and killin' and stuff." She shakes her head disapprovingly. "Gangs used to not be everywhere—they everywhere now."

I ask if there are more girls than ever in the gangs now.

"I'll put it like this: if there *was* more homegirls than they really is, I think it would be a lot better. Wouldn't be as much killin', 'cause lotta times a girl *will* try to talk things over, or maybe just get into it with fightin' and stuff. Guys"—she hesitates, needing to find the right words—"guys, they just be crazy-ass niggers too much. They want to be seen as the baddest, or the toughest. Or the killin'est. Guy'll pull out a gun and shoot somebody just 'cause they get irritated with 'em. Or 'cause . . ." She breaks eye contact and looks off for a moment. "My own brother's a crazy-ass nigger . . . got a big rep, and my sister damn near got killed from it." Her eyes swing back to connect with mine again.

"It happened in '82, when she was twenty years old. She was over at the L.A. County Jail, visitin' a friend, and these guys from an enemy set caught her down in the parking lot. That's when they didn't have no security, no lights, nothin' to protect people. She went to the car to get her coat, and they grabbed her down there."

"This set is known for doin' dirt, anyway, and they wanted to get back at my brother who was in the penitentiary at the time. They snatched her outta that parking lot, dragged her to some park or somethin', and raped her and stabbed her. Everybody took turns rapin' her, and when they got through with her, they dropped her off at Crenshaw High School, laid her out in the yard. The janitor found her there the next mornin'. My sister was conscious the whole time they was draggin' her and rapin' her, and she could hear everythin' that was goin' on. When they finally left her, they thought she was dead. And this one guy kept on stabbin' her, over and over again, even after his homies told him to leave her alone, she was dead. He just kept sayin', 'No, no, no, no,' and went on stabbin' her. She had to get, like, eight hundred stitches just in her neck when they got her to the hospital."

She is quiet for a long moment. And there is something there, something that is clearly bothering her beyond the horror of her sister's abduction.

"Like I say, these enemies did it to get at my brother. We tried to keep it from him, you know, 'cause we didn't want him to go off up there. We knew the minute he heard his sister had been attacked like that, by those guys, that he'd go off on the first one of that set he ran into. My brother was just about to get out, see, and we didn't want him gettin' crazy up there, and maybe killin' somebody. But, in the end he did hear about it, and when he did, he couldn't handle it. He went off on about four guys, and he had to be put in the hole. That's like eight years ago, and he still thinkin' about it to this day. He still say he gonna kill one of their prettiest homegirls—put the gun down her throat and blow her away. And knowin' my brother, there's no tellin' what he will do. He'll wait forever, but he will . . ." Bianca's composure, so brisk until now, has begun to dissolve. It is only noticeable to the degree that her voice has cracked a little, but it is unmistakable.

"I love my brother more than anything else in the world, but to tell the truth, that's a messed-up attitude. People's sisters and brothers and girlfriends don't do nothin' to you, so leave 'em alone. I try to tell my brother that sometime, you know, try to tell him things should not be done that way, but he got a mind like he don't care. That's what I mean when I call him a crazy-ass nigger."

Her voice assumes a faraway quality. "There's a lot I don't agree with, but I'm still part of a gang, you know what I'm sayin'? And I *will* shoot somebody if it come to that. So I can't really fault my brother or any other homeboy for doin' what he thinks he's gotta do. We all of us do what we gotta do in whatever way we gotta do it."

I ask Bianca if she wants to marry and have children of her own someday. She looks at me as if I had asked her if she might consider becoming a nun.

"I ain't never gonna get married, and for sure I don't want no kids."

I ask why she has made such a decision at sixteen.

"Sixteen don't have nothin' to do with it." She sets her knife and fork neatly on the plate and moves it an inch or so to her left. I noticed earlier that everything this girl does she does without excess motion. Whether it's picking up a wriggling puppy or reaching out for a glass, Bianca never seems to fumble.

"I made up my mind a couple years ago I didn't want no children. All this dope, and this AIDS and stuff. Life don't mean nothin' anymore, and why bring in more kids that you

probably gonna have to raise up by yo'self, anyway? My grandmother tells me that before, long time ago, when she was
young, a man took a real part in his life and his kids' lives." She
narrows her eyes, thinking about the words she wants to say.
"Man was there, not as bein' better or higher than a woman,
but to, like, have a say in what was gonna happen. Seems like
now, lotta men just be around to let their lives happen to them.
I don't want no part of that for myself, I got too much I want
to do. I wanna get out there and see the rest of the world
someday. I know it's fucked up out there, too, just like it is
here, but I want to see for myself."

She looks up and smiles as Quacker and Baby Track walk
back to the table. I pay the check and as we walk across the
street to the parking lot, each kid thanks me for the meal. Baby
Track is bothered about the size of the tip I left, though.

"Hell, you shoulda left that dude a quarter and give *me* the
five bucks."

I can see the security guard out of the corner of my eye
as we walk past him. He is leaning against one of the cars, arms
folded across his chest. As he leaves my line of vision, I hear
him speak in a soft, contemptuous drawl.

"You come back and see us again real soon."

Bianca hears it too, and her arm snakes around Baby
Track's waist, drawing him closer to her as she hurries him
along to the car.

Back in the neighborhood we make one last pass through
the street where the homeboys were congregated earlier in the
day. Evening is coming on now, but there are still groups of
guys standing in threes and fours on the sidewalk. The guy with
the Cadillac earring is there; the one with the teardrop tattoos
is not. Cars glide slowly by. People hover in the background,
most of them women, and every once in a while somebody will
approach one of the guys and launch a whispered exchange.
Bianca takes off to talk to some kids who are standing halfway

down the block. Quacker and Baby Track follow her.

I pull up to the curb and get out of the car; one of the guys I had spoken to earlier wants me to meet another home-boy. As I cross the street, a tall woman with unkempt, gray-streaked hair appears out of the shadows. She is perilously thin.

"Can y'all spare two dollars?" Her voice is a whispered croak, barely recognizable as belonging to a woman. But even in this half-light it is possible to see that despite the graying hair, she is not old. She is simply ruined. I hand her two one-dollar bills; they can make no difference in what is left of her life. She jams the money in a pocket and scuttles back to where a man stands waiting for her. He is close to seven feet tall, and he looks as if he might have been an athlete at one time. Now he is going to fat. I can see his face—it is sweetly addled, like the face of a not very bright child.

The guy I am crossing the street to talk to has been watching. He jerks his thumb toward the two people. "She his mother. He used to be one of the downest O.G.'s around, had a real big rep. Now they both cluckheads." He smiles grimly. "She always hittin' people up for money—gets it, too, most times. How much you give her?" I tell him; he nods his head. "Yeah. She know to ask for just enough so a person can't really say no." Now he peers past my shoulder, looking at something or someone behind me.

"Hey, Cuz. How you doin'?"

I turn to look. Wimpy, the guy who was stabbed earlier in the day, is getting out of J-Dog's car. He is moving carefully, taking it by degrees, but his face is impassive; not a grimace, not a wince is displayed. I move a couple of steps closer to him, trying to see without being obvious if he is under medication. He seems to be completely straight.

He moves slowly, almost majestically, toward his home-boys. As he passes me, I ask how he is feeling. He stops and turns his head to look at me—he is surprised, as if a car or a lamppost had spoken. I repeat my question.

"I'm doin' okay." He is looking at me the way a lion looks at an eland or a zebra when the lion isn't hungry: without interest or ambition.

I ask him, because I want to hear what he will say, how he has managed to keep from showing fear or even pain through this whole ordeal. His answer comes immediately—he doesn't have to think about it—but both of us know, in that instant, that I am not really going to understand.

"Hell, lady—can't be no buster."

■   ■   ■

Her voice, on the telephone, sounds as if it must be caroling its way up out of an imposingly voluptuous body. It is the voice of a very large, maybe even a fat, woman. The first time we spoke she was calling to give me some information about visiting a prisoner I hoped to interview at County Jail; he had given her my number upon his arrival in Los Angeles from San Quentin. He had been brought down to L.A. to appear as a witness in another prisoner's case, and Claudia was acting as unofficial go-between. She performs this task for several people in custody; telephone calls for prisoners are at a premium, men or women can wait in line for hours to make their call only to find that the person they are trying to reach is not at home. So Claudia has become a kind of one-woman relay system. She is almost always at home to receive calls. She was blinded by a shotgun blast to the neck eight years ago.

I learned about the blindness on our third or fourth conversation—it was simply a piece of information she handed me, along with the facts that she is thirty years old, that she lives with her mother, that she has two children, aged ten and thirteen. In other conversations I learned that she reads and writes in Braille and that she is trying to start a small business making tapes of golden oldies for inmates in prisons around the country. When I expressed an interest in meeting her, Claudia invited me to her home for her daughter Kaleesha's eleventh birthday party.

The small house is separated from the street by a chain-link fence that surrounds a patch of carefully tended grass. In the driveway is a ten-year-old, bright yellow Coupe de Ville; on the front porch are one of those old-fashioned gliders and a couple of kitchen chairs. Two kids are lounging on the glider, and as I park the car and walk toward them, the boy, who has a set of Chinese martial arts batons (wooden rods connected by a stout chain) slung across his shoulders, gets up and walks into the house. I stop when I get to the bottom step and ask the girl if her mother is home.

"That's me."

There is no mistaking that astonishing contralto; this is Claudia. I had expected a terrible, maybe even a frightening disfigurement. I had expected a pair of Stevie Wonder wrap-arounds and scars. I was unprepared for this childlike figure in faded size-six jeans and a Care Bear T-shirt. Her hair is braided in three parallel rows that meet in a thick ponytail. Her skin is a light olive tone, and even though one of her eyes is made of glass, even though the other wanders slightly in its sightless-ness, this woman is still attractive.

"I just been sittin' here enjoyin' the breeze. Kaleesha and my mother went out to buy a pair of shoes but my godmother gonna be here in a minute." Claudia gets to her feet, extending her right hand for me to shake. The right arm is even thinner than the left, and she holds it a little stiffly. The hand itself is a small bundle of bird's bones, but Claudia's grip is warm and firm.

"That's some nice smellin' perfume you got on." She sniffs the air appreciatively. Up close I can see, rising like serpents out of the neckline of her T-shirt, the thick, dark tendrils of scar tissue on her throat. There is a small diamond stud in her left earlobe with a pair of tiny gold circlets above it. The right earlobe has only the ragged edge of cartilage to show where the piercing holes used to be.

Now Claudia turns toward the heavily barred screen door that leads into the living room. The pinging beeps of Nintendo are coming from somewhere inside the house. Cupping both hands to her mouth Claudia leans against the screen and calls out, "Nelson! Come on and open the screen door, we comin' in now!"

Her son opens the door, which is on a deadbolt. He steps aside to allow us to walk past him, replacing the key to the bolt in a reinforced steel slot built into the living room wall. He is about to go back into the room where the Nintendo game is going, but Claudia reaches out and pulls him back to introduce him to me. He mutters a brief "hi," his eyes meet mine for an instant, then he looks down and away.

The living room, although not large, is airy. There is blue and silver paper in a swirling, waterlike design on the walls. A pair of plumply upholstered sofas and three matching club chairs are linen covered and plastic swathed. You can see the elaborately carved wooden frames and the pristine whiteness of the linen through the clear plastic sheeting. Along one wall a mirrored bar bears a boldly lettered inscription across the front: DOUBLE TROUBLE. Later, Claudia will tell me that it stands for her two kids; a friend had it made for her. There are shining, gold-colored platters and ashtrays on the tables and shelves. And there is not a speck, not a mote, of dust anywhere in the room.

Claudia asks if I would like a cup of tea. As I follow her through to the kitchen, her foot brushes up against a telephone someone has left on the floor. She picks it up and replaces it on a table. "I'm gonna break my neck one of these days if people don't be puttin' things back where they belong."

The kitchen is flooded with sunlight and rich with the dark-brown perfume of a cooking roast. Claudia motions me to a chair and fills the kettle. An embroidered sampler, wood framed and protected by glass, hangs over the stove—it shows a pair of clasped hands with fingers steepling up toward a rhymed prayer for a busy cook. A cast-iron frying pan with crumbs of scrambled eggs in it sits on one of the back burners; next to it is a little dish of cooked sausages. Claudia makes sure the fire is on under the kettle, then she goes into a small utility porch next to the kitchen. As she opens the door, a rangy dog trots in to sniff curiously at my legs. Claudia has mentioned already, on the phone, that she has nine dogs; now she calls out from the utility room that this dog is the mother of all of them and that the rest of the pack are outside in the backyard. The dog stands still for a pat on the head before she turns and goes into the room behind the kitchen where Nelson is playing. When Claudia comes back, she is carrying a tall wooden stool. I get up to take it from her, but she waves me away.

"Unh-unh. I like to do for myself when I can—but thanks for askin'."

She sets the stool down near the stove and takes an old-fashioned curling iron out of a drawer and places it across one of the front burners.

"My godmother gonna do my hair for me when she gets here."

As if on cue the sound of electronic chimes playing the opening bars of "You Can't Hurry Love" echoes through the house. Claudia goes to the front door, skirting the furniture like a dancer. She is back almost immediately with a tall man who looks to be in his mid-twenties. He is wearing freshly pressed khakis and a starched shirt with the sleeves rolled up. His hair, what can be seen of it under the edge of a black baseball cap, has been styled into a smooth, longish pageboy and enclosed in a net. Claudia introduces him as Junebug. He nods and reaches out to shake my hand; his face is unsmiling.

"How ya doin'?"

I start to tell him that I'm doing fine, but he has already begun to walk out of the kitchen toward the back room and the Nintendo game.

Claudia sets a flowered mug filled with steaming tea in front of me, then she opens one of the cupboards and brings out a matching sugar bowl and creamer. Her movements are deft and precise as she takes a carton of half-and-half out of the refrigerator and pours some into the creamer, checking by weight to see when it is filled.

When she sits down with her own mug of tea, I ask if she herself was a homegirl at one time. She smiles at the question.

"Yeah, sure I was. They used to call me 'Miss Sweet 'n' Sexy'—and I was hangin', 'bangin', and slangin' with the best of 'em. Even used to have some girls workin' for me. Sometimes I think I got shot as a punishment from God for some of the stuff I used to get into. Anyway, it sure seems like He had another kinda life in mind for me."

I ask if she used to carry a gun. The smile appears again.

" 'Course I did. Had a few of 'em—but my favorite was a trey-five-seven. Used to call it my three hundred and fifty-seven homeboys."

That surprises me—Claudia is so tiny to have wielded something with so much firepower. I ask how she managed the recoil of such a large pistol.

"Heck, you just hold it nice and easy with both hands and you brace yo'self real good. Jacked a few people with that gun." She shakes her head, chagrined at the memory.

"See, I got into it real early—I wasn't but thirteen years old when I got with my son's father. See, he was an O.G., had that big rep, and all my girlfriends was, like, 'Golleeee!' And I was just little Miss Innocent—I didn't become a homegirl 'til after he went to the pen when I was seventeen. Then it was like Dr. Jekyll and Mr. Hyde. My other side come out—'bangin', slangin'—all of it."

I ask where this man is now.

"Oh, he still stay in the neighborhood. He married with a couple kids now. He knows Nelson is his. You know, they see each other around. But their whole relationship is just, 'What's up?'" There is not a hint of wistfulness or of anything else in her voice. She is simply stating facts again.

The doorbell sounds again. This time it is Claudia's god-mother, Mrs. Dancer. She is a slender woman in her sixties, rather stern-faced. Bustling into the kitchen, she shakes my hand briskly, refuses the offer of tea, and gets about the business of doing Claudia's hair. She has brought an ivory-backed, densely bristled brush with her and she places it on a square of newspaper which she spreads out on the countertop near the stove. Reaching behind a lineup of canisters she brings out a large jar of VO5 and sets it down next to the brush. Then she inches the stool into the center of a puddle of sunlight and, patting the seat, orders Claudia to sit down.

Claudia settles herself on the stool, and Mrs. Dancer undoes the braids and brushes them out. Claudia's hair billows around her face, a cloud of glossy black ringlets. Then Mrs. Dancer scoops up a dollop of the VO5 with the tips of the fingers of her left hand and, parting the hair, begins to work the unguent into Claudia's scalp and through the strands, using the brush to spread it evenly. Then she applies the heated iron. She repeats this process every few minutes, straightening the hair by degrees.

Once Mrs. Dancer has established a rhythm, I ask Claudia to tell me about the shooting. She answers without hesitation.

"They said it was gang-related—but I don't think it was." She shifts to a more comfortable position on the stool, propping her left ankle up on her right knee. "I was over at a friend of mine's house, we was eatin' dinner, and what happened was, all of a sudden this guy jumped up on the front porch, looked in at us real quick and then jumped back down. And then, before we could even talk about it, he jumped back up again and started shootin'." She pauses for a beat. Behind her, just above her head, Mrs. Dancer presses her lips together in a small, silent show of unforgiving anger.

"The guy that he was shootin' at didn't get hit, but myself and another innocent bystander got shot at the same time. The cops said it was over some dope, but I didn't see no dope bein' transferred or nothin'. All I saw was this guy and the shotgun." Claudia's lips turn up in a grim little smile. "That's the last thing I ever saw—that guy and the shotgun." The smile fades, and her thoughts go inward for a moment; then, with a small shake of her head, she goes on. "Then I heard a big ol' boom, and I felt somethin' like a bee had stung me on the right side of my neck." Her hand lifts to touch the nest of scar tissue at the side of her throat.

"The way my head was turned, the buckshot broke my jaw and took out all but twelve of my teeth. It knocked my right eye completely out and left the left eye hangin' on my cheek. It collapsed my lung and paralyzed my right arm."

Mrs. Dancer makes a small, soft sound. It is clear that no matter how many times she might have heard this account, it is always going to affect her. Claudia reaches up to find her godmother's hand and finding it, her fingers squeeze softly.

"The doctors said the sight in my left eye wouldn't never come back, but I say different. 'Cause it's not supposed to hurt, and it does. And it's not supposed to drop tears, and both eyes cry real tears. I feel 'em on my face when I cry."

Mrs. Dancer is working the hair at the back of Claudia's head now; Claudia ducks a little with each stroke of the brush, and once again I am struck by the fact of her beauty, however flawed.

"I stayed at the hospital for about a month and three weeks. Had a trach in my throat for a month—they didn't know if I was gonna live or die. And since I got shot in the neck, see, and buckshot splattered all up inside my brain, they didn't know if I was gonna be a vegetable if I *did* live. It's still in the danger zone, 'cause some of that shot and stuff is still all tangled in there, and if it moves the wrong way"—she shrugs, shaking her head in a slight, diffident gesture, as if she were apologizing for shortcomings—"I can be retarded for the rest of my life. I'm not supposed to get upset and let things bother me, but most of the time I got that under control, believe it or not." She lifts her head toward my face—as if she could see. "I'm just maintainin'. Day by day."

The doorbell rings again, and this time Claudia shouts for Nelson to go see who it is. He comes back with a heavy-set young man with a beeper ostentatiously displayed on his belt. He is introduced to me as Ducky; he smiles intensely at both Mrs. Dancer and me, then he disappears into the back room with Nelson and Junebug.

Now Mrs. Dancer brushes Claudia's hair, which has straightened dramatically, back away from her face and secures it with a rubber band. Her cheekbones are accentuated attractively, and I tell her so. She thanks me, ducking her head again, this time in shyness.

"I didn't look like myself at all for the longest time after I got shot. I just"—she hesitates only for an instant, but several emotions travel across her face in rapid succession—"looked a total mess. My own mama didn't recognize me, and my son . . ." She breaks off again, takes a breath, continues. "When my son come in the room he just took one look and went yellin' out of the room. I could hear him screamin', all the way down the hall, sayin' how that wasn't his mama in that bed and where'd they take his mama to. He went runnin' in all the other rooms lookin' for me, just cryin' and callin' for me. Now he say he

100

don't remember any of that at all. But I remember."

Claudia shakes a cigarette out of her pack and lights it with a disposable lighter. She inhales deeply and sighs out a long plume of smoke, and I think about something I heard somewhere, that blind people rarely smoke, because most of the pleasure is lost if you can't see the smoke curling up from the cigarette or coming out of your mouth. Claudia seems to be enjoying it, though; she takes another deep pull before she speaks again.

"I didn't know I was blind for about a month. I mean, I knew I had patches on both my eyes, but nobody didn't tell me I was blind. They left that for my mama to tell me. Even the homeboys—they was all comin' to see me, but none of them wanted to tell me either."

I ask what kind of feelings grip you when you first learn that your sight is gone.

"I couldn't believe it at first. I kept thinkin' they'd take them patches off and I'd just see, like always. And then, when that didn't happen, I kinda lost it for a while. Thought about killin' myself . . . all kinds of stuff like that." She shakes her head, disapproving of the suicide she contemplated eight years ago. "That wasn't no kinda answer at all. Gettin' on with it was the answer."

I ask if there had been any retaliation for the shooting.

"They wanted to retaliate, you know. Because I was like a sister, or a mother to all the homeboys around here. All the different sets respected me—Grape Streets respected me, Main Streets respected me, Nine-Oh Mafias respected me, Hoovers—I took 'em all, like, as my little brothers or my nephews or somethin' when they'd get into little things, you know. They'd call me, and even when I was pregnant, I'd walk up to school and pick 'em up. And it hurt 'em to the heart to find out the true-blue homegirl had been shot.

"I had to talk 'em into not goin' out to do that, 'cause I

101

didn't want an innocent bystander to get shot or killed when nobody really knew what was really goin' on." She reaches out, feeling with the little finger of her right hand for the ashtray. She touches the edge, and then hits it dead center with the ash from her cigarette.

"You see, sometimes you have to remember your Bible. Bible says 'Revenge is Mine, says the Lord.' And, see, why should I just give up that attitude—you know, the gang attitude, of 'all for one'—this particular time to my homeboys, knowin' how crazy they are and knowin' how much I am loved, and have them go out and maybe get killed, and maybe kill innocent people, too. Then, even *if* the right person got killed, too, that would have been on my conscience."

While Claudia has been talking Mrs. Dancer has been tidying up, putting the jar of VO5 back behind the canisters, returning the curling iron to its place, wiping up the counters, even washing the mugs from which Claudia and I drank our tea.

Now she opens the oven door to check on the roast. A wave of heat billows out into the room, and the aroma of cooking meat intensifies. Claudia sniffs delicately at the air, just as she sniffed my perfume when we first met outside on the porch. Then she goes on talking.

" 'Cause they was like six stories about how I got shot, and they—everybody would say, 'Well, we don't want her to have to relive that night.' But it doesn't bother me. It was just like . . . like . . ." This is the first time she has really stumbled in the telling. "Like a . . . a joke to me. 'Cause if he wanted to have a shootout, you know, there was a gun in the house. I mean, he was about my size . . ." She chuckles softly. "I would've accommodated him. We coulda gone outside and acted like we was back in the . . . you know, the Western days."

Her smile is so narrow it might easily be mistaken for

something else. "See, I never had, and I never will have no fear of anybody in this world but my mama and Jesus Christ."

I ask Claudia what happened to the man who shot her, if the police ever got him.

"Nope. He got away with it. They said I was in a drug house and wasn't nothin' they could do."

What about the other person who was shot. Did he die?

"Nope. I'm the one who got it the worst. The other person just got some buckshot in his leg. It happened on a Monday, and he was outta the hospital the next Monday." No anger, no resentment in her voice.

And the police never tracked down the man who did the shooting? I can't help pressing this question.

Now, for the first time since we began talking about this, Mrs. Dancer speaks up. "They dropped it! Dropped the case. How's that?" Her voice is high and quavery with outrage, but as soon as she speaks, as though embarrassed by this small outburst, her mouth snaps shut and her eyes seem to lose focus.

"I feel like after they had told me they was droppin' it, they was like, 'Well . . .'" Claudia brushes her hands together in a fast gesture of dismissal. "'That's one nigger that *coulda* been home.' I really fought with the police about that, because I didn't get no 'victim of crime' support and I *was* a victim of crime. I didn't get no support from nobody except my mother and my godmother here. But everybody that used to hang around my house—I haven't seen any of them for almost nine years. That's when you find out who's your friend and who's not your friend."

Now I can detect a flare of well-suppressed anger in Claudia's voice.

"The O.G.'s, they still show respect—'cause I talk to 'em all, and when they come down from different penitentiaries to the central jail, they call me, and if I can, I get up there to visit. Or I write to 'em, send pictures and stuff. To let 'em know I'm still here. Regardless." She slides down from the stool and stretches, rolling her head from side to side to relieve her neck muscles.

" 'Cause every one of them O.G.'s used to hang out in that livin' room there." She is silent for a moment, remembering, perhaps, those better days. Then she turns toward where I have been sitting and smiles.

"You know what? It's hot in this kitchen. Let's go out and sit on the porch fo' a little bit." She turns toward Mrs. Dancer. "How you feel 'bout that, Mama D.? Wanna get some air?"

Mrs. Dancer says that she's going over to pick up the birthday cake now, before people start arriving.

Claudia and I settle ourselves on the front porch. She takes the glider again; I sit down on one of the kitchen chairs. It's hot out here, too, and from the side of the house I can make out the smell of fresh dog urine. Across the street two boys are washing a partially restored Chevy Impala; a portable radio on the curb next to them is playing a Ziggy Marley song.

"I just don't understand the people of today. But I guess it's all this dope, that's the main problem. Back then, in my time, people were, like undercover with they cocaine smokin'. And it was expensive back in them days. You couldn't go and get a five-dollar rock, or a five-dollar powder. Everything was twenty-five dollars and up back in them days. Now," a small shudder of disdain ripples across her shoulders, "everythin' is just so common. Prostitution is common, gangbangin' is common . . . when I first started 'bangin' in the early seventies, half the parents didn't even know their kids was in it. Mine didn't. And another thing—back then there wasn't no cowards like there is today. Back then you put yo' fists up fo' yours. Now you got a lotta cowards in gangs—they won't go one on one, they won't get 'em up from the shoulder. [5] Now they just pull a trigger. Slap a gun in they hand and they think they John Wayne."

A young woman with a headful of pastel foam rollers opens the door of the house directly across the street. She calls out something to one of the kids working on the Impala. He tosses the rag he's holding to the other kid and moves quickly toward the house, brushing past the girl who steps aside to let him pass. The other boy is hunkered down at the front bumper, polishing the chrome grillwork. The girl stands watching him for a moment, then she turns and goes back inside.

"It's all about getting a rep these days, and most of the kids don't have any street knowledge. They'll come up dead, tryin' to make those reps. And innocent people . . ." Claudia breaks off abruptly, starts to say something else, changes her mind, then changes back again. "I'll tell you somethin'—my godmother, Mama D.? Where she stay at, in her 'hood, you really gotta watch what you wearin' all the time. Can't *never* wear no red over there—not even a head rag, not even in the house. Now she old, she got nothin' to do with gangs, you know what I'm sayin'? But if she forget and put on a red rag to go to the grocery store, kids'll follow her and beat her up. And if she snitch to the cops, it'll go worse for her. That's why she so quiet all the time. She scared." The hinges on the glider squeak softly as Claudia pushes herself back and forth.

"I been a Crip since I was thirteen years old, I'm true blue, but them kids are scandalous. How about a two-year-old baby blasted outta her mama's arms 'cause she wearin' red shoelaces?! The *baby* wearin' red shoelaces! These kids just shoot anybody. But they gonna learn—the Man upstairs is watchin'."

[5]fight with fists

105

The kid who went into the house comes out again. He has on a clean T-shirt now, and a pair of baggy gray khakis. He slides in behind the wheel of the Impala and starts up the engine. The other boy leans in the window on the driver's side, and there is a brief, whispered conversation, then the first kid nods his head, the other one gets in the car and they take off, heading toward the intersection.

I ask Claudia to tell me the average age of the kids she's talking about.

"About sixteen, seventeen. Some of 'em be younger'n that, even. And most of 'em don't bother to go to school—they want fast money and some roller tells 'em, 'Man, I can give y'all more money than yo' mama ever give you.' So they drop outta school and work for him. And if they get picked up and sent to Juvenile, they get right out, 'cause they minors—and 'cause they ain't no room inside, anyway. Even if they do get locked up, by the time they let 'em out, they just leadin' on for the next kid."

I ask what the schools are like in this area. Claudia snorts derisively.

"What you think they like? Most of the teachers—well, you hear stories about some of 'em drinkin' or takin' drugs, but I don't know if that's just stories, or what. But . . ." she hesitates for a beat, seeking the right words to get her point across to me. "Look, it's like this—say I'm the teacher, and I have a room with twenty kids in it. Say fifteen of them kids wanna learn and five of 'em don't. Well, if it was *me* doin' the teachin', them five are gonna get escorted *out* of my room. But some of these teachers, a kid will say, 'Fuck you, bitch!' and all she'll do is say, 'Well, fuck you, too!' The *teacher!*" Her voice is filled with emotion now. "So, some of that, together with the home life—the way a child is brought up—or the influence of the streets because your child might be scared of people he

hangs around with, so he gets bullied into doin' something' . . ."
Her words trail off into a brief silence. When she speaks her
voice is soft again.

"My baby, Kaleesha, got the third highest score on a
national I.Q. test when she was in the second grade. The third
highest score in the country! Now she gettin' into fights at
school. I think it's 'cause she wants to get the teacher's attention. But the teachers down here, looks like they just givin' up.
It's like they sayin', 'Hell with it—I'm gonna get my paycheck
regardless if y'all learn a damn thing or not.' And the truth is,
how'm I gonna blame 'em? I chastise my kids all the time and
they don't listen to me, how they gonna listen to some
teacher?"

She brings up one hand to rub her forehead. She closes
her eyes, and her fingertips move lightly across the lids. Then,
surprisingly, she smiles.

"They don't even have to listen to me to do what's right
for themselves. All they really gotta do is take a look."

It is later in the afternoon. Pizzas have been delivered and
eaten. Birthday cake has been sliced, and presents have been
unwrapped and exclaimed over. Now the party has divided
itself, with grown-ups sitting in the living room and kids scattered throughout the house. The boys are riveted to the video
games in the back room, the girls have separated according to
age. There are pre-teens gossiping in the kitchen, nine- and
ten-year-olds playing a fast and intricate game of jumprope in
the front yard. Kaleesha is moving back and forth between the
two latter groups. She is a rather solemn-looking girl, already
taller than her mother and coltish without being awkward. She
is only slightly unsteady in her first pair of two-inch heels.

Claudia's mother, Mrs. Utley, is striking, with a shock of
pure white hair. It's deceptive, that hair; at first glance she

seems to be a plain-spoken grandmotherly type, stolid, even dull. But then she begins to banter with her daughter, and you look a little closer and see the glint of humor behind the lenses of her glasses. Her eyes are so brown that it is hard to see the pupils; this woman can watch people for a long time without their feeling as though they are being looked at. Between her daughter and herself a young and thriving friendship is being nurtured; this is the core of their relationship. It is impossible to imagine the private battles and finely wrought compromises that enabled Claudia and her mother to create the life they now share, but one thing is clear: tragedy has been hammered into strength.

Today Mrs. Utley is not feeling well. She was involved in a minor automobile accident earlier in the week and now the muscles of her neck and shoulders are out of whack. So, with apologies to Kaleesha and the guests, she has gone to her room to lie down.

It is an odd assortment of people here in the living room. Three young women, two of them holding infants, sit next to each other on one of the couches. Ducky and I are at opposite ends of the couch facing them. Junebug has taken the chair next to us; Mrs. Dancer is perched on a rocker near the front door. Nobody is really talking to anybody else; all the conversation seems to be filtered through Claudia, whose chair has been moved to the edge of both placements, as if it were at the head of a dining room table. It is Claudia who is keeping things going, smoking her cigarettes, one after the other, turning her head toward each person who speaks, reaching out to hold each baby in turn.

When Ducky's beeper sounds everyone turns to look at him. He grabs it quickly to stop the noise, then he mutters an embarrassed apology and lumbers to the door. Claudia gets up immediately to unlock the screen door for him and, as she does so, he tells her he'll be back as soon as he can.

"Uh-huh, sure you will." She is teasing him, laughing softly and without malice.

A portable cassette player next to Claudia's chair is running one of her golden oldie tapes: Gladys Knight, singing "Midnight Train to Georgia." Junebug leans forward and asks Claudia to turn up the volume. She shakes her head.

"Unh-unh. We got company, and you ain't gonna get me to bust their eardrums playin' this as loud as y'all like it."

He sighs and slumps back in his chair, resigned to boredom. Now a series of high-pitched shrieks come out of the kitchen. We all turn to look—Claudia jumps to her feet, clutching the back of the chair for support—but it is Junebug who bolts across the living room as the girls mill away from the thing that has scared them.

I have gotten up on my knees on the couch; I can look directly into the kitchen.

It is a small mouse, a hiccup of a mouse, brown with pink tissue-paper ears. It sits, frozen with fear, at the open door of the utility closet. The girls have welded themselves into a palpitating mass plastered against the sink at the far end of the room. It is left for Junebug to dispose of the intruder. His face is turned toward me, and I can see it clearly—he is afraid of this tiny creature, but he is ready to do what he has to do. He calls out for Nelson to bring in his baseball bat.

Without thinking about it, I get up off the couch, yelling at Junebug, telling him not to kill the mouse, begging him to take it outside and let it go. The women seated across from me are watching with idle curiosity; so is Mrs. Dancer, who has stopped the rocking action of her chair. Claudia turns to ask if it is a rat in there. I tell her it's a very small mouse and she nods her head. I know that she understands my sentimental and perhaps foolish plea to save its life; I'm not sure she agrees with it.

Junebug has swept the mouse into the box that held

Kaleesha's new shoes. Now he holds it out at arm's length and walks quickly out of the house with it. The girls in the kitchen return to their whispered conversation. The women on the couch go back to playing with their babies and making small talk. Mrs. Dancer begins to rock her chair again. Claudia walks into her mother's room to see how she's doing. When she comes back, she is carrying a box of dominoes. Somebody starts to set up a card table.

When I tell Claudia that I'm ready to leave she urges me to stay and play dominoes with them. She means it, too. It's not merely the polite suggestion of a dutiful hostess to an outsider. But I have things to do at home, so Claudia walks with me to the front porch. As we stand talking for a moment, Junebug bounds up the stairs. I ask him if he let the mouse go free, and, as he waits for Claudia to unlock the screen door, he looks at me and mimes the act of twirling a small creature by its tail before letting it sail through the air over his head.

As Junebug walks into the house, Nelson is coming out. He is wearing a baseball cap and a running jacket, and he is in a hurry. Claudia reaches out and places one hand on his arm.

"You still got them damn sticks 'round yo' neck? You better leave 'em home 'less y'all want to get arrested." She turns toward me. "The cops pickin' up anybody they see with them things—they callin' 'em lethal weapons."

Nelson is not wearing them, but he is clearly annoyed at having been asked by his mother. "They called Noon Chuks. And I ain't wearin' 'em, so can I go now?"

"Yeah—and you better be home by nine, or I'm gonna get someone to take me lookin'."

Nelson pounds away down the steps. Claudia listens to his receding footsteps, then she turns toward me again.

"I may be little, and I may be blind, but I can still slam that kid up against a wall if I have to. Did it the other night

when he started in dis'in' me about jumpin' in a set. I told
him—and I meant it—'I'll beat you like I'd beat a nigger in the
street, you start in 'bangin'.'" She stands quietly again, still
listening for his footsteps.

"I don't worry so much about the penitentiary no more.
I worry about the cemetery."

5 Camp Kilpatrick

I t's about five-thirty and dinner is over with—pork chops, applesauce, candied yams. D.P.O. Nancy Block is about to conduct the weekly meeting of her dorm group, the Falcons. Nancy is one of the two or three caseworkers on staff at Camp Kilpatrick, which means that, in addition to her regular duties, she handles extra cases, counseling the kids assigned to her, checking out their home situations, placing them in foster care when she feels it is necessary. Like the other Deputy Probation Officers she puts in three consecutive twenty-four-hour work shifts, sleeping in one of the small rooms assigned to staff members. It is hard and often frustrating work, but Nancy is happy in it, and she plays fair with the kids.

We are in one of the classrooms. Nancy is seated at the teacher's desk, and the boys have arranged their chairs in a semicircle facing her. The room itself is as typical as one you might see in, say, Flint, Michigan: American flag in one corner, penmanship figures tacked up above well-stocked bookshelves, basic science mobiles, NASA posters of the earth and moon, a photograph of John Paul II.

There are twelve kids here; two of them are Hispanic, the rest black. Nancy begins the discussion with a brief summation of the point system: each boy can earn up to twenty-five points a day toward the amount he needs to get out of here. He can lose that many—and more, depending on the infraction he commits. There has been a bad dorm inspection, and everyone got penalized for that one. Next is an announcement of some changes in the visiting rules: food can no longer be brought in from outside. She finishes with a reminder about the track team—there will be a meet in three weeks; anyone involved must keep up his points.

Now the floor is opened to the kids. Almost every hand in the room goes up, and Nancy calls each boy in turn. Everything is a complaint—the staff is unfair; the rules don't make sense; the point system is bullshit. Nancy listens patiently to each youngster as he rails against his confinement. Then she smiles and leans forward on her elbows.

"If you guys were out in the streets, you'd deuce it out in about three minutes. Most of you have been here for at least two weeks, and you're still complaining about rules. You know what? I think you just like to complain."

One of the kids makes a snickering sound in his throat. Nancy flicks a glance at him and goes on talking. "There's nothing I can do about these complaints about the staff. And the only thing you guys can do is learn to ride with it. Now, let's talk about some stuff we *can* do something about, maybe."

She looks around the lineup of kids. The boy who laughed earlier pokes a hand up. He is not a handsome kid, but his eyes shine with the light of intellect; the lids themselves are slightly oily, and they droop a little at the outer corners. He is probably fourteen years old. Nancy gives him a nod, and he brings his hand down to point at a boy sitting directly across from him.

The boy is very young-looking; I know that he must be at least thirteen to have been placed in this camp but he looks nowhere near that age. He is reed thin with a delicate, almost pretty face and large, very white teeth.

"That fool be talkin' and whisperin' *all* the time, losin' us points."

The kid sticks up for himself. "Oh, yeah? Well, lemme tell you about Lumbly, *he* just want to be boss all the time."

Lumbly continues to point. "He always insultin' me, talkin' about my mama smokin' drugs, talkin' about how my uncle be sellin' drugs and buyin' me clothes." He makes a snorting sound. "Hart can't even buy *his* own clothes."

"I *can* buy my own clothes, fool!"

Nancy interrupts this exchange to give the nod to another boy; he's sitting next to Hart, and he looks nearly as young.

"Today I was tryin' to break up a fight on the basketball court, you know what I'm talkin' about? And he"—he points at Hart—"started in cryin'."

Hart whirls in his chair to face his accuser. "Did you see tears in my eyes? You ain't nobody to break up no fight, and you just want people to kiss yo' little booty!"

Lumbly gazes imploringly at Nancy; for good measure he includes me as part of his audience. "See what we got to put up with? They just give us all the little immature people. Little thirteen-year-olds." He points at Hart again. "He only thirteen—he say he fourteen."

"I *know* how old I am, mummyhead!"

Now Lumbly speaks directly to me, as one adult apologizing to another for something beyond his control, secure in the knowledge that the other adult will understand the dilemma. "We afraid to tell Hart to shut up in Group. He have a fit." This gets a laugh from the others, which Lumbly acknowledges with a lazy wave of one hand. "He a crybaby."

Whatever Hart is about to say in rebuttal is lost as a

latecomer joins the circle. He's a Hispanic kid and Lumbly sees fit to introduce him. "Ah, here comes the smoker." To me, again, "He like to get high; talk about it all the time, like it was his girlfriend."

One of the other kids says something in the smoker's defense. I don't hear what it is, but it gets another laugh. Lumbly slides easily down in his chair, draping both arms across the back in graceful repose. He looks at the boy who just spoke, and one eyebrow lifts in an inverted vee. "What about you, homes? You always masturbatin' and tellin' us to look at you."

The boy who said he tried to break up the fight on the basketball court literally falls out of his chair laughing.

Hart looks down at him in outrage. "What's the matter with you, fool? You be the one havin' fits!"

Lumbly looks at Nancy and me. "There he goes, screamin' like a kid again."

"Someone hit him in the head!" Input from the other side of the circle.

"Okay, that's enough." Everybody looks at Nancy. "Now, look: you guys are here to try and get along. You don't have to love each other, we know you're in different gangs, but you *are* going to have to make an effort to act reasonably. Otherwise you're going to be stuck in here losing points and taking the long ride out."

Lumbly's hand is up before Nancy finishes speaking. "I can't make no camp program. I shoulda been outta here long ago, but I just can't make no damn camp program with all this school stuff and bein' with these damn babies. Why can't I do my time at Y.A.?"

"Come on, Lumbly, if you can't make it here, what makes you think you're going to do better at Y.A.? You were placed here because this is the program you need." Nancy nods to another boy whose hand has gone up.

"I thought we was gonna elect a group leader today. We needin' one so we don't be fightin' so much. I can't get to sleep nights with people hissin' under they breath at each other and cryin' and stuff. Some people even talkin' about killin' themselves." He looks down at the floor. "I ain't sayin' who."

Another kid pipes up. "I know who you talkin' about. He talk about suicide, but all he do, he be fartin' and wavin' it back in people's faces. He not gonna kill himself."

Nancy guides the discussion back to the election. A couple of names are mentioned, but the majority favorite is a tall, silent kid named Hooks. Even Lumbly likes him. The smoker says that he will "vote for anyone except Lumbly or Hart."

One of the Hispanic kids points out, needlessly, that Hooks is "the biggest one in the whole group." The boy sitting next to him pokes him with an elbow.

"Just 'cause he big don't mean nothin'. What's important is that Hooks don't go smackin' up to people."

Lumbly makes a snorting sound again. "Hell, ain't none of us do that. We don't even smack it up with our own families."

Finally Hooks, who has remained silent throughout this discussion, is voted in as group leader. He accepts the honor with shy good grace and mumbles his thanks. Hart takes the opportunity to tell Hooks to keep Lumbly and the others from kidding him about being a baby.

Lumbly laughs out loud. "Watch out, Hooks. He gonna be botherin' yo' ass now."

A Hispanic kid who hasn't spoken at all pipes up. "Beside, man, I'm the smallest one in this group."

Lumbly points at Hart again. "No, man. *He* always gonna be the smallest one. He always gonna be the retarded one. And he *always* gonna be the crybaby one."

The room erupts in laughter; it is not entirely malicious.

119

Hart narrows his eyes and glares at Lumbly. Then, under his breath, "Damn mummyhead. Think he a hard case."

■ ■ ■

"Okay—this is Gang Class. There's no sidebusting in here. Anything said in this room stays here. There will be no disrespecting anyone else's neighborhood. No sign-throwing. O.G.'s will help new members." A. C. Jones is speaking; he presides over this course, Gang Class, which is held once a week at Camp Kilpatrick. The boys assigned to the class are considered hardcore gang members, and tonight there are nineteen students in the room. G-Roc is one of them.

Jones moves across the room to pull down the shades at the windows and over the pane of reinforced glass cut into the door. This classroom is like the others I have seen: the desks are brightly painted and unscarred by graffiti; there are posters of the solar system, a chart of the human body, and large drawings of the four food groups on the walls. Books are neatly arranged on the bookshelves and, on a ledge under the windows, there are glass tanks that contain some of the wildlife indigenous to the area: a couple of lizards, a land tortoise, a tarantula.

Gang Class is a ten-week course in which each boy must accumulate two hundred merit points. Homework is assigned each week, and every completed task is worth twenty points. Last week the students were told to write their own obituaries along with a letter to their mothers explaining why it was necessary for them to die for their gangs.

When a boy has successfully completed Mr. Jones's class, he is allowed to make the choice of leaving it or staying on as an O.G. If he decides to stay, he is expected to act as an unofficial counselor for the newer kids in the class. There are five of these O.G.'s here this evening.

Camp Kilpatrick

Mr. Jones picks up a piece of chalk and writes, in large block letters, a single word on the blackboard:

KILL

The room goes very quiet; the only sound you can hear at this moment is the muted shuffling of feet under the desks. Mr. Jones faces his audience and waits for complete silence before he speaks.

"Okay, y'all know what that word means. Now I want each of you to give me a real good reason to kill somebody."

The words are barely out of his mouth when hands begin to jab the air. Jones nods at one of the kids.

"For the fuck of it."

Jones turns back to the blackboard, writes those words. "Okay, 'for the fuck of it.' Let's have another reason."

"Put in work for the 'hood."

Jones writes again. "Okay, that's a good reason. Next?"

" 'Cause he's my enemy."

"Yeah, that's righteous." Jones prints quickly. "An enemy."

"For revenge."

"Yeah, let's get that one down, that's a good one. Revenge." The chalk screeches against the board.

" 'Cause he said somethin' wrong."

"You mean like dis' you?"

"Naw. Just wrong—like, you know, *wrong.*"

"Yeah, okay. Because he said somethin' wrong and now you gotta smoke him for it, right?"

"Ye-eeeeeeeeh." The kid slouches back in his chair, grinning. He is clearly well pleased with himself for having made his thoughts so perfectly understood. Jones writes the words on the board, then turns back to face the kids. "Come on—let's get some reasons up here. Y'all supposed to be such tough dudes. Let's go."

Now the answers begin to come quickly.

" 'Cause he look at me funny, give me that mad-dog look."

" 'Cause I don't like him."

" 'Cause he asked me where I was from."

" 'Cause he wearin' the wrong color."

" 'Cause he gonna hurt a member of my family."

"For money."

Jones is nodding his head, scribbling furiously on the blackboard.

"So I can jack somebody for dope."

" 'Cause he give me no respect."

" 'Cause he a disgrace, he a buster."

"For his car."

" 'Cause he try to get with my lady."

" 'Cause he a transformer[1] in my 'hood."

"In self-defense."

" 'Cause he try to jack you—take yo' shit."

"For a nickel."

"For the way he walk."

"If he got somethin' I want and he don't wanna give it to me."

" 'Cause I'm a loc."

"For his association."

" 'Cause he called me a baboon—dis' me."

" 'Cause he fucked with my food—you know, like took one of my French fries or somethin'."

" 'Cause I don't like his attitude."

" 'Cause he say the wrong thing—he wolf me."

" 'Cause I'm buzzed—you know, all like, high and bent."

"Just playin' around."

[1] a spy

" 'Cause he fucked up my hair in the barber shop."

Jones chuckles as he writes down this one. "Fucked up your hair, huh? Well, I can understand that."

And still the reasons to kill keep coming.

" 'Cause he a snitch."

" 'Cause he hit up my wall, crossin' out names and shit, writin' R.I.P."

"If a lady don't give me what I want. You know—the wild thing."

" 'Cause they ugly."

" 'Cause he try to run a drag[2] on me."

All of the reasons are up on the board now, in three neatly lettered rows. Mr. Jones steps back, surveying the list for a moment, nodding his head. Then he turns to look at the kids again.

"Okay. Now. Which of this shit would you die for?" There is a beat of utter silence; the air seems to shimmer with the combined stares of shocked students. Jones stands quietly, staring back at them. "Oh, come on, now. If y'all can kill for something, y'all better be ready to die for it. So let's hear it: which of these reasons you gonna die for?"

One of the kids pipes up. "Hell, you can erase *all* that shit."

"No, let's go point by point, see what we got here. Okay, who's gonna die 'for the fuck of it'?"

Five hands go up. An Essay kid, he's one of the newest members of the class, wants to talk about it. "It would be like when you play Russian roulette, you know? Like if I got nothing else to do, because I'm bored."

Mr. Jones does not hesitate to put a finer point on it, "But that would be suicide, killing yourself, wouldn't it?"

The kid doesn't see it that way—the original premise was

[2]a con

123

"reasons to *kill*"—"it didn't say nothing about who." Now, surprisingly, it is one of the other students, one of the five kids who also raised his hand to defend this reason to kill someone, who argues with the Essay kid, telling him how wrong he is.

"We ain't talkin' about killin' yo'self here, fool—we talkin' about smokin' somebody else just for the fuck of it. You got the heart to kill somebody else?" The Essay kid assures him that he does. Now Mr. Jones interrupts to explain that it isn't just killing another person for the hell of it that is the subject here. He reminds the students that in killing the stranger, they must also die. That's the deal in this instance. You kill—for whatever reason—you die. The five hands that were raised go back down. The words "for the fuck of it" are erased from the blackboard.

As are the other reasons. There are some arguments, of course: "Putting in work for the 'hood" and "revenge" get some people yelling. But as Mr. Jones reads the reasons aloud, one by one, the show of hands gets smaller. Until he gets to "wearing the wrong color." Then every hand in the room thrusts into the air. Every kid here is willing to die for red or blue—the Essays are adamant about this one too.

We are at the heart of gangbanging.

Jones holds up both hands for silence. "Okay, I want y'all to listen hard and go along with this: I'm a madman with a fully loaded 'gauge. You all naked, sittin' there in yo' chairs with nothin' on. But they's some clothes *under* the chairs—three pairs of pants to choose from: pair of blue pants, pair of red pants, pair of white pants. Now—anyone puts on any color but white"—he hoists the imaginary shotgun, squints down the barrel—"Booyah![3] You dead." He turns, aiming dead center on a kid's chest. "What color pants you gonna put on?"

[3] a word used to emulate the report of a shotgun

124

The kid's eyes move quickly around the room—everybody is waiting. He licks his lips, "Red pa . . ."

"Booyah!" Jones swings toward another kid.

"Bl . . ."

"Booyah!" Jones shakes his head. "Maybe y'all didn't hear me. I'm a madman, I don't care about no loyalty. I just don't like any color but white, makes me mad if somebody don't like it, too. Mad enough to kill you." He nods at a kid who has his hand up. It's G-Roc.

"But if I choose the white pants instead of my set's color, that make me a buster."

The other boys nod their heads vigorously. Jones smiles sweetly.

"And if you put on the blue or the red, what does that make you?"

G-Roc shrugs.

"Make you dead for no other reason but a madman's whim. You R.I.P. because he like white pants. Now, how many of you gonna die for that?"

The kid persists. "Yeah, but if I do put on yo' color, I'm just a punk."

"No. I just like white. I don't care about no blue, no red, no pink, no green. I just like white."

G-Roc shrugs. "Okay. I'll put on the white." But he's not happy about it; you can see it all over his face.

"Anybody else gonna die for the red or the blue?"

No hands.

Jones erases the words "wearing the wrong color." Then he turns back to look at the kids again. "Lemme tell you somethin'—you can be down for your 'hood, you can go to jail for your 'hood, you can die for your 'hood. And if you do, if you die, you know what happens? *Nothing.* Nothing changes. The beat goes on. All your dead homeboys? Even *they* don't mean diddly. Because nothing changes."

Jones reads off the rest of the reasons that are still on the board. There is no show of hands, until he gets to the words "for his association." This was G-Roc's reason, and he is implacable now: he will kill and he will die because he does not approve of another person's allegiance. When Jones attempts to reason with him, he simply shakes his head, over and over. He remains unmoved even in the face of argument from a couple of the O.G.'s. The only thing that he will say is, "Y'all don't know me."

Finally only three reasons to kill—and to die—are left up there on the blackboard. There is "for his association," with one vote next to it, and there are "for my family" and "self-defense," both of which got a unanimous show of hands.

Now Jones clears the board entirely. Then he puts another word up there:

IRRATIONAL

"Who's heard this word? Irrational."

No hands. Jones writes again, two words this time.

NORMAL   SPRUNG

"How about these?"

Some hands go up. Jones gives the nod to one of the O.G.'s.

"Normal means like regular."

"That's right. And 'sprung'?" He points to another kid.

"It mean nutty."

"Right. And that's what that first word means—irrational. Irrational means sprung." Jones leans back against the desk, crossing both arms against his chest. "Most normal people have a kill-die equation. What that means is if your mother prays at church every Sunday at the Ebenezer Tabernacle and

126

somebody threatens her children, she will kill or die for them. Fathers too. That's what protecting the family is about. Self-defense and protecting your family is a normal kill-die equation."

The kids are listening hard now; Jones goes on. "At the beginning of class we were some abnormal, sprung motherfuckers." A mild laugh ripples through the room. "That's what people think about gang members—they will kill people for any damn thing. That's what people look at. If you decide to be normal, you have to be willing to kill only for that thing you are willing to die for. If you get to that point, you gonna make it—you won't be the kind of person whose numbers are so fucked up that I want him in the penitentiary forever. Forever. Because his numbers are too fucked up."

One of the younger kids—the one who was ready to kill the barber for a less than satisfactory haircut—pipes up.

"How many numbers was up on that blackboard?"

"Y'all gave thirty-seven reasons to kill."

The kid shakes his head. "Thirty-seven's a bigass number."

"Yeah, it is. And if you got more than two for two, then you're the kind of person other people are afraid of. People are afraid of you if you're abnormal."

Jones nudges his head forward a fraction. "Want to get respect? You don't gotta kiss nobody's ass, you don't have to smack,[4] you don't have to talk white. Just be a normal motherfucker. Because everybody—even you—are afraid of abnormal people. Abnormal just don't make it."

The kid who thought that thirty-seven was a bigass number nods his head solemnly. "It don't make no sense."

"That's right. It don't make no sense."

---

[4]kiss ass

6 South Central

The house is situated near a large commercial bakery. Near enough so that you expect to smell the comforting aroma of baking pies and cookies. And maybe you do, in the early morning hours when the plant ovens are going full blast, but now, at four o'clock in the afternoon, the only detectable thing in the air is the faintly metallic scent of an approaching storm.

The street is comparatively bare of traffic at this hour, but you can hear the rumble of heavy freight trucks from the industrial area nearby, and the wind carries a pulsing, thudding sound from one of the factories a couple of blocks over.

I am with Jim Galipeau, who has worked as a Deputy Probation Officer for the last twenty years, most of them with the Metropolitan Specialized Gang Unit. More than fifty kids are assigned to his caseload, and that number keeps on building. Galipeau has invited me along today for his initial visit to a seventeen-year-old girl who has just been placed with him. Recently released from Juvenile Hall where she spent five months on an armed robbery conviction, she will be on probation for the next four years. On the ride over to her house, Galipeau fills me in on the details of the case. Tashay Roberts, a homegirl affiliated with the Bloods, approached a woman at a public telephone and demanded that she hand over her purse. To further state her case, Tashay pulled a .38 revolver out of her handbag and pointed it at the woman's head. The woman yelled, grabbed the gun, and kept on yelling. Tashay wound up in custody.

Mrs. Roberts, Tashay's mother, meets us at the gate of the steel-mesh fence surrounding the scant patch of grass that is the front yard. Her face is as expressionless as a mask; she seems to look through Galipeau and me, rather than at us. As she unlocks the gate to let us pass through to the house, three little kids appear in the doorway. She calls out for the eldest, a boy wearing a Teenage Ninja Mutant Turtles T-shirt, to run across the street and fetch his sister. Then she herds the other two children, both girls, back into the house, standing against the door to allow Galipeau and me to walk inside. As I move past her I can see, at the periphery of my vision, the mask as it breaks for an instant, revealing a look of venomous resentment. By the time she shuts the door the disguise is back in place.

When Tashay walks through the front door, Galipeau and I are seated, with her mother, at the dining room table. Two young guys in their late teens or early twenties are seated in front of a television set in the living room. A movie is playing at low volume.

Tashay has another girl with her—her best friend from across the street. The friend sits down on a straight-backed chair in the corner of the dining room. From where I am sitting I can see into the kitchen—Tashay's grandmother is in there, seated at an old-fashioned white enamel table. The three smaller kids are clustered about her, one of the little girls is on her lap, and she is whispering to them, telling them a story.

After a minute or two of general amenities, Galipeau gets

to it. Leaning forward slightly, resting his splayed elbows on the table, he locks eyes with Tashay. He is a solidly built man in his mid-forties, wearing black jeans and highly polished cowboy boots. His head is completely shaven and he affects a fastidious bopster's goatee and a small diamond stud in one earlobe. His dark brown eyes glisten and smolder with the passion of a man utterly devoted to what he does for a living. His presence in the room goes beyond physical space; it is compelling and slightly disturbing.

"Okay, Tashay, let's get all the facts straight. First, you call in every Monday. That's how you report to me, and if the phone at the probation office is busy, you keep trying 'til you get me. If Monday falls on a holiday, then you pretend Tuesday is Monday and you call me then."

Tashay nods her head, and Galipeau looks at her mother. "Now, if she don't call, she messed up. Right?" Mrs. Roberts nods.

"And don't worry about coming in to see me. I'll come to you."

Both heads nod in unison.

"Okay, that's how you report. Let's move on. If you move, you tell me before you tell Bekins. Okay? I don't want to have to go all over lookin' for you."

"We ain't about to move. Been livin' here in this house since my oldest over there was a baby." Mrs. Roberts gestures toward one of the young men in the living room. There is an edge of anger in her voice.

"I know that, Mrs. Roberts. But I gotta tell you this stuff. That's how we make sure we understand each other." He looks at her for a moment, looks beyond the mask, making certain that this woman understands that he is not simply hassling her or her daughter.

His eyes move back to Tashay. *"No* engagement in gang activity. I know you got some good friends in your set, and I

133

know you're gonna want to see them, but if it even looks like you're gonna get involved in something you shouldn't, I want you to be smart enough to back off. You understand what I'm talkin' about? That means no picnics,[1] no chillin' with the homies. Nothing that even smells like a gang thang."

Tashay seems to be listening intently. She's a nice-looking girl, with enough baby fat still on her to make her look even younger than seventeen. Her hands rest gracefully on the table top. She is wearing a cluster of gold rings, both singly and in groups, on all of her fingers.

"Okay—school. Tashay, I want you to go to school every day. I want you to maintain good grades, and I want you to practice good citizenship. This is real important, and we're gonna come back to it later. But first we're gonna talk about curfew." Galipeau's eyes move back to Mrs. Roberts. One of the toddlers has wandered out of the kitchen, and she has pulled her up into her lap and is murmuring to her.

"You listenin' to this, Mom?" Galipeau's voice, although warm in tone, cuts across the table.

"I'm listenin'."

He looks at Tashay again. "Now, you been told that you have to be in every night by nine o'clock, right?"

"Right."

"You gonna be in by nine? On Friday? On Saturday?"

"Uh-huh." Tashay is looking down at her hands now, fiddling with the rings, changing them from one finger to another.

"Well, I think that's a little bit unrealistic, don't you?"

Tashay's head comes up fast. She looks straight into Galipeau's eyes, waiting.

---

[1] Gang picnics are just that: picnics in a park with hampers of food and beer or wine coolers. These occasions are often an invitation for a drive-by shooting.

"Got a boyfriend?"

"Yeah . . ." The girl's voice is very soft now. She's looking for the trap here; she wants to be ready for it.

"Well, no way can you go out on a date and see a movie, or go bowling and grab a bite to eat and still get home by nine."

He has the undivided attention of every person at the table.

"So . . ." He turns his gaze toward Mrs. Roberts.

"That's *your* responsibility. Tashay can go out on Friday and Saturday nights, and she can stay out 'til midnight. *Sharp.* As long as she goes . . ."

". . . in a car with insurance and a licensed driver!" Both Tashay and her mother chime in, speaking in sing-song, to complete Galipeau's sentence with him.

All three of them chuckle, then he gets back to business. "I don't want this girl ridin' on buses, and I don't want her picked up by some homie in a stolen car on his way to a drive-by. And, I don't want *you* cuttin' her no slack, Mrs. Roberts, if she shows up at midnight on a Wednesday." His eyes swing back to engage Tashay's eyes again. "And I mean what I'm sayin'. Because there *is* no slack at Juvenile Hall.

"No guns. Ever. If your boyfriend has a gun, he better not be in the car with you. It'll cost you three years of your life if you're with anyone who's packin'.

"You're to submit your property to Search and Seizure at *any* time of day or night. With or without a warrant—and anyone who lives in this house lives under that condition." Galipeau glances over at the young men in the living room, and then he raises his voice slightly, talking across the space that separates him from them.

"So you two guys—*be cool.* No pot. No coke. And *no guns!*"

"Her brother here about to become the Man."[2] The guy doesn't turn around as he speaks. His voice is lazily insolent.

Galipeau doesn't miss a beat.

"That's good. Then you can look out for your sister."

Now he refers to the list of requirements printed up by the probation department.

"Okay—'cooperation with the probation department for psychological testing.'" He looks at Mrs. Roberts. "Think she's crazy?"

Mrs. Roberts smiles and shakes her head. She is more relaxed now; her face is no longer a mask.

Galipeau smiles, too. "She don't look crazy to me, either." Then his face sobers, and he turns to Tashay again. "But if you start runnin' with gangbangers, I *will* think you're crazy, and I *will* order you to a shrink."

Now he begins to talk to both mother and daughter, looking into each face in turn. "Now, the good news is, when she goes back to court in six months, if she's doin' what we're talking about here, and she does it right, I'll recommend that your camp order[3] be dismissed. You can give me and the court the finger. And you're outta all this—all you gotta be is eighteen, and dismissed. Your case is sealed."

He lets what he just said sink in, then he moves on to the next subject. "Do you drive, Tashay?"

She nods her head. "But I don't have my license yet."

"Do not drive *any* car without a license. For *any* reason. No drivin' to the market if Mom here forgets the mustard for the hot dogs. No cleaners. No liquor store. *Nothing.*" He looks hard at Tashay. "You understand all this stuff?"

[2]a member of law enforcement

[3]Camp order is short for "camp community placement order." It means that the custody of a minor is taken from the parents or guardian and placed with the probation officer. This gives the power to the P.O. to commit the minor to camp placement if any of the terms and conditions of probation are violated. In Tashay Roberts's case she was given four years custody time with Jim Galipeau.

Another nod of her head.

"Okay, let's talk about school." He looks at Mrs. Roberts. "I think it would be smart if she went to a youth intervention program and got some credits." The woman nods in agreement. "Or she can go over here to one of the schools that have good security. Or a school enrichment program. It's up to you guys, but . . ." He pauses and looks seriously at Tashay; "I don't want you just layin' up. You gotta choose the program you feel is right for you, and then let me know what that is. By next Tuesday. That's a week from now."

Mrs. Roberts reminds him about a part-time job that Tashay is being considered for.

"Oh, yeah. That's the job in the park, isn't it? Workin' with the little kids? I think that would be *wonderful.* That would fulfill all my conditions—*if* you also remember to call me every Monday."

The three of them talk about various school programs, trying to decide which one will be the best for Tashay. Galipeau reminds them about the National Guard Program, where kids on probation can earn their G.E.D. equivalency diplomas and get jobs that pay six or seven dollars an hour. Neither Tashay or Mrs. Roberts seem very interested in anything that has to do with the National Guard.

Now, for the first time, Galipeau turns his attention toward Tashay's girlfriend. She is extremely pretty, with the graceful angularity of a model. Her hair has been extended with long braids which are swirled across her forehead in a curious fashion, like some kind of organic cap.

"You're her best friend, huh? What do you think of all this?"

"If she had listened to me in the first place she wouldn't be in this damn trouble. But no-o-o-o-o-o . . ." She grins ruefully at Tashay, who shrugs and grins back at her.

"What did you say to her that she didn't listen to?"

"I told her not to start messin' with them gangbangers. Told her to go to school and get some good grades, try to get into junior college, make some kinda life for herself."

"What about you? Do you take your own advice?"

"Look, mister—these two little girls here belong to me." She gestures toward the toddlers in the kitchen. "My husband got a steady job, and I'll be graduatin' from high school next month. I don't deal in gangbangin'. Never did, and with these two children I got, I sure don't need for them to start messin' with it when they a little bit older. So I try to do what's right. You know what I'm talkin' about?"

Galipeau nods his head in approval; he's clearly impressed with this young woman, and he doesn't try to hide it.

"Then you can help your friend here out, you sound like you got good sense. Hire her to babysit sometimes. Keep on givin' her good advice." He winks at Mrs. Roberts, then looks at the girlfriend again. "Do you approve of her boyfriend?"

"Which one?"

Tashay giggles; her mother smiles tolerantly. Then Galipeau gets serious again.

"Okay, Tashay—here's what I want you to keep on your mind from now on." He leans forward in his chair. "The last week before you got out of the Hall, let's say some homegirls sneak in with some bud. They tell you it's awesome. You gonna take a hit?"

"Naw!" Tashay is honestly surprised by his question.

"Why not?"

" 'Cause I don't wanna lose my go-home date."

"Right!" Galipeau's voice booms across the table. "Now you keep that attitude, you'll do just fine. Any time somebody offers you a toke, or a late night out beyond the times we agreed on, any time somebody wants to take you out and they don't have a driver's license, or they do have a gun—all you need to do is think about goin' back for three and a half years."

A silence falls across the table. Tashay fidgets a little in her chair.

"So, you just keep on remembering, for the next few years, that all the rules are different for you. If you smoke weed— three and a half years. If *she*"—he points at Tashay's girl- friend—"smokes weed, she gets a sixty-five-buck fine. If *she* stays out too late, she maybe gets yelled at. If you stay out . . ." He raises one eyebrow in a minute gesture.

Galipeau has great timing. He knows there isn't any more to be said today. He will keep his end of the deals he cut with Tashay today; if she welches on any of them, he will come down hard on her. Tashay Roberts is one of his fifty kids, and he will play fair with her, the same as he does with all the others. But if being nice doesn't work, he'll be a hammer. He'll do what he has to do.

We are at the front door when he turns around and walks back to look into Tashay's face again. His voice, when he speaks, is very soft.

"Use your head, Tashay. Just use your damn head."

7 Camp Gonzales

Camp Gonzales is the last stop before juvenile jail—California Youth Authority—and making the point with silent impact is a ten-foot-high concrete wall. You can feel the difference in this camp, even though the boys go to school and play sports and get to see videotaped movies. Even though the food is well seasoned and plentiful. Somehow the air seems different here. Colder. More inhospitable. A neatly lettered sign on the camp director's desk reads, "Make my day."

I am assigned another small office where I can talk to the inmates. Like the rooms at camps Miller and Kilpatrick, this one is next to the D.P.O.'s bullpen too, but the sound of voices and the ringing of telephones is, by some trick of acoustics, much louder. And I am told that in this camp I must keep the door of the office open at all times for my own protection. It is also suggested that it might be better if only one boy at a time is in here with me.

The first kid is seventeen years old, a Crip. He is enormously fat, like a young, unsmiling Buddha, and his eyes are flat and reptilian. He settles himself into the chair opposite me and leans forward, hitching himself as close as possible. He is willing to talk about his career as a high roller, his condo at the beach, and his cousin on Death Row. But what he really wants to tell me is why he is here. He has been sentenced to do time for rape and sodomy. As he talks one of his hands brushes against my knee, and I move it a fraction—slowly, as though I hadn't noticed the touch. We continue to talk and his fingers are there again, brushing, tickling.

Now I must say something. "Hey, don't be tickling my leg." I'm keeping it light, leaving him room for a dignified retreat.

He sits back in his chair, and now he's smiling. He'd like to ask me a question. Do I think masturbation is harmful?

I tell him that this is not an appropriate subject for this interview, that I am not the right person to ask about it. I smile when I say it because, even with the open door, even with four staff members only a few feet away, this kid scares me. I want him out of here.

I get to my feet and begin to thank him for his time. I tell him that I have to go over to the building where the lockup is so that I can talk to the guy in charge. I tell him I'm late. He points to the window; that's the lockup, over there, see? And as I turn my head to look he grabs my ass with both hands. And I do the only thing I can think of, short of screaming. I whirl on him and, in as strong a voice as I can muster, I ask why he dis'ed me. It is his language, and it backs him off. He begins to stammer an apology, and I am able to herd him out into the bullpen where someone will collect him and take him back to class. There is another boy waiting to see me, sitting on a wooden bench near the door that leads to the main campgrounds. I tell him to wait a minute more, and I go back into the small office. I don't want him to see that I'm shaking. It is the first time that I have been frightened by any of these kids. This was one of the abnormal, sprung motherfuckers that A. C. Jones was talking about and, like Jones, I want him to be kept inside forever.

I go to the door and beckon to the kid who is waiting. He is sixteen years old; this is his third time in a detention camp. His gang moniker is Steel, and he is here for aggravated assault with a deadly weapon—a nine-millimeter automatic—and conspiracy to sell drugs. He is a second generation Crip, and he has been active in his set for eight years.

I ask him how he feels about killing another person.

"When you shoot somebody, and you wanna kill 'em, you aim for the head, you shoot 'em—bam—in the head. But if you wanna shoot 'em and just let 'em live, you shoot 'em in the stomach. So that they will live, see, and just be like all messed up for the rest of they life. Have to wear a shitbag for the rest of they life. I got a homeboy who was writin' on the wall and some of our enemies came and blasted on him, shot him in the back. Now he's paralyzed and I know that whoever shot him aimed to cripple him. That happen more than you think, 'cause people get crazy sometimes.

"I'll tell you, though, some of the guys I know, they're born messed up already. They crazy, like . . . just automatically crazy. They don't take drugs or nothin', don't drink—but they just loony. They just—all they thinkin' about is killin' some-body . . ."

Steel sits easily in his chair, hands crossed calmly on the desk in front of him. There are dozens of narrow scars on his fingers, pale pink tissue shining against the dark skin there. A series of holes has been punched into the lobe and cartilage of one ear to accommodate the earrings he wears on the outside. He has explained that the earrings are sapphire and diamond studs, in honor of his gang colors.

"Just gonna shoot somebody. They're nuts right from the start, those dudes, just always want to do somethin' wrong.

145

They like to stay in trouble—lotta guys like that. And some-times it rubs off on you when you kickin' with 'em. That's one of the reasons I try to stay outta jail. Every time you look around the pen, it's 'Where y'all from? Who you claim?' Like that. And you can't really fight or nothin', not in here. You just gotta sit around and get mad. Unless whatever enemy shot one of my homies comes in here. Then he'll get got. No doubt."

I ask him what he thinks would happen if, by some mira-cle, the gangs stopped waging war on each other. He narrows his eyes, thinking about it, taking it seriously for that moment. But a little smile flickers at the edges of his mouth.

"We would never call a truce with the Bloods. Never. That just won't never happen, so there's no point even playin' around with the idea. But if all the Crips stopped fightin' each other, I'd give it six months. It would stop, everything would be cool, and then," he shrugs, "they'll find somethin' else to do. Either fight with the police . . . or just go out and harass people. All that robbery and stuff'll still be goin' on. It's just like certain people—and everybody, *everybody* got these same type people in they 'hood—just *got* to get shit started. Just for the hell of it. Like they'll be kickin' it one minute, and they'll get high, or drunk or somethin', and they'll like, 'I remember the time we didn't get along with that set . . .' and 'That homeboy killed our homeboy, so *fuck* that 'hood!' So every-thing just kick back up again.

"From what I know out there on the street, there's some crazy people out there—and not only the ones who smoke sherm [PCP]. I know some people *want* to be crazy and they smoke sherm so they can get that way. See, just drinkin' and everythin', you know, that just chillin' with the homies, every-thin' cool and all—and that include smokin' bud—weed. That just chillin', you don't gotta go shoot or nothin'. That be just kickin' with your female, or whatever. But some people be smokin' sherm 'cause they *like* it. And they . . . ." He hesitates, searching for the words that will describe exactly the way he feels about this. "They be like the livin' dead. In a way I'm glad I never smoked it. It scared me, tell you the truth. 'Cause I got an uncle who smoked it, and he got to trippin', tearin' the house up, takin' off all his clothes. He"—Steel allows his lips to droop a little, at the corners, and he shakes his head, remembering—"my other uncle have to hold him down. Tie him up and bring him down. Scared me, tell the truth."

Later he talks about the conflicting feelings he has developed in the past few months. "There's some people in here, like, they just don't wanna touch reality. They think the 'hood is everything. They think the 'hood is gonna take care of them the rest of they life. They damn near *worship* the 'hood. Like, 'My homeboy gonna kick me down lotta money, he gonna do this, he gonna do that . . .' What about when all that run out? When it all run out what you gonna do? You gonna take it on down to Skid Row, build you a box house, that's what you gonna do. I just look at it, like—there's my gang life, and there's my real life." He looks down at the desk for a long moment; his hands clasp, unclasp, clasp again. "I'm startin' to pull away, I guess . . ." He looks up at me for a couple of seconds, then looks away again. "And the funny thing is, I don't really know how I feel about that. One thing for sure, I'm not feelin' as good as I maybe should be about it. It's right, pullin' away, you know? But I think I'm gonna miss it."

■   ■   ■

Conversation between four inmates at Camp Gonzales:

"You wanna know how gangs started? It was way back when the old Mexican gangs was out. You know, the ones who used to kill everybody? Rob banks and like that?"

"Well, the Crips has been out for a long time. Like forty years."

"Naw. The Bloods was the first gang, man. Bloods was out first."

"Nunh-*unh!* Crips was out first, man!"

"I'm tellin' you, man. First it was the Bounty Hunters, and then everybody started."

"Naw. Naw! Listen, homes—my mama and them stayed in Nickerson Gardens before I was even born, you know what I'm sayin'? And when they was stayin' in Nickerson Gardens, they was all together. They wasn't no Bloods, homes. Everybody just stick to they own front steps."

"You all wrong. It started with the Watts riots."

"The what?"

You're never going to get a precise history; nobody ever wrote anything down. What you do hear are the myths. Jim Galipeau tells one of the best.

Galipeau figures the whole thing really got underway in the late fifties, early sixties, with the black social clubs—young guys who got together and ran around and hung out, like the Chicano guys did in their car clubs. The Chicanos, traveling generationally back to the early East L.A. *pachuco* gangs, took great pride in their appearance, their sense of machismo, and the ownership and maintenance of customized cars known as bombers. These Chicano cliques, with names like the Pharaohs and the Counts, formed up in Wilmington and San Pedro after the war. And, even though the black youngsters couldn't really identify with the *cholo* kids, with their Mexican-American accents and carefully constructed ducktail hairdos, they *could* relate to the way those kids walked the walk and talked the talk.

Before long the Pharaohs and the Counts had their counterparts in South Central Los Angeles. The new outfits had names like the Businessmen, the Slausons, the Black Cobras, the Gladiators, and the Boozies, and the membership was made up of guys who banded together for camaraderie and, to a certain extent, for protection. Whatever fighting went on had to do with a guy from one club getting pissed off at a guy from another club. It was all about one-to-one combat with fists. Sometimes there would be weapons—stuff like chains, tire irons, bumper jacks—but guns were a rarity.

In 1965 the Watts riots broke out, and from the ruins sprang the militant political organizations: the Black Panthers, US, and others. They tried to give black youngsters a sense of pride and of nationalism, but too many of these kids weren't political enough—or sophisticated enough—to align themselves with Elijah Mohammed or Malcolm X. And even though these young people heard what Martin Luther King had to say, his unswerving allegiance to nonviolence wasn't all that appealing to them either.

Then, in 1968, 1969, somewhere in there, a kid named Raymond Washington pulled together a little gang of kids at Fremont High School in Watts. At the same time the 77th Division of the L.A.P.D. and the Firestone sheriff's office were throwing the block club concept into high gear, encouraging neighborhood residents to organize and protect themselves against property crimes and violence.

As it happened, a large percentage of neighborhood residents in the Watts area were Japanese, many of them older people—sixty and up. The police advised them to travel in groups whenever possible and, if attacked, to yell as loud as they could, to make a lot of noise, to wave their hands. That way, the police explained, they would attract attention to themselves and help would come.

The night arrived when a bunch of these older folks went to a block club meeting, and after it was adjourned, they decided to go for coffee before they walked over to catch the bus on Central Avenue. And they were toddling along toward the corner when here came Raymond and a bunch of his homeboys, bearing down on them like a pack of wild dogs. The old people did what the cops had told them to do: they yelled, they screamed, they carried on. And, sure enough, two things happened: the kids, scared off by all the commotion, ran away after grabbing only a couple of the women's purses, and the police arrived on the scene very quickly. Everyone started talking at once and things got funny when the officers asked for a description of the assailants. Because to these older Asian-Americans, all black people looked alike. Except for one lady. She kept repeating, over and over, that one of the kids was "a crip. A crip with a stick." The cops were finally able to make out, through this torrent of fractured English, that what the lady was trying to tell them was that one of the boys who attacked them had a game leg and that he was carrying a cane. A cripple with a stick. Whatever police reporter was hanging around the station that night picked up on that word, *crip,* and bam, Raymond's little gang of thugs had a name.

They kept on intimidating people. Kept on striking fear into them. Kept on scaring the hell out of other kids. At the same time, over in Compton, a sixteen-year-old called Tookie, a sophomore at Washington High, along with three other youngsters, started up the West Side Crips.

Pretty soon other people felt like they had to organize too so that they could stand up to the Crips. So some kids over on Piru Street formed up the original Pirus.

By the time the Pirus got together to oppose the Crips, Tookie and his boys had adopted the color blue, from the blue-and-white railroad bandannas they used to cover their faces when they went out on what they referred to as "missions." These bandannas were also manufactured in red and white, and the Pirus took them up, claiming red as their color. It was right around this time that the Pirus began to call themselves "Bloods." That was a word African-American fighting men in Vietnam had coined; it was what they called each other. The Pirus picked up on it and it stuck.

Low-income, government-subsidized housing projects provided the spawning grounds for early Crip and Blood sets. In Watts, at the Jordan Downs projects, the earliest resident gang was predominately Mexican-American. They called themselves Varrio Grape Street Watts. But as more and more black families moved into Jordan Downs and as more and more black kids infiltrated the gang, it ultimately became a Crip set known simply as Grape Street Watts.

At the same time another Crip set, the Imperial Courts Crips, fired up at the Imperial Courts projects. They got along fine with Grape Street, and together they began to prey on the kids from another nearby project, Nickerson Gardens. The youngsters from Nickerson got sick of getting the shit kicked out of them, so they pulled together their own gang, a Blood set called the Bounty Hunters, and they declared war on the Crips.

But in the middle of these territories a whole bunch of kids remained unprotected. So they organized too and became the Alley Bishops and the Block Bishops—Bloods. A little bit farther north, in a project called Pueblo del Rio, the Pueblo Bishops, also Bloods, formed to fight the Crips who had organized there and were intimidating people in those projects.

Meanwhile, back in Watts, from Central Avenue up to Compton Avenue, the Kitchen Crips began—so named because that part of the city was nicknamed, unaccountably, the Kitchen. And the Kitchens and the Block Bishops as well as some of the newer sets that were springing up fast began the long fight for possession of the park that separated their territories.

The factions continued to spread. Soon there were the Outlaw Crips, around Central Avenue and Vernon; the Hoover Crips, covering the blocks from Forty-third to 112th streets between Hoover Boulevard and Budlong; the Rollin' Sixties on the other side of the freeway, controlling the streets that roll up from Fifty-second through Tenth Avenue and over from West Boulevard past Western to Crenshaw and from Florence Boulevard to Slauson; the Athens Park Boys—Bloods—from 120th to 135th, north and south, from Avalon Boulevard to Figueroa, east and west; the Denver Lanes Bloods, from Imperial Highway and Century Boulevard to 109th Street. Then, over in Compton, on the other side of Piru Street, past the blocks belonging to the Piru Bloods and the Lime Hood Bloods, you had the Compton Crips, the Southside Crips, the Santana Block Crips and the Atlantic Drive Crips, to name only a few of the sets.

The Crips always outnumbered the Bloods with a ratio that evens out at about seven to one, but it wasn't until the early seventies that the first conflicts between Crip factions began. Nothing too serious at the beginning—usually it was just one guy mad at another guy but—in 1973 or '74 something happened that changed everything: a member of the Rollin' Sixties got into a fight with a guy from Hoover, over a girl, and there was a killing. That conflict goes on to the present, with other Crip factions taking sides.

In 1974 the Eight-Tray Gangster Crips got underway, and they maintained close relations with both the Sixties and the Hoovers until 1979. Then there was a fight over a girl from Eight-Tray territory. The Eight-Trays cover a lot of ground: from Sixty-seventh to Century Boulevard on the north and south, from Vermont to Western on the east and west, then across Eightieth Street to Eighty-third, from Vermont to Van Ness Boulevard. They are considered to be a "deep" set—with lots of members—and yet the actual head count is no more than 350 people.

The way the story goes, it all started at school—Horace Mann Junior High. The girl in question was going out with a kid from the Rollin' Sixties, but she broke up with him and began to date a boy from Eight-Tray named Bootsie. The girl—no one seems to remember her name—started to wear Bootsie's jacket, a satin job with his name on it. A little horsing-around jacket. One day, at lunch time, the kid from the Sixties, the one she had dropped, walked up to her while she was wearing Bootsie's jacket. Apparently the sight of his rival's scripted name was too much for him because he said, in a loud voice that carried to kids nearby, *"Fuck* Bootsie!" The buzz about disrespect got underway, and next thing you hear, there was a fight at a party that was being given that weekend. No weapons, just fists and a lot of yelling. But the following Monday the fight continued at school, and one of the Eight-Trays, looking to build up his rep, went and got a gun, shot and killed the younger brother of a Sixties O.G., and wounded another youngster.

The Sixties mounted up and rolled on into Eight-Tray territory, but they were looking only for the shooter. He was gone (the police'd already gotten him), but emotions were running high. There were some skirmishes and fist-fights, but nobody really wanted a full-out war.

The O.G. whose brother had been shot called a meeting between the two factions. The Eight-Trays went into the Sixties neighborhood for the talks, but things erupted into a full gang fight—fists, bats, knives, and finally guns. The police helicopters converged, and things quieted down for the moment, but a couple of days later, an Eight-Tray youngster was ambushed on his front porch. He was shot six times in the face.

It was automatically assumed that the assassins were the Rollin' Sixties, because threats had been made the night of the meeting when things got so crazy. That was later found to be untrue; the kid had been killed by another gang, but by then it was too late. The war was on.

Since that first "Fuck Bootsie!" in 1979 there have been twenty-five deaths between the Rollin' Sixties and the Eight-Tray Gangsters.

At just about the same time you had East Coast, which is on the east side of the Harbor Freeway, and West Coast—the Hoovers again. They started killing each other across the freeway, and to this day it is one of the deadliest Crip rivalries going, and nobody even knows for sure how it got underway. It is generally believed that, like so many of the interset wars, somebody dis'ed somebody else at a party and things just went from there.

Now, going back a little bit, you had the Six-Deuce Brims Bloods, whose territory extended along Sixty-second Street, going all the way across to the other side of Western Avenue. They got started back when the Crips still got along with each other, and they needed to defend themselves against the Hoovers and the Sixties. The Brims were completely surrounded by Crips: they had the Hoovers on the east, the Rollin' Sixties on the west, the Rollin' Forties on the north, and the Seven-Four Hoovers on the south. At about the same time, the V.N.G.'s— the Van Ness Gangster Bloods—started up near Crenshaw High. But Crenshaw was, by sheer numbers, basically a Rollin' Sixties school. So, right up to the present time, V.N.G.'s attend classes at Dorsey High, which is close to an area near Baldwin Hills that is known as the Jungle. The Jungle is held down by the Black P Stones, who began with the Blackstone Rangers, out of Chicago, and Blood affiliated.

The kids in Inglewood went to two schools: Morningside High and Inglewood High. So what they did was join up with the Bloods to defend against the Sixties on the east side and an offshoot set that came to be known as the Inglewood Village Crips on the west. A club that had memberships at both schools—the Family—became, in the early seventies, the I.F.'s, the Inglewood Family Bloods. The Crip set there, which started up at the beginning of the eighties, is the Inglewood Village Crips.

There are now, at the beginning of the nineties, thirty-eight known Blood sets and fifty-seven Crip sets. The largest Crip set, East Coast, boasts a membership of over one thousand; some of the smaller sets claim twenty kids, maybe less. The average head count of any Blood or Crip set that is considered to be deep is about three hundred members.

CRIP SETS IN LOS ANGELES

52 Hoover*	98 Main Streets
59 Hoover	Broadway 52
74 Hoover	Broadway 112
83 Hoover	Front Street
92 Hoover	Back Street
94 Hoover	357
107 Hoover	Raymond Crips
112 Hoover	Shotgun Crips
Rollin' 30's	Pocket Hood
Rollin' 40's	Front Hood
Rollin' 60's	P. J. Watts
Rollin' 90's	Kelly Park Crips
East Coast 1	Venice Shoreline Gangsters
East Coast 59	Compton Crips
East Coast 62	Kitchen Crips
East Coast 69	Eight-Tray Gangsters
East Coast 89	Inglewood Village Crips
East Coast 97	Grape Street Crips
East Coast 118	Ghost Town Crips
East Coast 190	Watts Baby Loc Crips
83 Main Streets	Playboy Gangsters
94 Main Streets	Schoolyard Crips

*Street names are usually pronounced not as numbers but as words, e.g., Five-Deuce Hoover, Eight-Tray (sic) Gangsters, Broadway One-Twelve, East Coast Six-Deuce, and so forth. The rolling numbers are pronounced as seen: Rollin' Sixties, for example.

Water Gate
Marvin Crips
Santana Blocks
Nutty Blocks
Schoolyard Cs
Gear Gang Crips

Insanes
Lantana Blocks
102 Budlong Gangsters
105 Underground Crips
106 Playboy Style
99 Mafia

BLOOD SETS IN LOS ANGELES:
(Note that capital letter *C* has been changed to letter *S* or *K*)

Athens Park
Black P Stones
Bounty Hunters
8-9 Families
Inglewood Families
Swans
West Side Pirus
Ludas Park Pirus
Rolling Twenties
Outlaw Twenties
Miller Gangsters
Be-Bop Watts
Treetop Pirus
Holly-Hood Pirus
Denver Lanes
Pasadena Devil Lanes
Pablos
Five-Deuce Villains
Fruit Town
Lime Hood

Thirty-Seventh Street Fruit
  Town
Kompton Fruit Town
Van Ness Gangsters
Ujima Village Bloods
Skottsdale Pirus
Karson Pirus
Kabbage Patch Pirus
Bell Haven Bounty Hunters
Nine-Deuce Bishops
Sirkle Sity Pirus
Sirkle Sity Bounty Hunters
Pomona Island Pirus
Mid-Sity Gangsters
Senter Park Pirus
Neighborhood Pirus
Avenue Pirus
Krenshaw Mafia
Six-Deuce Brims
Five-Nine Brims

8 South Central

art has been released from Camp Kilpatrick. I spoke to Nancy Block, and she told me that he will not be going back to his mother but will be sent to live with his grandmother, in Compton.

Since I first met him at the dorm group meeting I have come to know Hart rather well. Intrigued by his youngness and his fierce need to defend himself, impressed by the sheer cussedness he displayed in the face of that storm of disapproval from Lumbly and the others, I went back to Kilpatrick to speak privately with him.

We sit outside on the same picnic bench where G-Roc and Tiny Vamp talked about trust and loyalty and drive-by shootings. On his own, with his hands folded on the table in front of him, Hart looks even younger than he did in group. There seems to be something of the choirboy about him: the smooth, unblemished skin, the narrow shoulders, and the skinny kid's arms. You look at him and you want to tell him not to worry, that everything is going to be okay.

He is excited about this visit, and he tells me that this is the first time in the two months he has been here that anyone has come to see him. He's telling the truth—Nancy Block told me the same thing.

Hart was not sentenced to detention camp for gang activity, although he claims baby homie status in one of the larger Crip sets. He is here because he hit an undercover cop who was trying to get the goods on Hart's mother. She has her troubles with drugs, crack in particular, and she does what she has to do in order to assure herself of her daily pipefuls. Hart was with her when she was confronted by the officer; he accused her of solicitation, and when she argued with him he called her a whore. Hart flew at him and actually landed a couple of punches before he was subdued and taken into custody.

"That dude come into our 'hood flyin' a blue rag so's we'd think he was with us. And then he started in askin' my mama all kinda silly questions. And then he talked crazy to her, called her a ho'. She just doin' the best she can, like everybody else, and I ain't about to let nobody call her no ho'. So I socked him."

Hart goes on to explain—even though I haven't asked—that the reason his mother never comes to see him is because she doesn't have a car. Nobody in the family has a car, he tells me, although he admits to having stolen more than a few fancy models. He tells me that he joyrides the cars, then strips them of all the parts he can sell. It's difficult to imagine this little kid behind the wheel of a high-powered engine: his voice is high and reedy, and he doesn't stand much taller than five foot four, but he boasts that he's been driving for years. "Hell, I taught myself how when I was eight, nine years old. Just scootch the seat up and go—ain't never got in no accident in my life." He is quiet for a beat or two, thinking about it. "Everybody I know start in drivin' young—you know, just havin' fun and also puttin' in work drivin' for the O.G.'s." I ask him if that includes drive-by shootings. He shrugs. "That include anything."

For the remainder of the time we talk about nonessentials—movies, cars, favorite foods. Hart's dearest wish is to have dinner at a Sizzler when he gets out. Just before I leave, I ask him why he has been targeted for so much teasing. I ask if he knows why Lumbly seems to dislike him so much. Hart looks at me, and an expression of amused tolerance builds on his face. "Me and Lumbly friends, we from the same 'hood. He my homeboy."

And that makes it okay for him to pick on Hart?

"Naw, it ain't like that. That's just his way, he like to carry on sometime. I gets on him, too. That just be the way we do with each other, always like that—even on the outs. But we good friends, always got each other."

We walk to the locked door that opens into the main lobby. As the D.P.O. in the bullpen buzzes me inside Hart asks, in the softest of tones, if I will be coming back to see him again. He quickly adds that he will understand if I am too busy to make it. I tell him that I'll be back.

The next time we meet he's got Lumbly in tow. The two kids sit side by side facing me across the picnic table. Hart's manner toward me today is slightly possessive, as if I were a newly discovered relative. He and Lumbly are eager to talk about themselves. They both admit to selling dope; Lumbly claims to have made as much as two thousand dollars a day, but something about the way he says it gives me serious doubts. I remark that two thousand dollars is a lot of money.

Hart shakes his head. "That ain't a lotta money. Two million is a lotta money."

"Ye-eeeeh. Stay out from mornin' to night, just sellin', stackin' up the money. Pockets be bulgin' with bills."

Remembering what some of the other kids have said about stashing the bulk of their dope in a safe place, I ask these two if they hide their merchandise. They answer together, assuring

161

me that they are too tough to have to hide any of their stuff.
Hart is ready with an example.

"I was out there one night and this little dude come up
to me, stuck a gun in my side, said, 'What you think about this,
motherfucker?' " He snorts in derision. "I look down at this
iddy-biddy thing he got and it's *plastic* so I pull *my* gat outta
my pocket—big ole .38—and stick it in *his* face and say, 'What
you think about *this,* motherfucker?' " He giggles. "Dude almost pissed his pants."

I ask if either of them has ever gotten high on crack.

"Hell, no!" Hart's voice resonates in the stillness of the
afternoon. It's Saturday and there are few visitors here today;
most of the boys' families come up on Sundays.

Lumbly volunteers that he and Hart "mostly get high by
smokin' weed and drinkin' beer."

"Ye-eeeeeh." Hart nods his head. "Sometimes we get a
bottle of Silver Satin, mix it up with some Kool-Aid, make a
good drink. Sweet."

The boys swap tales of prodigious drinking feats until
Lumbly reaches around behind and good-naturedly swats the
back of Hart's head. Hart giggles and I take the opportunity
to ask Lumbly why he rides Hart so mercilessly at other times.

Lumbly looks over at Hart and rubs his chin with one
hand as if he were feeling for beard stubble. "Well, he like got
that squeaky voice, it irritate me . . ." Hart snorts out a small
chuff of sound and Lumbly grins. "But, you know, he got a
bad temper. Last time I was with him in the Hall, we started
messin' around and there was some innocent person sittin' on
a bench there in the day room and Hart just jumped up over
the table and started sockin' that dude for no reason."

I glance at Hart and he shrugs. "I didn't like the way he
was lookin' at me."

They are both eager to discuss their lives on the outside.
Hart begins: "On the outs, see, I get up in the mornin' . . ."

He pauses. "Well, I don't really go to sleep sometimes, so it just get to *be* mornin'. Anyway, I tell my mama I goin' to school, or whatever. She don't never . . ."

Lumbly cuts him off. "I don't tell my mama *nothin'*. I just go on out. See, me and Hart be together, livin' in one house or another lotta times. His mama's house, my mama's house, wherever. Anyway, we go out and, like, we'll be hungry, want some breakfast, but we be broke and we wanna go buy some food, or some bud or somethin', you know, so we go sell some dope for our homeboy. Like he give us a hundred dollars' worth, tell us to bring him back fifty and he give us fifty. So that's twenty-five for Hart and I get twenty-five. And then, you know, we can buy some food to eat—like, hamburgers, potato chips, and sodas and stuff. For when we get the munchies."

This sounds much closer to the truth than Lumbly's earlier story of pockets bulging with big bills. In view of what I know about Hart's mother's problems with drugs and what Lumbly said about his own mother in the group meeting, this image of these two little kids dealing piddling amounts for food money is one that is easy to believe.

I ask them about school. Lumbly says that he has "enemies in every school I get sent to." Hart says he likes to go to school sometimes but that when he does he gets chased home. He sits up straight on the bench and strikes an attitude of narrow-eyed menace. "Maybe I do get run off, but I tell you one thing—I done my share of shootin', and I'm not done yet. Still some people to be dealt with."

Lumbly reaches out and cuffs him on the back of the head again. Only this time he does it with greater fondness. "This little dude ain't afraid of nothin'."

The next time I go back to see Hart, Lumbly is gone. He has injured his shoulder playing ball and has been sent to the hospital for treatment. Hart admits that he misses Lumbly, but he figures that he'll be back before Hart himself goes home. This time I have brought a few things with me: magazines, toothpaste, skin lotion, deodorant. (Hart's caseworker has told me that neither kid ever received from their respective families those items classified as "personals" at the camp.)

Hart is touchingly grateful for the stuff I give him. One of the magazines is about cars and he begins to riffle the pages, exclaiming over the photographs. I ask him to read one of the descriptions aloud; he shakes his head vehemently. I ask again and his eyes remain fixed on the page.

"I don't know how to read too good." I can hear the apology in his voice.

I ask if he's working on that here at the camp school. He nods his head.

"Yeah, they tryin' to teach me, but I ain't all that interested, you know?" Then, as an afterthought, "I'm good at art, though. Teacher say I know how to draw real good, got a talent for it."

He seems to feel the need to make up for his inability to read because he asks for a pencil and flaps open his new notebook. In rapid succession he makes a stylized sketch of a sports car, then an ornately lettered, graffiti-like rendering of his gang nickname, and finally a drawing of a tombstone with carved letters spelling out R.I.P. To the side of the tombstone he makes a list of his enemies' names, about twelve names in all, then he draws a thick line through each one.

"That's how we do it on the walls in our 'hood. Do it in they 'hood, too. Line through his name means that person gonna die." He is swaggering a little, for my benefit.

He doodles idly for a few seconds and I sit watching him. Then he makes an unexpected move: without raising his head he reaches out and places the tips of his fingers on the back of my hand. His touch is feather light. We sit like that for a moment, nobody saying anything, and then I feel a slight movement as Hart allows his fingers to feel my hand. His fingertips make tiny ovals on my skin, caressing with such diffidence it occurs to me that this must be the way a blind person reaches out to a newly minted page of Braille, eager to read the words but bitterly aware that the raised code is often sharp enough to slice into the skin.

"Can I ask you somethin'?" Like many of the other kids he pronounces it "ax." His voice is very soft.

"Sure."

"Can I call you 'Auntie'?" Before I can reply he rushes on. "That way it be like you come up here to see me 'cause you care about me."

"I do care about you."

He is quiet for a moment, thinking about it.

"So can I call you 'Auntie'?"

"Yeah. I'd like that." I turn my hand over so that our fingers can mesh. He allows his to rest there on my palm, unmoving, but when I curve my hand to clasp his, he squeezes back timidly.

Another boy, a Hispanic kid, slouches up to the table. Hart shows him the car magazine, and the kid sits down to look through it. Then he looks up at me.

"Hart told us you was his auntie comin' to see him today. Is that for real?"

I don't even have to glance at Hart to see the look on his face.

What the hell. "Yeah. I'm like an auntie."

This time when Hart walks me to the door, he reaches out for a hug.

The next time I visit I bring a couple of books so that Hart and I can work together on his reading. He's not thrilled about anything that looks remotely like schoolwork, but he is touching in his willingness to try for me. We work together for an hour or so, and then we begin to stroll around the grounds.

Hart takes my hand, pulling me along the covered walkway toward one of the classrooms. It is locked and the shades are drawn over the windows, but Hart moves in close to stand on tiptoe at the glass pane that is set into the door. He gestures for me to look inside too.

"See that picture of the tree up there over the black-board?"

I cup my hands at both sides of my face and peer into the gloom. Finally I spot the drawing, a large tree in full leaf casting its shadow over a riot of brightly colored flowers.

"I made it for you. They told me I could take it with me to give you when I leave." I can feel the movement as he turns to look at me.

"Are you still gonna see me when I get outta here? You still gonna be like my auntie?"

"Yep. Guess I got a soft spot for the hard cases." He snorts out a little laugh; he is enormously pleased.

"You like the picture I drew, huh?"

"Huh? Huh?" I put my arm around his shoulders and we turn away from the door. He knows I am teasing and he giggles, leaning in close to my side. "Maybe I'll get it framed so I can hang it up in my house." We are nearing the locked door that leads to the bullpen.

"You gonna let me come over and see it hangin' on the wall?"

"No way. Think I let mummyheads in my house?" There is a split second of silence before he unlooses a real laugh.

When I reach the far end of the bullpen, just before I walk through the swinging doors that lead to the outside world, I turn to see if he is still standing on the other side of the windowed door. He's there, watching me, and when I turn around he smiles and lifts one hand in a solemn little wave.

On my next visit Hart is eager to read aloud, to show me the progress he is making. He tells me that he has been working at it in his spare time, and it's clear that he has made progress. He is beginning to recognize common words, and he is learning to sound out and connect syllables. I ask how it's going with the other kids; he shrugs. I ask when Lumbly is due to return to camp. He shakes his head and tells me that Lumbly was sent to another detention camp after his release from the hospital. Hart talks about his own release; he is eager to see his mother again. He misses her and is worried that she might not be doing so well without him. He has been told that he might be sent to live with his grandmother, but it's clear that he would prefer to stay with his mother in his own neighborhood.

During the following week I call Hart's caseworker and ask when Hart is to be released from camp and where he will be sent. The caseworker tells me that Hart is being held at Kilpatrick only until they can place him. His mother is completely unfit and his grandmother is reluctant to take him.

The thought that has been formulating in my mind simply will not go away. I think about making vast and inconvenient changes in the pattern of my life. About tough-guy writers who, caught in the grip of missionary-like zeal, offer themselves up as safe harbors for parolees who have caught their fancies and touched their egos. About misplaced ambitions and dangerous sentimentality. I think about what I might reasonably be able to offer Hart.

When I call the caseworker, he tells me that Hart cannot be released to my care. That even if I were qualified, the fact is that Hart has a blood relation—his grandmother—who has been approved.

I call Nancy Block at Camp Kilpatrick, and she tells me that she has spoken to Hart's grandmother, that the woman has finally agreed to take him in. Nancy tells me that he will be leaving camp the next day; she herself will be taking him to his grandmother's house. But she has spoken to Hart's caseworker and has gotten permission to let me have the grandmother's telephone number. She also gives me the name of the probation officer who will be taking on Hart's case once he is out of camp.

I wait a couple of days before I call Hart at his grandmother's house. I make the call in the late afternoon; no answer. I try again at seven-thirty or so and the grandmother answers. I introduce myself and ask if I may speak to Hart. He's not there. I ask when he is expected. She doesn't know. Can I call back later? She guesses so. At nine-thirty a man picks up the phone and he is annoyed. He doesn't know where Hart is and people are trying to sleep. I call the next morning. This time it's a young voice on the other end; Hart's eighteen-year-old brother, Brian. He tells me that Hart has already left the house. I ask if he has registered for school; Brian doesn't know. I ask him to give my telephone number to Hart. He tells me that he'll make sure that Hart returns my call.

I call back in three days. The telephone rings endlessly. When I call again I make sure that the grandmother writes down my number. When I come back from the market there is a message from Hart on the answering machine. When I call his grandmother tells me that I have missed him by minutes.

The next call comes in at nine o'clock the next morning. It's Brian, and he tells me that Hart was picked up last night on a street corner in his old neighborhood. Brian wants to know if I will drive him out to Los Padrinos Juvenile Hall so that he can get Hart and take him back to their grandmother's house. He does not try to sell me on the idea that the arrest may have been unjust; rather he expresses anger that Hart has fallen back in with his old homeboys so soon after his release from camp. Without being asked he assures me that he himself no longer associates with members of his set. We make arrangements to meet in front of the apartment house where Brian and Hart live with their grandmother.

The gang graffiti emblazoned on the walls of the two-story, gated building proclaims this to be the territory of one of the biggest—and most notorious—Crip sets. Hart has described the members of this set as his "worst enemies," and he has expressed some degree of fear at moving into their neighborhood. As I pull up to the curb a tall, rather nice-looking young man disengages himself from a group of three or four other young guys and waves at me. He is quietly dressed in well-pressed gray trousers and an expensive-looking shirt of muted beige and gray checks. His hair is cropped close to the scalp. Nothing about his appearance suggests gang affiliation; he might be a student at any good school.

The conversation is desultory during the ride to Los Padrinos. Most of the time we talk about Brian's fiancée who has recently joined the army. He tells me they plan to be married in a month or so and that he is seriously considering a stint in the service. The possibility of being stationed overseas appeals strongly to him. He gestures languidly out the passenger window toward the barren landscape of auto body shops and dingy apartment buildings that is unrolling next to the car.

"I don't wanna stay around here, no way. This place just eat you up alive you stay here."

Los Padrinos Juvenile Hall is located in the unyieldingly conservative city of Downey. The Hall is situated next to the lush grounds of a city-owned golf course so that what you see from your car as you pull through the main gate is a verdant stretch of perfectly manicured grass punctuated here and there by groves of shade trees. I have been told, by an amused and somewhat outraged county juvenile probation officer, that although the dormitory windows do not look out over the course itself, they do, in fact, give onto an area where several peacocks strut and shriek near a large swimming pool.

A bored young woman plugged into a switchboard tells us to wait for Hart in the lobby, a cheerless plain of plastic chairs and metal tables. He spots me the instant he walks through the glass doors that lead from the main body of the Hall, but he covers his surprise quickly. What he cannot hide is the fact that he's happy to see me; his hug is immediate and all-enveloping. He is carrying a brown paper bag with his belongings—a new lightweight jacket and some change, eighty cents or so—inside. On the walk to the car Hart pulls the jacket out of the bag to show us where the arresting officer grabbed him. The jacket is stained and crumpled on both sides of the neckline.

It is almost one o'clock now and we are all hungry, so I suggest a meal at the nearest Sizzlers. Brian says he knows of one that's located in the neighborhood where they used to live. Hart asks if he can ride in the front seat next to me, explaining that he tends to get carsick in the back.

As we walk into the restaurant it is impossible not to notice the change of attitude that washes over Brian. His step modifies itself into a subtle but definite swagger; his eyes flick back and forth over the people standing in line with us; he mutters something inaudible under his breath. Hart is aware of this too, but his interest is in the salad bar, the steaks, the complimentary desserts. We place our orders and find a table in a quiet corner of the room. Brian is scowling now, and I go with Hart to fill our salad plates, hoping we can eat quickly and get out of here without incident. When we return to the table, Brian is staring at two elderly women sitting nearby. I sneak a glance at them; they are quietly eating their food.

"They're not even looking this way, Brian. Let's just enjoy our meal, okay?" My voice sounds thin and strained in my ears.

"They not lookin' this way, huh? Them two black bitches been lookin' crazy at me ever since I walked in here. Think they better than me. Think they better than you, too, 'cause you in here with me." His voice is filled with barely suppressed rage. "I don't even feel like stayin' in this place."

Hart is shoveling cherry Jell-O and whipped cream into

his mouth. His face is completely without expression, but I can feel the tension steaming off him. Brian pulls a cigarette out of his shirt pocket, lights it, and hisses a plume of smoke toward the two women. I glance over at them again; they begin to flap their napkins in front of their faces a bit more strenuously than might be necessary.

I signal the waitress and ask her to pack up our order to go.

Back in the car, on the way to his grandmother's house, I notice that Brian keeps shoving his arm, fist raised high, out of the open window. He does this every time we pull abreast of any car with young guys inside, and he does it any time we pass young guys on the street. He is, of course, throwing the hand sign of his set. In almost every instance the gesture is returned.

Hart's grandmother's apartment is very small, very clean. The furniture in the living room is protected by neatly arranged clear plastic sheeting and every available flat surface, every wall and table, is covered with framed family photographs and ceramic knick-knacks. There are several pictures of Hart as a baby and two or three of Brian in prom and graduation finery. A tinted studio portrait of a smiling young woman with her hair in the Afro style of the seventies sits alone on top of a large TV-stereo console. A cut-glass vase of pink paper rosebuds has been placed to one side of the frame.

Four people—Hart, Brian, their grandmother, and her son, Clarence, a taciturn man in his mid-forties who has recently been released from prison—live here, sharing the small, single bedroom, taking turns in the bathroom and at the kitchen sink. The grandmother is a reed-thin woman in her late fifties. Her hair is laced with gray, and there are teeth missing up near the front of her mouth. She might have been pretty once, but now all that remains of her looks lies buried deep in a structure of fine, high-riding bones. She is not surprised to see a stranger bringing her grandson back from Juvenile Hall;

171

she is used to strangers coming into her home—caseworkers, probation and parole officers.

She is happy to see Hart, happier with the food that we have brought with us. Brian, Hart, and I dish out the portions. Clarence accepts his plate and continues to watch a game show on television. The grandmother perches on the edge of the couch, lifting little dabs of food to her mouth in short, furtive movements and talks about the rigors of her job as a factory maintenance worker. She says that she doesn't know how she's going to manage to take Hart to school to get him registered for classes. She says she doesn't know how she's supposed to take him to meet with his probation officer when she has to catch a five-thirty bus every morning. As she talks her eyes move, again and again, to the portrait on top of the TV set. When she sees that I am watching her she smiles crookedly.

"My daughter sick, you know, she bad off. Otherwise her children be with her—she a good mother."

Clarence makes a sound that could be a muffled cough and Brian turns his head to look at him. There is bad blood between these two; Hart mentioned it to me when he was still in camp. They have already come to blows.

Hart has finished eating and now his eyelids are beginning to droop. He smiles at me in apology and slides down to rest his head on the arm of the couch.

"I didn't get no rest last night. Can't get no sleep in the Hall, too much noise." I ask him where he sleeps here at home and he points down at the spot where he is now slumped. He is already more than half asleep.

Brian walks me down to my car and thanks me for having driven him to rescue his brother from Juvenile Hall. He closes the door for me and locks it, then leans in the driver's window.

"You know, it ain't no good stayin' here. That ol' lady don't care nothin' about us, she just want money all the time. Complains about everythin', threaten to call the police on you and then she ask you fo' the money you make."

As I drive away I can see him in the rearview mirror as he moves slowly toward the corner and the shadowy figures of his friends who are waiting for him.

The telephone has been disconnected at Hart's grandmother's house. The tinny voice of the computer gives me the information when I call about a month and a half after the Juvenile Hall incident. I try again in about a week and once more a week or so after that. Then I place a call to Hart's probation officer; Hart never made it in to meet with him.

It is Saturday, and hot. The front door of the apartment is open and I can see the flickering light of the television through the screen. I call out Hart's name and his grandmother gets up from the couch and unlatches the lock, stepping back to let me into the living room. A young woman is sitting in a club chair next to the couch; she's holding a baby on her lap. The baby looks to be about nine or ten months old, and she is dressed in a pink sweatsuit with tiny matching running shoes. Her hair has been sectioned off into braided pigtails with pink and lavender barrettes at the tip of each braid. She looks up at me, dimples briefly, then goes back to gnawing the piece of Zweiback she's got gripped tightly in one fist.

The grandmother introduces me to the young woman, who is the baby's mother and Hart's half-sister. Her name is Bijou and she tells me, with some pride, that she has another child, a two-year-old son.

The grandmother can tell me very little about Hart, only that he is out of the house most of the time, hanging around with boys from his old neighborhood. She doesn't think he ever did get to school because she wasn't able to manage the registration process which demanded proof of address. She doesn't know where he is now; he hasn't been home for two or three days. Brian hasn't been around either, and she's angry at him because he ran up her telephone bills with long distance calls to that girlfriend of his, the one in the army.

Hart's sister interrupts. She knows where Hart is, and she will take me to him if I want to wait until she fixes her hair. She leans forward and parts the hair on one side of her head to display a battery of stitches on her scalp.

"Got in a fight with this dude two nights ago. He dis'ed me, you know what I'm sayin', and I got a knife in his shoulder, so then he hit me with some kinda damn bat. Shoulda stuck the knife in his stomach." Her voice is casually conversational; she might just as easily have been discussing a scene on a television show.

She hands the baby to her grandmother and rummages around in a large shoulder bag. She comes up with a pack of Towelettes, pulls out a couple and dabs gingerly at her scalp. In spite of the purplish bruise on her temple, she is startlingly pretty, with prominent cheekbones and a short kitten's nose. Finishing with the Towelettes she pats her hair into place and gets to her feet.

"Let's go."

The grandmother and the baby are both watching an old movie when we leave the apartment.

As we drive to Hart's old neighborhood, Bijou tells me that she was a hardcore homegirl until she had her first child. She also tells me that she is nearly three months pregnant with a third. The father of this baby is a fifteen-year-old homeboy in the neighborhood where she lives.

"He really want the baby and all, but I ain't gonna have this one. I ain't but nineteen myself and I know he just too young to be any kinda father. He just excited about *bein'* one, that's all, just like the other two was. You know, braggin' to the homies and all like that."

Then, with a sudden shift of subject, she asks me if I know anyone who makes commercials for television. She tells me that

174

she was chosen to appear in one for a fast-food chain when she was eight years old, and she wants to do it again. Maybe I can help her meet some people?

"I just need to get a bunch of money and get outta this neighborhood. Can't raise no good kids around here." In a sudden, fluid move she turns all the way around in the seat to look at a car that's parked on a side street.

"Had a car stolen off me last week. Dude said he'd pay me a hundred bucks if he could use it in some movie, then he just took off with it. Pretty good car, too—Honda. Only had it a couple days."

We have been driving along a major boulevard in South Central. The sidewalks are teeming with people, the sun is blazing off ugly concrete buildings and smudged glass storefronts. Bijou directs me to turn onto a residential street.

"There he is."

She points to a knot of teenaged boys standing in front of a ramshackle house halfway down the block. Now she leans out the window and shouts her brother's name. He turns, squinting for a clear look at whoever might be in the car with Bijou. When he recognizes me, he lifts one hand in a listless greeting.

I get out from behind the wheel and he takes a couple of steps toward me. Hart has changed dramatically since I last saw him. He is taller, his chest and shoulders have broadened, he is leaner in the waist. He swaggers a little as he walks slowly toward me, and I notice that his hair has grown out and that he is wearing it swept back from his forehead. He is carrying a huge portable radio with twin speakers; I can hear the solid beat of rap music playing.

I move quickly to hug him, but he tenses so visibly that I lower my arms and we exchange nods instead. Bijou walks past us and disappears inside one of a series of rundown bungalows that form a court next to the house where the kids are standing. As we head toward them I ask Hart if he has seen Lumbly.

"Naw. He still inside—he at Y.A. now." His voice has deepened to a smoky rasp.

There is an array of stitches at the corner of Hart's mouth, six or seven of them. The skin around them is puffy, and it looks infected. I ask him what happened.

"Some fool stuck me with a screwdriver. I headed up with him because he tried to pull me outta a car I was drivin'." It appears to be difficult for him to talk, and he keeps spitting out of the other corner of his mouth, as though his saliva tasted too bad to swallow.

We have reached the group and Hart makes a halfhearted attempt at introductions. There are five boys in all, and not one of them looks any older than Hart. One kid is at least fifty pounds too heavy for his height and frame, and he keeps cadging bites from a taco the boy standing next to him is eating. They begin to tease each other about skin color—the boy with the taco is very dark. Hart jumps in with a comment to the fat kid. "You be talkin' about his color, you the funniest lookin' nigger around here. You red, look like a damn apple."

The others laugh. The fat kid's light brown skin does, in fact, have decidedly rosy overtones. Now he turns to look at Hart. "Yeah? Well, *you* just orange all over."

At that moment Hart's sister comes out of the bungalow. She has two guys with her, seventeen- or eighteen-year-olds. They are both wearing the low-slung dungarees, oversized white T-shirts, and broken-down houseshoes that proclaim their gang affiliation. The taller of the two has on a plastic shower cap that covers all of his hair and rides low on his forehead. The other boy is sporting a headful of glistening jheri curls.[1] They are rough-looking kids, unsmiling and suspicious.

[1] term for a hair process, like the one worn by Michael Jackson

They slouch to the edge of the patch of dirt that separates the bungalows from the pavement and stand staring at me. Hart edges a couple of steps away from where he had been standing at my side.

"Y'all from the county?"

The kid with the shower cap has asked the question. I tell him my name and give him a few fast facts about the book. He remains unsmiling and unimpressed. Bijou has been carrying on a whispered conversation with the other kid, and now she beckons Hart to join them. She is gesturing with swooping motions, and her eyes have a glittering, unfocused cast to them. Suddenly she reaches out and pushes hard on Hart's chest.

"What y'all call me, nigger?" Her voice is suddenly shrill.

Hart mutters something about the car; it is clear that he blames her for the loss of the Honda.

"I'll kick you in yo' place, you call me that again! Don't you *never* call *me* no bitch!"

Now Hart's voice gets louder. "How about I call you a dick-eatin' 'ho?!"

All conversation has come to a halt; everybody is watching these two. The fat kid giggles.

Bijou's lips pull back from her teeth. "You just a little buster showin' off for yo' friends. I'll kick the shit outta you, you think you so down, you dick-eatin' little homo!"

With great care Hart places the radio on the ground, making sure that it is well out of the way of people's feet. Then, in a lightning move, he shoves his sister hard enough to send her staggering back several steps. The kid in the shower cap laughs out loud and punches his buddy's shoulder gleefully.

Bijou regains her balance, and now she goes after Hart with everything she's got. She lashes out with fists and feet, her earrings fly off to land unnoticed in the street, and a couple of her punches must have hurt him pretty bad because now Hart is crying. Bijou isn't even breathing hard.

"Fuckin' homo! I'm gonna cut up all yo' clothes!" Her lips are flecked with spittle. "You stink! When you wash last?"

He connects with a right to the jaw and she drops to one knee, shaking her head to clear it.

A couple of older guys, men in their thirties, have drifted over from across the street. One of them wags his head in disapproval.

A heavy-set woman comes out of one of the bungalows and leans against the door jamb, watching the fight with idle interest. A small, untrimmed white poodle has followed her outside, and it runs, yipping loudly, toward the action. The woman calls out in a piercing voice and it trots back to her side.

Another flurry of blows is exchanged, and now Hart is bleeding from the stitched-up corner of his mouth. He is losing this fight, and he knows it; the frustration—and the shame—are all over his face.

Bijou dances around him. "Yo' mother a cluckhead 'ho! She don't want *you* no way!"

"Eat dick and die, 'ho!" He spits a stream of red at her face.

She swipes at her cheek with one hand and looks around wildly. Her eyes settle on the radio, and suddenly it is in her hands, and she is hoisting it high over her head. Hart's hands go up reflexively, but there's nothing he can do as she hurls it, with all of her strength behind it, into the street. It shatters on the pavement, and a cassette pops out and breaks, spewing a ribbon of tape.

There is an audible intake of air from some of the onlookers. Hart stands still, looking down at the ruined portable; the expression on his face is like that of someone who has just seen his dog run over by a car.

He stands like that for a moment, and then he whirls and

charges her, hitting her anywhere he can land a punch. They are both breathless now, sucking in air in great sobbing gasps. Finally she decks him with a solid left hook. Then she turns and saunters off.

Hart lies there on the ground. He blinks his eyes once, again, then he props himself up on both elbows and looks over at the wreck of his radio as if he could will it whole again.

Then he does an amazing thing: He gets slowly to his feet, walks to where the radio is lying, and begins to jump up and down on it. His feet come down again and again as he crushes and mangles it beyond any recognition. He sobs in rage and humiliation. Not only has Bijou whipped him in physical combat, she has struck with unerring accuracy and lethal force at his every vulnerability. She has, in effect, rendered him impotent in front of an audience of his peers.

And she's not through with him yet. Hands on hips, she struts back to stand in front of him, giving him a slow, insolent once-over.

"You ain't so tough now, are you?"

He throws a wild haymaker; she sidesteps neatly. Now the others are laughing. There is a beer bottle in the gutter; Hart picks it up and slams it against the curb, but this is real life, not the movies, and he has to repeat this process several times before the bottom half shatters leaving Hart with the jagged neck of the bottle in his hand. Only now the timing is off. Bijou has already begun her walk away from him. He follows her, holding the bottleneck out at hip level, jabbing it toward her in short, threatening moves.

"Look out, girl—he comin' to get you!" The guy in the shower cap is enjoying himself.

"Only thing he gonna get is his ass whipped again." And she keeps on walking, heading first into the street to scoop up her earrings and then straight back to disappear again into the

179

bungalow at the back of the court. The two young guys follow her inside.

Hart stands there with the broken bottle dangling from his fingers and looks around at his circle of friends. Each boy, in turn, looks away from his gaze. They might be feeling pity for him, they may even know how he is feeling right now, but for the most part they seem to be embarrassed for him and perhaps a little bit angry at him for having allowed himself to suffer such ignominious defeat, for not having used the broken bottle on his sister.

It is left for me to approach him. Cautiously. Because he is holding that broken bottle and because he is lost. The thing I had seen in him at camp, that small, unwavering glow of inner spirit, is gone. And his eyes have dimmed with its loss.

"What you want?"

I tell him that I want him to put down the bottle. That it frightens me.

He looks at me for a long moment before he loosens his grip on the bottleneck, allowing it to drop to the ground.

"Why you come here again, anyway?"

I tell him that I have come to see him, that I care about what happens to him. He is shaking his head in a slow back and forth movement before I finish speaking.

"What the fuck you care about what happens to me? You white."

"I do care about you, though." I reach out to touch his arm. He jerks away as if I had taken a pass at him with a razor.

"Ain't nobody can care about me. And I don't care about no fuckin' person on earth." And he turns his head away to stare off toward the sluggish stream of traffic moving across the intersection at the end of the block.

9 | South Central

It is easy to imagine how a Christmas tree would look in this room. The color scheme is all warm beiges and deep russets and browns. The chairs and sofas are wide and comfortable. The wood surfaces have been polished to a gleaming patina; you can smell the faint aroma of furniture wax. There are two large baskets of toys and children's books in one corner. It is chilly today, and in spite of the sunlight that falls in slits and rods through half-open blinds, there is a fire blazing in the brick hearth.

This is G-Roc's home. He lives here with his mother and stepfather, Reverend and Mrs. Lunceford, his older brother, and his younger half-sister. Mrs. Lunceford is a gently pretty woman with solemn, watchful eyes. Her voice is calm and even, but runnels of emotion course beneath the surface of her demeanor.

"The thing I'm learning now is not to blame myself for Jeffry going into a gang. I'm beginning to accept the fact that I didn't make that choice for him. He did, and it's a bad choice. Of course, I have to live with it." She reaches out to pour more coffee into the cups on the table in front of us. She and I are sitting on the couch; her husband sits facing us. G-Roc—Jeffry—has relaxed into an easy chair at the far end of the table. He is listening to his mother with idle interest, as if her words have nothing to do with him. His expression is blank; only his eyes give him away as they flick back and forth from her face to mine.

Mrs. Lunceford goes on. "I'm against the gangs, but I have to say that the system is really trying to sock it to these kids who are involved with it, especially the black kids. Because nobody considers what kind of backgrounds many of them come from, or if a boy is really a good kid underneath it all. I just talked to another mother whose seventeen-year-old is being tried as an adult. Not for murder, either. For robbery. Well, he started out early, gangbanging, and now it's completely out of his mother's hands. That kid might go to jail for the rest of his life. She asked me what I'd do if that was my son, and I told her, 'What would I do? I wouldn't even go to the courtroom.'"

She sees my look of surprise and holds up both hands in a gesture of surrender. "That's just the way that kid's mother looked at me when I said that to her, but I told her, 'Look, those were the decisions he *made*, he made his choices. If you have a son who's going in and out, in and out of that kind of trouble, and you've done the best you can with him, if you've been giving, if you've tried every way you know to work it out with him and he *still* chooses the gang, then you have to accept that that's the way he wants to go. But you still have to have a life. Why keep putting yourself through this?'" She is really speaking for herself and for G-Roc now. "You can't just say, 'Okay, forget about the rest of the family,' and just totally dedicate yourself and your life to that one kid. Not if that kid has made the choice that that's what he's going to do. It doesn't matter a bit how carefully you raised him and how much love you gave him and how many times you begged him and warned him and prayed for him. Because that kid *will* do what he's going to do."

The front door opens and the Luncefords' eight-year-old daughter, Theresa, comes into the room. She has been playing outside with friends but now, she tells her parents, it is the time that she and her father agreed upon when he would take her to the store. She holds up her wrist to show him the time on a brightly colored plastic watch. He looks at the watch with a show of exaggerated solemnity and drops a fast kiss on top of her head. Then he excuses himself and goes to change his clothes.

The little girl moves to stand next to G-Roc's chair, rubbing her shoulder against his affectionately as she listens to her mother's voice.

Mrs. Lunceford picks up her train of thought. "It's like with Jeffry. This week has been great, but some weeks I've just said, 'Forget it, I don't want to do this anymore.'" She takes in a deep breath. "Right now, though, let's face it—Jeffry has been breaking curfew every night. One night somebody called to tell me where he was—middle of the night, way past curfew—and I got up and went to get him. I don't even know who it was called me, all I know is he wasn't supposed to be where he was in the first place, you know what I mean? I got up and went, but the truth is I'm getting tired. I'm not going to do it anymore. I'm not going to get up out of bed and run . . ." Her voice breaks, and she looks at me with a little half-smile of apology. "I have to be at work every morning. I'm just not gonna run and . . ."

Her words fade away. She looks over at her son, and when she speaks again her voice has regained its strength.

"You know what time you have to be home. You know where you're supposed to be and what you're supposed to be doing. So if you can't do that, if you do get picked up by the police, I am not coming to get you." She brushes her hands together in a swift gesture of dismissal. "It's simple as that, Jeffry. Because I cannot . . ." She lowers her head and gives it a hard little shake, as if she were trying to dislodge a stubborn notion. Then she looks back up, at me this time. "I myself have not chosen, for my life, to keep running down to the police station. I don't want to do that. If Jeffry has chosen that life for himself, I can't stop him from living it. I can only say for myself that I don't want to go to sleep every night with my heart pounding in my throat waiting for that phone to ring with terrible news."

Mr. Lunceford has returned and is standing in the archway that separates the living room from the entrance hall. Now he gestures to Theresa, and she walks quickly across the floor to take his hand. As the front door opens Mrs. Lunceford calls out, reminding Theresa to take a sweater with her. There is some doubt about the location of the sweater, and Mrs. Lunceford goes to fetch it. I look at G-Roc; he has slid all the way down in his chair with both legs splayed out in front of him. We talk briefly about A. C. Jones and Gang Class, about Tiny Vamp and a couple of the other kids at Camp Kilpatrick. Mrs. Lunceford comes back into the room at the tail end of the exchange and sits listening. With her entrance G-Roc's voice has dropped a couple of notches, and his answers have become monosyllabic. Finally the conversation jounces to a stop, and there is a long beat of silence.

G-Roc fidgets in his chair.

I ask Mrs. Lunceford if it had been difficult for her to accept Jeffry's sentence to detention camp. She glances past his head out the window and almost, but not quite, smiles.

"Honestly? Honestly I feel that it was justified for Jeffry to be sent away to camp. He *didn't* know how to behave at home; he *didn't* want to do the things he was supposed to do; he *did* take my car without permission. It wasn't just the gang-

banging that got him sent away. Maybe I sound hard sometimes, but if you're a parent you know that we only want to save
our kids. And until you *have* a kid who's acting out, you just
can't know what his parents are going through. No one who
hasn't gone through it can possibly know how disruptive that
is in a home."

Wordlessly G-Roc gets to his feet and walks out of the
room. His mother watches him until he disappears through
the archway. Then she turns her head to face me again. "I took
Jeffry to a psychiatric hospital because I thought he needed
some counseling. But," she shrugs eloquently, "he didn't like
it, he didn't feel comfortable, blah, blah, blah." She looks
down at her hands; her fingers are long and slender with beautifully manicured, almond-shaped nails. She is wearing several
narrow, Victorian-style gold rings. Now she begins to twist one
of them around and around on her finger. "Some of those
places are really good." She mentions one that advertises regu-
larly on television and in print. "That place does a heck of a
good job even though the prices are outrageous." Then,
amending, "Well, at least there are some good counselors that
work there, and some of them have volunteered to work with
kids on the outside for free."

G-Roc walks back into the room—he is chewing something, a cookie or some kind of chip—and drops heavily into
his chair.

"One particular counselor said that he had been in a gang
himself"—G-Roc begins to shake his head in a slow but emphatic back and forth motion—"and this was just in general
conversation, it wasn't a counseling session at all. He said he
didn't think Jeffry needed residential care. He said that Jeffry
needed to be . . ."

"Let go. He said I should be let go." His voice has sliced
through his mother's.

"Okay, okay. Of course, *he*"—she indicates G-Roc with a

nod—"picked up on that single phrase, 'let go.' But there's a . . ."

"Don't try to protect yourself. If you gonna say somethin', say what the man said." It's the same tone of voice he used when he talked to Tiny Vamp in that small room at Camp Kilpatrick.

She whirls to face him. "I took you to that hospital for evaluation because I needed some peace of mind!" Then, turning back to me, "And that's just the bottom line. I took him because I had already talked to one counselor, and I wanted a second opinion. Well, the counselor at the hospital suggested that Jeffry—that all of us—come back for some counseling and . . ."

"*I* ain't goin' back."

". . . the bottom line is I think we *can* all use the counseling. See, what I try to do is help Jeffry make his own decisions, but when he chooses *not* to make them, that's when I'm forced to use the system."

The front door opens and shuts. Mr. Lunceford and Theresa are back from the store. They walk into the kitchen, and the little girl shouts to her mother that they were able to find a certain kind of cereal that Mrs. Lunceford had asked for. Mrs. Lunceford nods her head absently, as if the child could see her.

"See, what I'm trying to do is . . ." She stops, starts again. "I don't want to have to go to Jeffry's probation officer with this."

G-Roc leans forward in his chair.

"She ain't gonna make me go to no counseling. I can't be made to go to no counseling if I don't wanna go."

"Fine. Fine." She looks steadily at him. "We can do this the easy way or we can do it the hard way. That's the bottom line."

G-Roc unleashes the same hiss of contempt he used at

camp. "Whatever it is. Just don't threaten me—I ain't no punk." He looks defiantly at his mother. "And I ain't goin' to no counseling regardless. Don't matter if I go crazy. I ain't goin' to no counseling."

It is a few minutes later. Mrs. Lunceford and Theresa have left the living room, and I am sitting with G-Roc and his stepfather. Mr. Lunceford is an imposing looking man, tall and solidly built. His voice rumbles up from his chest when he speaks; it is easy to imagine how it must sound during a sermon.

G-Roc hitches his chair a little closer to where his stepfather is sitting as Mr. Lunceford begins to talk.

"One of the biggest problems that I see in all of this is that almost every middle-class black forgets that they have been in some situation in their own life where society looked down on *them*. Maybe it wasn't gangbanging, maybe they didn't shoot people up, but it was something, there was some situation in their life where society looked down and pulled back." He shakes his head and smiles. "But let them get up and out of the ghetto, out of the neighborhood, and they forget *that's* where they came from. They forget *that's* what they went through. And they condemn the kids coming along today. The average middle-class black today forgets that at one time they *were* those kids.

"There are not many black Americans, even in the higher echelons, who are real role models. If they've gotten away from hard times, they're sure not coming back to work with these kids, and if they never had hard times, how are they going to be able to understand?"

G-Roc nods his head in a slow and solemn movement. He is sitting forward to listen; with his mother out of the room he is much more relaxed, he's not simply striking nonchalant poses now.

189

Mr. Lunceford continues: "Another big problem, of course, is the media. You pick up a newspaper, you turn on your television, and all you hear about is the youth gangs in South L.A., East L.A. Nobody ever mentions the gangs in Beverly Hills or Sherman Oaks. If a kid writes on a wall in Brentwood or Palos Verdes, he's expressing himself. That same writing on a wall in South Central or East L.A., that's gang related only. If a kid lives in a deprived, rundown area—Watts, Downey, Inglewood, Compton—no matter who that kid is, he's automatically perceived as a gang member."

But Jeffry *is* a gang member.

"Yes. And I can understand how our children can become affiliated with gangs, even though my son tells me I don't comprehend." He lights a cigarette, one of many. The air is thick and blue, and he motions for G-Roc to open a window. "You talk to a boy and he might tell you, 'I didn't start out to be a gang member, but things just went along and grew, and then I realized that if I got in trouble my homeboys were there to support me.' But, of course, that love and loyalty becomes, in many cases, detrimental. These kids are killing each other when they could be consolidating and building a real power in the community. When I talk to Jeffrey and his friends, I try to get them to understand that violence breeds only more violence. I try to get them to understand that sometimes, by suffering unjustly, you can gain attention and have others who notice begin to wonder *why* you are suffering. I try to show that even though we, as black Americans, are in a so-called revolution, we must first band together as a people and move forward from there. The black movement in the United States is going to have to undergo a very severe undertaking before all the factions can come together. Right now we have too many blacks up there who are still pressing down on blacks who have not risen to meet their standards of success." His voice is strengthening and lifting. It resonates with the accrued passion of years of Sunday sermons.

"We need to guide our young men to join together, to focus—not on certain territories or gang affiliations—but on the injustice of the present system. That's what must be fought against." He turns slightly in his chair, and now his words begin to stream like tracer bullets toward his son.

"You have to fight against the fact that the system doesn't want you to rise above the job of machinist. You have to fight against injustice. Fight against the laws that can keep you from raising your own child. You can't rise against any of this by going out and joining a gang. You must make your choices—the right choices—now."

"You can't tell me, like right now, 'You should quit gang-banging and make the choices, woo-woo-woo . . .'" G-Roc's tone of voice, even though he is disagreeing with his stepfather, is still respectful. "I might feel it's not that time and you might say, 'Well, if y'all wait, it's gonna be too late.' Well, tomorrow I might feel it *is* that right time, you know what I'm tryin' to say? Ain't *nobody* can tell me *when* I should change. If I don't feel it's that time, then I ain't gonna change."

"But my purpose is only to tell you, to let you know that there has to *be* a time of change. Not to tell you when."

"You could try to help me, but until I feel it's the time"—G-Roc shrugs—"I ain't changin' nothin'."

Mr. Lunceford crushes out his cigarette; he has smoked it all the way down to the filter. Then he looks at me. "The biggest problem I see—and you heard it just now—is communicating and understanding. If I can only put across the idea of a need for change, then maybe they can just start to think about that possibility. But most young blacks now"—his head moves back and forth in a slow, solemn movement as he shakes another cigarette from the pack—"are so hostile that their understanding is nil."

G-Roc uncrosses his legs, crosses them again. He arches his back, stretching moderately. He darts a slightly annoyed look at his stepfather.

Mr. Lunceford glances at him and continues. "And the young women? I can't tell you how many of them are as militant as the young men. When I get the chance to talk to them, I tell them that I am just as much a man if I can accept a slap in the face, if I can take some verbal abuse, to affect a greater change. I choose to fight my battles that way, and I ask these youngsters not to glower at me—the way my son is probably glowering now . . ." G-Roc makes his hissing sound, but he smiles slightly as he does so, as if he were the parent, indulging a child who prattles about unrealistic dreams.

Lunceford goes on. "Our ancestors were slaves, they were shackled hand and feet, but they used their minds more than today's young black men whose minds are shackled." He turns to point an index finger at G-Roc. "As long as that man—the man who's running things from the top—can force you to get out there and act the way he wants you to act, do the things he wants you to do, as long as he can hold you down, then *you're* defeating your purpose and *he's* laughing at you. He can give you maybe sixty blocks, or whatever, and say, 'This is your territory.' He'll put the dope out there, he'll put the guns out there, and he'll say to you, 'Now, you gonna hold onto this whatever way possible, and if it means killing, that's okay too. You've just got to hold onto it.'"

Now G-Roc is really fidgeting in his chair. His foot jiggles up and down in frantic meter; his fingers drum on the floral upholstery; his eyes roll up toward the ceiling. He has heard all this before. From the dining room I can hear the sounds of tablesetting and the low murmur of Mrs. Lunceford's voice as she talks to Theresa.

Mr. Lunceford looks at me again. "The Man will tell the young black: 'I'll make you rich beyond your wildest dreams if you do it this way, with the dope. It sure beats the minimum-wage job, don't it?' "

I ask him who he thinks the Man is. He shrugs. I ask if he thinks the Man is black. He smiles humorlessly. "In this country? At this time?" He takes a beat. "Oh, sometimes there's a black face who mouths the Man's words, but the real Man got too much power to be black." He points his thumb at G-Roc. "I tell Jeffry all the time, 'He's brainwashing you without sitting you under a faucet twenty-four hours a day and letting the water drip. You're being brainwashed and you're going to have to open your eyes. Because you're being put in a position where you kill yourself as you kill others. Then he gets you in court and he sticks you in the gas chamber or the electric chair, or he puts you in prison for the rest of your life and he wipes his hands and says, 'Well, that's one more we don't have to worry about.' " He gets to his feet and moves toward the windows at the other end of the living room. As he turns he touches G-Roc's shoulder for an instant. "That's your real enemy, son."

G-Roc is silent for a moment, then he shakes his head. "Anybody can be my enemy. Whoever try to stand in my way of progress is my enemy. Whoever stand in the way of me doin' what I want to do is my enemy. They can say they tryin' to help me, but if I get the slightest little fear that they can't be trusted"—he looks away for a beat—"they're an enemy. I can be around 'em, but . . ." The rest of his statement goes unsaid as his eyes stray into the distance again. He shakes his head in a slight movement.

"Like a counselor?"

His eyes snap back to my face. "Exactly." His lips curve into a narrow smile. "But if I could trust you, I got no problem with you—you all right with me. But if I get that fear of distrust, that's an enemy, and I'm prepared to do what I gotta do at all times if they try to trip me."

Mr. Lunceford has resumed his seat again. He listens intently as G-Roc continues.

"The big enemy is the system. Not white people, per se; I'm not prejudiced—and the majority of gang members is not prejudiced. But this system, this government—whew." He leans forward to tap one finger on the tabletop. "They say they want to help you, they say they *are* helping you but then, really, they ain't doin' nothin' but killin' you off with words." G-Roc leans back again, gripping both chair arms. "The government plays a big part in why we kill our own kind."

I ask him to tell me what that means. He thinks about it for a moment.

"Say, me—and these around here." He makes a sweeping gesture toward the street. "These all around here is my enemies, they Bloods, but the same thing is happenin' to us all. The government don't want any of us to get no kinda good jobs. And that's based on the color of our skins, and that's even if there wasn't no gangs. They *say* they'll help, but the truth is you can't get no job that'll pay you enough to take care of yourself. So you feel as though—'Well, I need money and I need it now.' So you will go out and try to hurt whoever you can get it from. I see another black person walk down the street and if he look like he got more than *I* got, then I'm gonna try to get him for it."

"What if that was a white person walking down the street?"

"Yeah?" There is a slight edge of impatience in his voice.

"Would you hurt a black person faster than you would a white person?"

"Nope. Not really. Not faster. 'Cause I feel if you black and you not involved with no gang, and if you white and you not involved with no gang, and I want what you got, I rather go for the white before I go for the black. 'Cause that black person my own kind."

"You mean like a member of the Bloods is your own kind?"

The edge of annoyance turns into a flare of anger. "Blood ain't my kind. Blood my enemy."

■   ■   ■

It is later in the day, and G-Roc has agreed to take me to meet a couple of homeboys in his old neighborhood, the one where he lived until last year. All his allegiances are still anchored in this small industrial center that lies at the end of a twenty-minute freeway ride down the line from South Central. If you were seated in a low-flying plane and you looked down at this outlying edge of the sprawl that is Los Angeles, you would see block upon block of one-story, ranch-style houses, each with its pocket handkerchief of lawn leading down to the street. Many of the cars parked in the driveways that separate the houses are shrouded in nylon or plastic covering. During the week, when the factories are in operation, a visible effluvium spreads out over the area; you don't want to think about the quality of air that gets breathed here.

We turn off the main boulevard and drive a couple of blocks into a small cul-de-sac. I wait in the car as G-Roc sprints to the front door of a bluish-gray, shingle-roofed house. A wedge of light cuts through the early evening darkness as the door opens, and I can hear the buzz of voices. Then the door closes with a soft thump, and G-Roc and another boy are walking slowly toward the car. I get out from behind the wheel and take a couple of steps up the walkway. G-Roc starts the introductions.

"This is Sp . . ." The other kid makes a fast gesture, cutting him off mid-word.

"Eric. My name is Eric." Unsmiling, but not necessarily unfriendly. Watchful, that's the word. He is about the same age as G-Roc, maybe not quite as tall, and he is wearing the same kind of clothes: gray cords, dark sweatshirt. The sleeves have been cut off Eric's shirt, probably to display the definition of his biceps. I reach out to shake his hand, and he hesitates for a beat or two before he decides to return the gesture.

"Hey, Cuz—I told you, she cool." G-Roc opens the back door for him; he nods without enthusiasm and settles himself in the corner of the seat directly behind G-Roc. G-Roc turns to look at him.

"We goin' to get Cyco Mike."

"Ye-eeeeeh. But I got to be home by eight-thirty. I got early classes tomorrow, and my mom is takin' me to school at seven o'clock. So I wanna try and get some sleep tonight."

"Hey, Cuz—don't worry. We have you home." G-Roc faces front again, directing me through the neighborhood streets. Eric sits wordlessly in the back.

Cyco Mike lives close by in a monolithic apartment complex. G-Roc and Eric go inside to get him, and I sit waiting. Two young men, probably in their early twenties, are walking slowly up the street. One of them has on a leather jacket with the Lakers logo emblazoned on it. As they near the car, the guy in the jacket looks at me and says something to the other guy. He glances over and nods his head in idle greeting. I nod back. They walk on past my car and get into a black Cadillac that's parked a couple of spaces behind me.

As the Cadillac pulls out and moves down the street, G-Roc and Eric come back out of the complex. The third boy, Cyco Mike, is with them. He gets into the back seat with Eric, nodding pleasantly as G-Roc introduces us. I have been told that he is eighteen, two years older than G-Roc and Eric, but there's something about him that makes him seem younger than either of them. Not the way he looks—he's only a little taller than Eric and his face is no less impassive. It's just something there, some indefinable aspect of kiddishness the other two have lost already. He's wearing dark cords, too, and the anonymous sweatshirt.

I ask if anybody is hungry, adding that I'm ready for cheeseburgers and fries.

"Ye-eeeeh. I could go for somethin' to eat." Eric's voice sounds as if he might be relaxing a little bit.

I had spotted a McDonald's on the way to Cyco Mike's; we head back there. G-Roc volunteers to go in and get the food, but all three kids end up going inside to stand at the counter in various attitudes of coolness.

We drive to the corner of a residential block to eat, picnic-style, in the car. Cyco Mike places the largest of the empty bags on the seat between himself and Eric, propping it open against the back rest.

"Y'all can put yo' wrappers and trash in here when you through eatin'."

We eat in silence for a couple of minutes. G-Roc holds his burger delicately, between thumb and first two fingers; he takes careful bites, and he chews quietly, with his mouth closed, as do the other two boys. He polishes off his first bag of fries and turns halfway around in his seat.

"So, Cuz . . ." The two in the back seat repeat the phrase and all three of them laugh. Eric has mentioned, on the way here from McDonald's, that there were some Bloods he had met and liked. He referred to them, however, as "slob niggers." Now I ask him about that again. Cyco Mike cuts in before Eric has a chance to say anything.

"Them slob niggers, they busters."

Eric makes the same short gesture he used earlier when he stopped G-Roc from giving me his gang name. "Wait a minute. Wait a minute." He sets down his carton of French fries. "For the record: as far as we all human, right? and we all black, then that's when I could look at a nigger—a member of my family, say—and I could see *him* just as a person, even if he was in a gang which was opposite of mine. Then I could just judge him as a person, you know. If he's down or not. But, you know . . ." He has wound down, out of words for the moment, caught up in an eddy of conflicting emotions.

Cyco Mike reaches over and cuffs Eric's shoulder lightly. "But *fuck* slobs. That's what he's sayin'. Right, Cuz?"

Eric grunts. G-Roc's features split in a wide grin. "Ye-eeeeh. Regardless—fuck slobs, that's what we all sayin'. Fuck all snoops,[1] nigger!"

Now Cyco Mike slaps G-Roc's shoulder.

"B-one-eight-seven!"[2]

I look at G-Roc and ask him what that means.

"B-one-eight-seven." He says it in a sing-song delivery. "Means they murderers."

Who, the Bloods?

"Naw." He jerks his thumb at the back seat. "Them. Us. B-one-eight-seven means we kill Bloods."

I ask if any of these kids thinks there will ever be a chance for solidarity between Crips and Bloods. G-Roc shakes his head.

"Not as it's goin' now. I don't think anything can be changed. I mean"—he lifts his shoulders and shakes his head in a slow movement—"we'd be unbelievably powerful . . ."

Eric breaks in, "We'd be overwhelming. But it can't happen. Too many people have died, and nobody wants to give up their grudges. People's brothers have got killed, you know— that's gang members I'm talkin' about, but they're still family. Brothers. Sisters. Sons. Daughters. And people are like, *'Fuck* that togetherness. Bring it *on!'*"

Suddenly Cyco Mike erupts in a cascade of giggles. "Bang! Bang! Mighty West Side Crip gang! Unnhhhh!" He repeats

---

[1]disrespectful term for Bloods; like "slobs," "oo-lahs," and so on.
[2]police code for homicide (187)

the name of their set over and over, winding up with, "and everywhere I go, it's West Side through and through! I'm from the mighty West Side!" It sounds like a high school cheer set to a rap beat.

On an impulse I ask these kids if they know the name Monster Kody. I have asked this question to other boys—on the streets and in the camps—and the answer is almost always in the affirmative. Even kids in the Bloods will usually respond to that name. Monster Kody is, at twenty-six, a living gang legend. An O.G.'s O.G. I met him through his younger brother, Kershaun—Li'l Monster—shortly after Kershaun took part in a round-table discussion involving both Crips and Bloods that I conducted for *Harper's* magazine in October 1988. Shortly afterward Kody was convicted on a parole violation and sentenced to two years in prison. The mention of Monster Kody brings an immediate response from Eric and Cyco Mike.

"I know him. Well, I know who he is."

"He cool. *He* cool! From the notorious Eight-Tray Gangster Crips! The Eight-Trays down with us!"

I ask if their set is friendly with all the other West Side sets. They glance at each other and giggle—dumb question. Okay, then—who *is* their worst enemy, and why?

Eric answers quickly. "We don't have no worst enemy." He leans forward to look into my face. "Let me get this straight, Cuz—we ain't got no worst enemy. Just a list . . ."

Cyco Mike cuts in, "Oh, we got a main enemy we diddlin' with right now." He says it coyly, with a little lift of eyebrow.

"Naw. Naw. *Naw.*" Eric shoots a warning glance at Cyco Mike. "End of discussion, Cuz."

With the air of someone saving a difficult moment, G-Roc speaks up. "Just the pigs."

Eric nods his head, smiling thinly. "Ye-eeeeh. The pigs."

But Cyco Mike is unable to contain himself; the words

come bubbling up in an ecstasy of rage. He fucks the name of the enemy set over and over, as if he were repeating a mantra. He caresses the name with insults. "They busters and they all gonna die—*fuck* them niggers!" In his excitement he has over-turned Eric's carton of French fries; the sight of them scattered over the back seat brings him back to the moment, and he grins slyly. Then, surprisingly, he winks at me. "Look at this mess." He turns to Eric. "Don't just be eatin' on that shit and throwin' it around the lady's car. She gonna think we savages—clean up after yo'self, Cuz."

The tension in the car evaporates, and we begin a flurry of clean-up activities. G-Roc takes the bags of trash to a dumpster behind a nearby apartment house and lopes back to the car. We are just pulling away from the curb when there is a flare of red and blue lights in my rearview mirror, and I am momentarily blinded by the beam of a searchlight. A voice, made hollow by a loudspeaker, orders me, as the driver, to step out of the car with my hands in view. I ease slo-o-o-o-wly back to the curb. In my nervousness I graze the bumper of a parked car. The three boys groan and then go very still.

I open the door and get out of the car. I don't actually put my hands up over my head, but I am damned careful to keep them in sight. I move toward the police car, trying to walk in a normal fashion, wondering why I am as scared as I am. I know only that I am not going to say, "What seems to be the trouble, Officer?" or any other impossible cliché. I am going to keep my mouth shut and let them start this conversation.

"Do you know what city you're in? Do you even know what planet you're on?" He is backlit against the lights, but I can see enough to tell that he is short, white, redheaded. His partner is standing on the driver's side of the squad car. Taller, also white. They are both young, mid- to late twenties.

I take my driver's license out of my wallet and hand it to

the one with the red hair; he's the one doing all the talking. I have not yet answered his questions, so he asks them again. His attitude is even more truculent this time.

I tell him the name of the city. My voice sounds high and strained in my ears. It sounds once removed, the way it does on my answering machine.

"What are you doing with these guys? You driving them around or what? Know who they are?"

I tell them that I am a journalist, that I am writing a book, that I am interviewing these kids. I tell them that we have been sitting quietly in my car, eating Big Macs.

"Oh, yeah? Where was this McDonald's you say you went to?"

I tell him.

"How long were you there?"

I tell him.

"And you been sitting here on this dark street just talking and eating Quarter-Pounders ever since?"

I tell him that's right. Why does it sound so fake when it is all true?

"Well, I'm gonna tell you what probably would have happened after you finished your hamburgers. These 'kids' would have taken you to a darker street and then they would have raped you, one after the other, and after that they would have killed you, dumped your body, and driven away in your car. That's what would have happened. That's what these 'kids' do." His voice is leaden with contempt.

His partner speaks now. "We're just trying to protect you, ma'am. This is a real scary part of town, and these are bad kids. I know these three"—he gestures toward my car—"and they're nobody to fool around with." There is no sneering overtone in his delivery; maybe I can talk to him. (Good cop/bad cop? Never mind—maybe I *can* talk to him.)

"Listen—Officer, do you find yourself trusting your instincts much in this job?"

"You bet, ma'am. All the time."

"Okay, then you'll understand when I tell you that so do I. I know that these three kids are not looking to hurt me." The redheaded one sniggers softly behind me. "I know one of the boys from Camp Kilpatrick—I just spent the afternoon in his parents' home. The other two are friends of his."

"Okay, ma'am. Like I said, we're just trying to do our job. This really isn't a place where you should be alone." He glances over at his partner. "Now we want you to stay right here while we go over to your car and talk to your passengers. Just stand where you are."

Both policemen walk to my car and tell the three kids to step outside. They are then ordered to lean up against the hood, and the officers pat them down for weapons and/or drugs. I can hear the indistinct hum of voices as questions are asked and answered.

The redhead saunters back to where I am standing. "Your little friend, the one you spent the afternoon with, is flying on crack. The other two are out of their skulls on something else."

"I don't think so, officer. Did you find any drugs on any of them?"

"I'm telling you they've been smoking something."

"Not in my presence, officer. I'll back them up on that, and my publishers will back me up."

Finally it is decided to let us go. But not before they check the car in front of mine for damage. The tall cop sweeps his flashlight beam across the bumper once and then again to make sure.

"Nothing here. Absolutely clean."

Unsatisfied with this information his partner goes up to the front door of the house nearest the car and rings the doorbell. A youngster answers, peers out at the small group of people standing near the black and white, shakes his head no, shuts the door.

The redhead is not about to let it go at that. He walks back to me. "I want you to leave a note with your name and address and the name of your insurance company. Otherwise I'm going to take you in on a hit-and-run charge."

I fill out the information on a page from my notebook and hand it to the tall cop. He tucks it under the windshield of the car in question. For some reason I do not ask if he thinks it's such a good idea for my name and address to be left on the windshield of a car that's parked in such a dangerous neighborhood.

The squad car remains still, engine idling, as I pull away from the curb. I drive very carefully.

As we round the far corner I breathe out a loud sigh of relief.

"Those guys tried to scare me to death." The three of them break up into giggles. Eric is the first to get serious again.

"That was some heavy little shit, Cuz. Now you know."

We drop off Cyco Mike, and then we take Eric back to his house. This time he shakes my hand warmly. I tell him it was nice meeting him, and I thank him for having come out with us. He leans in the car window, talking past G-Roc.

"Call me Spider. Nice meetin' you, Miss Hit 'n' Run."

And he's gone. G-Roc laughs softly as he rolls the window up on his side. "Miss Hit 'n' Run, huh? Looks like you got yourself a gangbangin' name."

Heading back toward the freeway I take a wrong turn, and suddenly we are in another neighborhood. G-Roc goes very quiet, and even though I suspect what might be the trouble, I ask him.

"We in an enemy 'hood." He names the set. Bloods.

I tell him I have friends in that set, that I can mention names. He looks at me like I'm nuts.

"You ain't gonna have time to mention no names. Names don't mean nothin' to a bullet flying in the window." He has slumped down a little in his seat, tilting his head toward the floorboards. And now I know that he is really not kidding.

"Do you honestly think somebody is going to recognize you sitting here in my car?"

Again he gives me that look. "Hell, that's what gangbangin' is all about. Yo' enemies know yo' face as good as yo' homies do."

We pull up to a stoplight. Another car rolls up next to us in the adjoining lane. G-Roc's head ducks a little lower. Not much, but noticeably.

"Shit. I ain't prepared to die." His voice escapes through clenched teeth.

I stare straight ahead. I can't believe that things can happen this fast. I know that they do.

"I'm not either. So we're just going to try and handle this the best way we can. We're going to stay cool." I'm talking for myself more than to G-Roc, who is not even listening. What I'm thinking is that those two cops back there had a point: I *am* taking chances in a dangerous part of town. I *am* gambling on instinct or luck or whatever you want to call it, trusting, too, that the fact that I'm not a bad person will keep me alive and undamaged. Believing blindly, as always, that whatever the peril, nothing bad can happen to me. Knowing, sitting here, that it can.

I remember something Li'l Monster said in another conversation; I can almost hear the words now, here in the car: "That's my worst fear, to be sitting at a stoplight. That middle lane is no man's land. I seen that shit happenin', man. I *be* that shit happenin', and I don't *never* want that to happen to me. Just to be sittin' at the light and they take your whole head off."

And I remember another guy—B-Dog—saying, "Bullet ain't got no name on it. Bullet hit whatever it hit."

I sneak a fast look at the car next to us. Three young guys; they are unmistakably gang members. They're talking and laughing; the one in the passenger seat is turned all the way around to face the guy in the back. The image imprints itself on my mind the way a flash bulb sticks an image to your cornea.

The light finally changes to green. I force myself to pull away at a normal speed; to do what I want to do, which is to jackrabbit the hell out of there, would not be smart. Only when we make it to the freeway does G-Roc allow himself to sit up straight again. Then he looks over at me and grins.

"We was on a straight mission, girl."

I ask him what that means.

"A *mission*. Like drivin' through an enemy 'hood, bein' in danger of yo' life." He looks out the window for a long moment; it is very quiet in the car.

"Gangbangin' don't lie, girl. It's *real*. Niggers is out there to get you. Niggers is out there to *kill* you. It's fun in a way, but you got to look at it as a life-threatenin' situation, too. Every minute. And my homies and me, we be on the lookout, too. We be like—" he sighs, "whatever, Cuz. Whatever."

There is a drive-in movie next to the freeway. As we move past the screen, we catch a glimpse of flickering images. G-Roc cranes his neck to watch, then he turns his attention back to me.

"You ever see that movie *Colors?*"

I nod my head.

"Lemme tell you, girl, that was some dangerous shit in that movie. That shit just fired niggers up. Niggers saw that shit, they went out there just straight for the kill. You know, like no mercy *whatsoever* for anybody. That shit was just a green light to kill or be killed. Devastation just took over."

205

I ask him to tell me why that particular movie should have such an effect.

He makes his hissing sound. "Because that movie just made up a lotta bullshit. Talkin' about gangbangin', tryin' to show people how gangbangin' is. And *we* was like, 'That's bullshit! We gonna show how gangbangin' *really* is.' Like, 'Kill, buddy! Get yo' artillery weapons up! Show yo' armed forces!' Lotta people got killed behind that movie. 'Cause it tried to show drive-bys, but then it would show like niggers killin' Essays and shit, and that ain't like it is. And the Bloods, too—they felt like they got dis'ed 'cause all Bloods did was get killed in that movie, so they tried to have it a little bit, too, show some force—but the Crips just overpowered 'em."

But what about now, I ask. Isn't just as much killing going on now between gang members, with or without the challenge of a movie?

"It's still goin' on. We still *doin'* it, it's just we keep undercover from the police. They don't catch us as much because we just got our little secret creeps."

"Wait a minute, what's that supposed to mean?"

G-Roc shakes his head and looks out the window.

Okay, I tell him, but shooting is shooting and dead bodies are just that.

"Ye-eeeeh. But they ain't always shot. And the police, they don't find the mysterious killers. All this mass murderer stuff goin' on, and I tell you this much—ain't that many killers in the world. It's gangbangin'. It's *on,* buddy. Whatever you want to do, it's *on. Gangbangin'* is *on!*"

We have pulled onto G-Roc's street. The houses have that look about them that you see in any middle-class neighborhood on an early Sunday night. Lamps are lit behind carefully drawn shades; television shows are being watched. I can see the silhouette of Theresa's bicycle leaning up against the wall at the side of the front porch of the Lunceford house.

We slide up to the curb, and G-Roc opens the door on his side of the car, but before he gets out he turns to look at me again.

"It don't matter what you say about gangbangin', you know, don't matter if anybody understand it or not. We just bringin' home the hate. 'Cause everybody one-eight-seven. That's the kind of world we live in."

10 The Jungle

I saw B-Dog on television the week before he came to my house. One of the networks did a three- or four-minute segment on the six o'clock news of a Blood funeral and, sandwiched in between the long parade of stretch limos moving in stately procession along Imperial Highway and the image of a sobbing woman being carried down the steps of a chapel, there was a shot of B-Dog at the grave. He was framed against a bank of red and white roses, dressed in gray silk that matched the stainless steel structure of his wheelchair. He looked directly into the camera, his face rigid with anger. This expression was described, by the disembodied voice of the network anchorman, as a show of murderous rage for the enemy Crips who had murdered B-Dog's seventeen-year-old homeboy.

At my house the following week, he explained that the anger was, in fact, directed at the man holding the video camera because he had invaded B-Dog's privacy without permission. B-Dog further explained that the funeral was not, strictly speaking, a gang affair. The ceremony had been held for the brother of a member of B-Dog's set; the young man was not seventeen years old, he was twenty-three, and he was not affiliated with the Bloods. He died as the result of a motorcycle accident.

I first met B-Dog in 1988 when I interviewed him and three other Bloods for *L.A. Weekly.* At that time he was just approaching his twentieth birthday, and he had been with his set for eight years, during which he was shot nine times. The last bullet sheared his spine, leaving him paraplegic, bound to a wheelchair for life. B-Dog blames only himself for what happened to him: "I wanted to do what I wanted to do; I always knew which way I wanted to go. I wanted to 'bang with my neighborhood and put in work. I wanted to campaign."

One of the other men at the table that day was Rider. He is two and a half years older than B-Dog, and they have been friends since childhood. During the preliminary conversation that took place before that first interview, Rider told me, with some pride, that he was an active member of his set. He spoke openly about the Uzi stashed behind the passenger seat of his Jeep four-by-four. When Rider talks, you hear two distinct voices: one belongs to the college student with one year at Riverside City College and two at Cal State Long Beach; the other is that of the street kid from the Jungle. The tone of both voices is unhurried and thoughtful. These personas extend to the way Rider dresses, too: some days he looks like a young professional, an architect, maybe, or a third-year surgery resident, with his conservative haircut and carefully unstructured clothes by Liz Claiborne and Georges Marciano. Other times he wears the low-slung, knee-length shorts, the brown T-shirt and brown and orange baseball cap, the clunky, untied patent leather oxfords that proclaim his allegiance to the Bloods. He shows no jewelry except for a wristwatch, a wafer-thin Patek Philippe.

In 1988 Rider spoke openly about the benefits he and his

family were deriving from his participation in the booming drug trade. He talked about being able to spread the money out in concentric circles that extended from his wife and new baby to include grandparents, aunts, uncles, and cousins. Although unapologetic, he did admit that the flood of crack was tearing down his own community. Genocide, he called it, but he was quick to state that for every twenty people who went under, there was going to be one person who would make it out. In his case, he explained, it meant that he, Rider, would be able, within a couple of years, to "go legit." He said the money he was making in drug sales would enable him to realize his slice of the American Dream.

Now, in the summer of 1990, it looks as though that dream has been brought to fruition. Rider is no longer an entrepeneur in an illicit market; now his money comes to him in the shape of dividends from the investments he made two or three years ago. He pays taxes, he lives in a nice house with his expanding family—two children now. He has a forty-foot power cruiser, and he collects classic cars; the boat is named after his closest friend, a homeboy who was killed last year.

B-Dog recently became a father for the first time. He and his family still live in the heart of gang territory, and, like Rider, he is considered to be an O.G. of impressive legend. Both men are concerned about the new generation of gang members, and it is one of the subjects they have come to my house to talk about today.

Rider opens the discussion.

"I guess you could say that me and B-Dog here were latch-key kids. It was like, Pop's workin', comin' home, maybe ten, ten-thirty at night, and Mom's workin', too, leavin' at six in the mornin'. So I see 'em, you know what I'm talkin' about, but I don't see 'em." He has asked for a cup of tea, and now he takes a sip.

"I was goin' to private school, playin' football, doin' the

whole scholastic thing. But when I'd get home, it was *on*. Back to the 'hood, knock off my little homework and hit the corner. Go up to the park and hang with the homies—people I love, you know? That's how it was. I'd do all the stuff I was gonna do, put in whatever work, but by the time Mom comes home, all she sees is me in bed. She don't know. I mighta just did this, mighta just did that, but if she hears about it, she like, 'Hell, no! Not my boy!'"

B-Dog nods his head and laughs softly. Rider sticks out his right hand, clenching it into a loose fist; B-Dog reaches out and, making a fist out of his right hand, taps the top of Rider's fist. Then they reverse; Rider taps B-Dog's fist. Then Rider's face sobers and he returns to his subject.

"But a lotta these youngsters today have no resources, no guidance. There just isn't anyone around at home who really gives enough of a damn about 'em to care what the hell they do. Hell, look at their environment. I'll bet everythin' I got if you took half these little homies and just switched their environments for a couple weeks, you'd see real changes. But when you wakin' up to the same shit every day, the whole routine cycle of your life"—he begins to clap his hands for emphasis, cracking them together as he makes his points—"you wake up, steppin' over people on the floor of your house, Mom's smoked out, she don't care 'bout nothin', for sure not you. You roll up out on the street, same ol' homies. And no father around at all."

B-Dog has been listening intently, nodding his head in silent agreement. Now he speaks.

"These days yo' father is yo' mother's latest boyfriend. And usually yo' mother's switchin' boyfriends every other month."

"Or every other night." Something is burning away deep inside Rider, like a massive dose of radiation.

"It's that hard." B-Dog pauses, thinking about it. "Hard.

And a lotta these young kids, you know, look up to the O.G.'s." He pauses again. "I try to fix it so's they can get to somewhere sometimes, like Magic Mountain, somewhere like that. You know, hire a big ol' bus and just take 'em on out. Let 'em go on rides and shit, buy 'em T-shirts, let 'em eat all the hot dogs and pizza they want. 'Cause they don't even get to do little stuff like that . . ." His voice trails off for a moment. "And, you know, they kids, no matter what else they is. And, like I said, they look up to the O.G.'s, and if the O.G.'s turn they backs, them kids ain't got nobody." He looks down at his hands for a few seconds. They are broad in the palm with long, muscular fingers tipped with deep, rounded nails. "But the O.G.'s don't always have time for the little folks, you know?"

Rider has finished his tea. He takes the cup and saucer to the sink, rinses them, and places them on the rack to dry. Then, leaning both hands on the countertop, he stands looking out the window at the house across the driveway.

"We see these youngsters—the youngest, handsomest little motherfuckers—just hangin' around. Gettin' younger every year, goin' down further every year. Sometimes you just gotta say somethin'." He turns away from the window, walks back to the table. But he doesn't sit down right away; he stands looking down at me. His stance is easy, hipshot, and he begins to talk to me as if I were one of those kids.

" 'Thirteen fuckin' years old. Man, what're you trippin' *off* of?!' "

He sits down again. "And they look at us, like, 'Shit, I wanna be like y'all, and you tellin' me I ain't got what it takes?' "

B-Dog leans forward in his chair. "And that make 'em want to go out and *prove* themselves."

Prove themselves with guns? It is the obvious question. Rider smiles sourly.

"Not always. Sometimes they prove themselves with baby

215

rituals. Just bein', like"—his shoulders lift in a delicate shrug—
"you know, bad. All depends what's goin' on in your particular
neighborhood, or your particular block. It's not like they just
go get a gun and go prove themselves. Usually an incident has
to come up. Or maybe they'll just go across to whoever their
number-one enemy is, and they might bust a few caps without
doin' any damage." He shakes his head, smiling tolerantly, as
if he were a parent discussing some mild behavioral problem.
"It's a trip, though."

I mention the youngsters I have seen standing on street
corners in South Central Los Angeles and in the Jungle. Standing endlessly. Simply there, waiting for . . . what? Rider begins
to nod his head the moment I mention these kids.

"That's what I see, too." He looks off for a beat. "Out of
time. I asked a little male lok about that. Know what he told
me? 'Man, I stand out on this corner, and I watch time pass,
and I watch traffic pass.' " Rider's voice has reached for a higher
register in unconscious imitation of the young homeboy. " 'I
watch the Mexicans go to work at the factories in the mornin',
and I watch the same ones go home in the evenin'!' " Rider
shakes his head, and the next time he speaks his voice has
returned to its normal pitch. "They're just waiting, standing
there without knowing what they're waiting for, or why they're
waiting for it."

B-Dog has brought out a pack of cigarettes and a lighter
from one of the pockets built into the sides of his chair. Now,
as he shakes a cigarette out of the pack, Rider holds up both
hands in a warning gesture.

"Come on, Blood. Don't be firin' that thing up in the
house. Take yo'self outside, y'all need to be doin' that shit." He
has slipped back into the vernacular, allowing himself the
softer, slangier delivery of the streets.

B-Dog looks at me, grinning, making a show of being

helpless in the face of Rider's demands. "He won't let me smoke in the damn car, either."

I open the doors leading to a small patio, and B-Dog maneuvers his chair outside, stopping at the entranceway to turn back around to face us. Then he lights his cigarette, exhaling with obvious relish before he begins to talk.

"The majority of youngsters, they don't know nothin'. They go out, try to get some money, try to get a female, try to get . . . somethin'. All they know is they neighborhood. Just like . . ." He takes another deep pull on his cigarette, allowing the smoke to drift in a thick cloud from his mouth before pulling it back in through his nostrils. I watch the procedure, remembering how I tried to do it when I was a teenager first beginning to smoke in secret. We called it French inhaling, and I never did get it right.

B-Dog's voice goes on. "Just like when *I* was comin' up. All I knew was my set and the Jungle. If anybody want to kill me right now, they know exactly where I be at. All they gotta do is roll past."

As if by some bizarre cue, B-Dog's legs begin to jitter in spasms. He grips both knees, holding on tight, fighting the involuntary movement. His eyes squeeze shut, his head drops toward his chest. B-Dog keeps his head completely shaved, and a mist of perspiration is forming there now. A series of soft grunts escape from his throat.

I glance over at Rider. He is watching B-Dog the way a mother would watch a child, wanting to help, unable to do so. He catches my look and tells me, softly, that B-Dog will be okay.

I remember something Rider said in that first interview, two years earlier, about B-Dog: "This Blood, he live in pain twenty-four hours a day, seven days a week. He don't take nothin' for it, and he don't say nothin' about it to no one. A lot of the homeboys don't even know that."

The moment passes; B-Dog lifts his head and swipes at his face with both hands, brushing away the sweat.

I ask if they had it to do all over again, would these guys still pledge themselves to a gang?

Rider nods his head in a slow, serious motion. "Yeah. Yeah, I would. Not because of the way my life turned out, but because of some of my homies. I'm a reflection of them, just like they are of me. I'm proud to be a Blood."

B-Dog is more defensive. "What the fuck I want to change for? I don't feel like I done nothin' wrong in my life." His eyes slide over toward Rider. "Except not graduatin' from high school. I regret that." He looks at me again and nods his head in Rider's direction. "He big on education."

"These youngsters today, most of 'em don't even go to elementary school."

B-Dog reaches out to touch Rider's forearm. "But wait, lok. You know what? The schools these days, they only teach little shit, anyway. To me, the street gangs're better than school. Lemme say it this way—little motherfuckers be out there, they gotta learn how to *survive*. School ain't gonna teach 'em how to do that. They out there in the street, sleepin' in cars, sleepin' on somebody's floor, sleepin' wherever. They gotta do somethin', you know what I'm sayin'?" B-Dog has crushed out his cigarette, and now he rolls forward a few inches, talking fast. "Lookee, if a kid ain't got no money, if he can't get in his house 'cause it locked up on him, if he hungry, if he can't even find his mama, then he got to do *somethin'*. And that somethin's gonna be to rob. He gonna *learn* how to get his money. 'Cause if he don't know how to get his money, he goin' to jail."

Wait a minute. What kind of logic is this? If that kid starts in robbing people, he's going to be caught at some point, and he's going to jail anyway.

B-Dog throws me a look of disappointment, as if he had not expected me to be so naive.

Rider picks up the conversation. "See, people say street gangs into a lotta petty crimes." His lips twist into a grim little slice of a smile. "The average little gangster ain't out there snatchin' no motherfuckin' purses, he ain't grabbin' no television set. He's robbin' a jewelry store, you know what I'm sayin'? And if the Man come, he'll shoot it out. Whatever." Rider shifts position in the chair, scraping it back along the tiles so that he can poke his legs out beneath the table. He is well over six feet tall, and my wooden dining room chair seems too small for him. "You got to look at the scale of how things are."

B-Dog nods his agreement. "That's what I mean by tryin' to *survive*. Mama's smoked out. Daddy's smoked out—if they *is* a daddy. Little brother needs Pampers. Lemme tell you one thing: the average young brother who's out there, if his mama's on that shit and he got any little kids in his family, he gonna go out and try to get a grip[1] for his sisters and brothers. For his mama, too. He got to do somethin' to take care of his family." He glances at Rider, who delivers a short nod of his head. B-Dog looks back at me. " 'Cause, lookee, what would I look like, goin' to school every day, knowin' that my mama and my daddy is smoked out, knowin' that I got a little homie brother and sister at home? What I look like goin' to school and they not really even teachin' me nothin'?"

"Yeah, but that's not the only thing. Lemme tell you another part of the story." Rider folds his hands on the table and leans in toward me, like a moderator at a seminar. "Okay, the parents smoked out, right?"

In some cases, yes. But I can't go along with such a blanket statement; I've met too many parents who don't smoke

[1] a stake, some money

219

crack. Yet as I say this to Rider, images rise up in my mind: Hart. Faro. Lumbly.

"Okay, but we talkin' about a big group, a majority group of parents who do not give a damn. And we talkin' about a rest of the city who these kids are invisible to. Nobody could give less of a damn if these kids go to school or not. But even *that's* not the problem why they ain't goin'. A kid may *want* to go to school. But he don't wanna go all fucked up"—Rider begins to clap his hands again, as he makes his points—"with dirty shoes, dirty ol' clothes, dirty same shit 'cause he don't have nothin' else to wear, and everybody else"—his voice has risen with his passion; he takes a moment to calm himself, and when he begins to speak again, he is back in control—"is all clean and everything they wearin' is labeled Nike and Fila and Reebok, and your mama's smokin' and got you *shit* to go to school. Fourteen years old and gettin' shit from your parents. Oh, maybe a pair of khakis now and then, maybe you got two T-shirts to yo' name, gotta keep washin' 'em out just so you don't stink too bad. And they want you to go to school? Every day, wearin' the same shit and everybody talkin' about you, sayin', 'Oh, yeah—he got a smoked-out mama. Look at the way he dress and shit.' So that kid just stayin' home, standin' on corners, watchin' the Mexicans go to work at the factories and watchin' his life pass by with the traffic."

Hart. Faro.

B-Dog waits for a minute before he speaks. "We help where we can, you know. Give up money; give up clothes and shit, like tennis shoes. Hell, I got tennis shoes in my closet and you *know* they ain't gettin' wore out. Pants, shirts, shoes. I pass that stuff on to the little homies. Or to the homies comin' out of the pen who ain't got nothin'." His eyes connect with Rider for a second, then he looks at me again. "But I'll be damned if I give stuff to somebody who's got the potential to do they own. Some brothers got potential to do for theyselves, but they lazy. Some of 'em be like, 'Fuck that. I'm just gonna lay back and let the O.G.'s do for me.' They'll lean on me, they'll lean on Rider 'cause they know he makin' money."

"Ye-eeeeeh. People who never 'banged in their life. Just hang around us and look to get taken care of. We only down to take care of our own people. Like the little homies we been talking about, those kids on the streets. I try to tell them, 'Let your mama and daddy know where you are. Even if she's on crack, don't let her worry.' But there's only so much you can do without just breakin' your ass. I'll tell you somethin'—the churches could do more." Rider pins me with an intense gaze. "Lemme tell you somethin' I see way too much of: sometimes I'll be in a mall with a couple of the homies, and we'll be loked out in khakis and shades and stuff, and we'll see some church people there. Folks'll be walkin' by and the church people will walk up to them"—Rider alters the pitch of his voice slightly—" ' 'Scuse me, brother—can I talk to y'all for a minute 'bout Jesus?' And they'll always grab onto someone who's real clean-cut to witness Jesus about. You know what I'm sayin'. And then here we come . . ." Rider's shoulders perform a slight weaving motion, rolling from side to side as if he were walking. "But they won't say *nothin'* to us. Won't even get caught lookin' at us. So I walk on up to 'em and I say, 'How about me? I'm not worthy of God? How come y'all don't witness to me?' "

He shifts wearily in the chair; he looks sad suddenly, and older. "To me, they should be lookin' for the so-called sinner instead of the clean-cut one, probably already a Christian. I tell preachers this all the time, 'cause when they see us, they quick look the other way." Rider mimes a person shrinking away from something that repels and frightens him. His action is purposely overstated, and it merits a laugh from B-Dog. But Rider isn't playing it for laughs. He continues to look at me, and his voice assumes a plaintive tone. "I ask 'em, 'Isn't Christianity about savin' souls? Or are you only lookin' for people who already converted?' I ask 'em if they such strong Christians, why they so afraid of us? It ain't like gangbangers is the lions in *this* coliseum."

It is later in the day, and we have taken a break for lunch. Rider is a vegetarian, so I make lettuce and tomato sandwiches for us and stick a chicken pie in the oven for B-Dog, who has asked for something more substantial, something with a little meat in it. After we eat I begin to ask questions again. What about the money that is being made in the drug trade? It is widely quoted that approximately forty billion dollars is made each year on the profit of illicit drug sales in the United States. What percentage of that revenue finds its way to the gangs?

B-Dog and Rider exchange amused glances. Then Rider's eyes drift lazily toward me again.

"Understand, I'm not in that business anymore." His voice has assumed the barest hint of silken menace. "I don't do that kinda work now, you understand what I'm sayin'. But lemme tell you this: if that's a motherfuckin' *world* of money, then I wasn't makin' even a pebble of it. Shit . . ." He looks off for a long moment, staring past B-Dog's chair, out into the patio. His eyes follow the progress of a white cabbage butterfly as it makes its rounds through the flowerlets of an azalea bush. "Whoever controls international affairs in the government was makin' the real money." His head turns toward me again. "Who else could it be? Gangbangers not the ones goin' down to get the shit and bring it back here. Gangbangers like the grunts in the Marines, that's how you got to look at it, with the officers as the ones makin' the real bucks. It's the shotcallers who gettin' rich. The politicians. And the grunts? They don't even know the officers' names."

B-Dog allows his mouth to curve into a gentle smile. "Y'all heard some of the names when Ollie went on trial."

"Aw, hell, lok—let's get real with it. We got people out there, twenty-five years old, sellin' dope 'cause they just want to pay their bills. They're not out there tryin' to get some fancy car! They just want to keep their lights on, keep their gas on!" Rider's voice has lost that thoughtful edge; he's talking loud. "Them people can't nail down no decent jobs, and you tell me about any baller who's gonna tell 'em 'no' when they come lookin' for work." He lifts one hand and makes a gesture in front of his face as if he were brushing away flies.

B-Dog shifts uncomfortably in his wheelchair. It is a hot day, and the air outside is oppressive. He wheels himself forward, reaching back to slide the door shut. We sit quietly for a moment, and then Rider begins to talk again. His voice has returned to its normal tone of casual conversation.

"When you a kid, after you take care of the basic needs, all that money does is enhance your life a little bit. It lets you get around, lets you branch out, if you play it right, lets you go out and buy, like, a good car, go different places. And then"—his shoulders lift in a little shrug—"your artillery gets a little heavier. Because now you can just go *buy* a Mac 10 if that's what you want, instead of burglarizing somebody's house to get a weapon."

He leans his face against one upraised hand; the fingers tap lightly against his cheek. "See, every household keeps a gun and so when we"—he points his chin at B-Dog—"were young, that's how we got our guns." Both men grin at the memory. "Need guns fo' the homies? Somebody go break in a house, come away with, like, three, four guns for the neighborhood. But then, when the cocaine thing came around—shit, just go *buy* a gun. And then, as the cocaine came around more and more, most of those people whose houses you used to break into, they started in smokin', so they bringin' the guns to you now, to trade." Rider's voice slides into an impression of someone eager to make a deal, selling hard. " 'Oh, I got this nice, fresh nine millimeter for y'all!' " He goes back to his own delivery. "And people jump on that shit for real. Guns? Wo-oooooooh!"

As if he were talking about scalped tickets for a sold-out concert.

B-Dog has been peeling an orange. Now Rider reaches out for a couple of sections. He chews thoughtfully for a few seconds, then he leans back in his chair and looks solemnly at me.

"I'll tell you somethin' that gets me mad, and that's the notion that youngsters 'join up' with gangs. Like they was, I don't know, decidin' to join some damn fan club. Hell, half the time they ain't even got a choice." He turns his head to talk to B-Dog. "Tell her about the Drifter, Blood."

B-Dog nods slowly, grinning. Then he begins to talk about a youngster from his neighborhood who earned the nickname of the Drifter because he hung out with a group of baby homies from the set that B-Dog and Rider claim. This kid was a dot, a satellite at the periphery of a circle of twelve- and thirteen-year-old gang members. He was, as B-Dog describes it, "not *in* the gang, but he *with* 'em."

One day these kids, all of them, were making a slow procession up to the swap meet, a mammoth new and used clothing market that sits on a square block between a Blood neighborhood and a Crip neighborhood. This vast barn of a place is a repository of style for gang members; it is where they come to buy the clothes they favor, the khaki pants and Pendleton shirts, the oversized T-shirts and cords, the high-priced running shoes and unstructured house slippers.

The knot of homeboys moved along the busy street, attracting mildly curious looks from some passersby, covert and hostile attention from others, friendly greetings from still others. The Drifter tagged along, enjoying all of it. Maybe he raised his hand to return a wave, maybe he swaggered a little, in unconscious imitation of the loose-limbed g-ster amble.

Then, just like that, a kid with a gun in his hand stepped out of a doorway. There was a short series of popping sounds, like firecrackers exploding underneath an upturned cardboard carton. The boy next to the Drifter crumpled to the sidewalk, blood spurting from a quarter-sized hole in his throat. His homies, the other kids in the group, scattered, melting past the little knots of people who stood frozen in place in front of shop windows and at the doors of parked cars. The Drifter looked right, looked left, saw his friends disappearing, saw the kid at his feet lying in a widening pool of red. And he knelt down to comfort him. He leaned in close to the fallen boy's face to whisper softly to him, telling him that he was not alone, that everything was going to be okay. He didn't see the gun come up again, he didn't hear the report, he only felt the impact of the bullet as it plowed into his shoulder, hurling him across the torso of the dying boy he had chosen to stay with.

Later, when the Drifter talked about it with B-Dog, he said, "I didn't know whether to run or stay, but I saw him fall and I was with him. The second before we was laughin' about somethin' he said. So how was I gonna leave him layin' there, bleedin'?"

That action put the Drifter in the gang automatically. The thing was, he wasn't so sure he wanted in, so he thanked them and told them that he figured he'd stay on his own. But the decision was no longer his to make. The homeboys told him, "If you don't wanna be in it, you shouldn't be 'round it. But you chose to hang 'round it, and by doin' what you did, you showed us, right there, that you be loyal to us. So now you one of us."

B-Dog laughs.

"I told him, 'If you *had* ran off, they'd be beatin' up on you now. If you had run, you'd be the motherfucker who ran that time. But you stayed, you showed heart. So *that's* what you gonna be known for.' "

Rider nods his head in agreement. "Everything you do parlays to the next day. All your life. And that's the jacket you got to live with. Forever."

I ask B-Dog about the attack that paralyzed his legs. "July 3, 1985—I was fresh outta Y.A. for grand theft auto, seventeen years old. Just standin' in the park, breathin' in free air, and the dude shot me. I wasn't wearin' no colors or nothin', but my enemies knew I was out."

"He ended up in Martin Luther King Hospital. That's where everybody goes when they get shot. There or Cedars-Sinai. Without those trauma centers people'd be dyin' in the streets. For real." Rider narrows his eyes in concentration. "For real. Anyway, B-Dog's layin' up in Intensive Care and . . ."

B-Dog interrupts to mention that he was lying in bed, groggy from medication, unable to move below the waist and getting progressively angrier because he felt his homeboys were not retaliating for him.

". . . we all started tearin' up shit, sendin' the bodies right to where he was."

Two Crips were brought in on a Code Yellow, followed that same day by four more, also Code Yellows. B-Dog overheard two nurses talking about it.

"We was hittin' 'em up on street corners and in front of hamburger stands. On the steps of their houses." Rider is doing that thing with his hands, clapping them for emphasis as he lists the attack zones. "We was usin' AKs—we called 'em ARs back then. Nobody had really heard anything about 'em yet."

Rider goes on to explain that the people actually involved in the attack on B-Dog were "ghetto stars"—O.G.'s with very, very serious reputations. It took a week or so to get the first one. He was brought up to the floor where B-Dog was, and B-Dog spotted him as they wheeled him in on the gurney from Emergency. Saw the kid just before he died, saw the blood bubbling out of his nose and mouth and the tubes snaking out from under the sheet that covered him. There was a moment when B-Dog and the kid on the gurney looked at each other in recognition. They had grown up together, these two, they knew each other by name, there was a history of childhood between them. When B-Dog saw the rolling eyes and heard the wet, ominous sound of air as it was sucked into failing lungs, the only thing he remembers thinking about is that this was "one fucked-up kid layin' there. This was a kid I went to school with, and now he was dyin' in front of my eyes."

Later, when B-Dog was well enough to travel through the hallway in his wheelchair, another boy—one more victim of the wholesale slaughter—asked B-Dog why he, the boy, had been shot.

"B-Dog, I didn't shoot you. Why y'all shoot me?"

And B-Dog remembers trying, in that brief time out of war, to explain the rules to this youngster who had become his enemy by chance of address.

"You know, I can't walk no more because one of y'all shot me. And you know how the gangs do—once y'all shoot somebody, we gonna take it out on everybody in yo' set. Y'all do the same thing, that's just how it goes in gangbangin'." B-Dog's voice is earnest in the retelling.

Now Rider talks about how it went during visiting hours at the hospital. He describes the bristling hostilities, the face-to-face encounters in hallways and elevators when enemies came together. He tells me how he himself, brought to a fever pitch of rage by a comment from the girlfriend of a member of a visiting Crip set, challenged each guy by name, inviting them to take it on down to the emergency room, promising that they would need to avail themselves of its services when the battle was done.

"You gotta understand, everybody in most rival gangs knows each other's first and last names. You know why? We all grew up with maybe only one street separating us. Went to the same elementary school. Played stickball together."

B-Dog takes up the thought. "The split usually comes in junior high, 'cause that's when the gangs come more into it." He shakes his head and grins, the way somebody greatly amused by a private joke would. "It's a trip. I had a buddy who was a straight Crip—69 East Coast—and do you know, he chose to stay friends with me, so they kicked him out. And to this day, right now, he still deals with it like me and him is brothers. I'll never forget that. He say, 'Man, you cool. Fuck what anybody else say.'"

I ask Rider and B-Dog how they feel about their own children getting involved with the gangs. The replies come quickly, almost simultaneously.

"Hell, no!" B-Dog's lips turn down in a grimace of distaste as he shakes his head in an emphatic gesture. "That shit is really crazy now. Everybody in jeopardy."

"That's right. Everybody's at risk. That's why I'm thinkin' about movin' my family on outta here. There's just too much dangerous shit goin' on around here." Rider looks at me for a long moment. He seems to be weighing something in his mind, making some decision whether or not to say more.

"Look, I have regrets, no doubt. There are some things I'd change about my life if I could. Some people who wouldn't have died when I was busy cleanin' out streets that didn't really belong to any of us no way." He is vamping for time. B-Dog sits watching from his wheelchair with what seems to be a tiny flicker of uneasiness behind his eyes.

The three of us sit like that, nobody saying anything, then Rider clears his throat with a sudden scratch of sound.

"But then I think, hell, that was straight wartime. Get up, brush yo' teeth, roll the shit out and don't slip."

Another stretch of silence. I can see him making up his mind.

"There's another war goin' on right now, and it's on another level. They got it goin' on in my neighborhood and in other neighborhoods. It's in the older generation, the so-called O.G.'s—the ones that have the money. And it isn't just about, 'He's a Crip, let's kill him—or, he's a Blood, let's smoke *him.'* This is all about 'He's a baller, [2] let's go kidnap him and hold him for ransom.'"

This is the first time I have heard anything like this; it catches me by surprise. I glance over at B-Dog, and he is nodding his head, affirming what Rider has said.

Rider continues. "That's what's goin' on right now. That's the new warfare. One of our homeboys got kidnapped, and the people who took him paged me, told me they had him and to meet 'em with two hundred thousand dollars."

Rider brings up his right hand to rub the skin on his forehead. He uses his thumb and first two fingers to massage the temple and eyebrow areas with small, circular motions.

"They had it all planned out, every move. Where I was supposed to make the drop, denominations of bills, everything." He takes a beat or two; his fingers continue to move over his forehead.

"I wasn't about to do anything 'til I talked to my home-boy, Erik. So I told them to put him on the phone or to forget it. Well, you know how everybody got their own little language? How somebody's 'yes' can really mean 'no' if you know 'em well enough to read the tone behind the words? Well, when they put Erik on the phone to me, and I asked him if they was really gonna let him go after I brought the money, he said

[2] Blood term for a big drug dealer

229

'Yeah, man . . .' " Rider draws those two words out until they form a slender thread of hopeless resignation. "Those were the last words I ever heard from him.

"Erik's mother got wind of it, see, and she called the police. They got into it and fucked the whole thing up real bad. Came in and wanted to make the drop." His eyes are bright with sorrow. And rage. "I called the F.B.I. after that, but they said they couldn't come in on it unless the cops asked for them. And the cops said it wasn't necessary, they'd handle it." Rider places both hands on the table in front of him, lacing his fingers together tightly. His head drops slightly, as if he were studying some unseen book. When he looks up again, his eyes focus on a spot just to the side of my face.

"They let Erik go, all right. They let him go." His eyes flick back to meet mine again. "He was so fucked up he died the next day. They tortured him, burned him on the back and on his hands with a red hot butter knife. Stabbed him. Shocked him with live wires. And he was shot up, too. They shot him in the face when they first grabbed him to put him in the van and he was fightin' with 'em. They had him three days." He taps the table top lightly with his index finger. "And Erik was a ghetto star, so you can imagine what they was doin' to him."

"In L.A. right now? The nineties? The name of the game is kidnap and ransom." Then, in afterthought, "You ask Monster Kody about this—he'll verify it, 'cause for sure ain't nobody talkin' about it."

B-Dog edges his chair a couple of inches forward. "Some Crips over in the projects kidnapped one of their own and blamed it on us. That one's goin' on right now. Did they own people and blamed it on us."

Rider picks it up. "The homie was ballin', and he was rich. They figured he wasn't givin' back what they deserved, you know, they felt he was keepin' back on them, so they snatched him and killed him. And then they put out the word that the

Bloods did it. They said *our*"—he makes a fast, circular motion that includes B-Dog and himself—"set did it. And *that* guy was a ghetto star, too. So that made a big war break out, and it's goin' on right now. It's on an older level, too. Our age." His index finger performs that tight arc again, between himself and B-Dog. "And it's all about money."

"It's not just 'bangin', see. It's not just affiliations. This is about grabbin' somebody, callin' his people and tryin' to get that money. 'Cause you *know* he's got that money, you *know* he's ballin'. They call and tell you to bring that money, that two hundred thousand, and you better *do* it, boy, you better call 'em, better pay somebody."

I ask if any youngsters are ever involved in this kind of structured move. Both men shake their head vehemently, but it's Rider who continues speaking.

"This is upper level warfare; a G won't even take a youngster with him when he sets out to grab another G. You set out to kidnap a real gangster, you know you better be ready." He gets to his feet in a sudden move; his chair scrapes noisily against the tiles. He picks it up to move it closer to the table, then stands over it for a moment, with his hands resting lightly on the curve of the back.

"This is the new nineties shit. And it's gettin' worse."

He walks over to the sink, turns on the taps, and splashes his face with water. Then he pulls a paper towel from the roll on the wall, and as he blots his face and neck with it, he begins to speak again.

"Tell you the truth, when they had our homeboy, we got wind of where somebody lived, and we thought about grabbin' his son."

He turns to look at B-Dog.

"You remember when they had Erik . . ." B-Dog nods his head. "Well, we thought about snatchin' one of those guys' fathers."

231

He reaches down to open the cabinet under the sink so that he can toss the crumpled towel into the trash bin. When he turns around again he is looking at me, and his voice is rougher, colder, as if he were talking to his enemy.

" 'You got our homeboy? Well, now we got your father.' " Rider is staring hard at me now. "How you feel if somebody call you . . ." His voice changes, he is that faceless enemy now. " 'We got Erik, but he can't come to the phone right now. We gonna play a little game with him, we call you back later.' "

He jerks the chair away from the table and sits down again. His eyes are shining with tears.

"Make me crazy right now just talkin' about this shit." He brushes his fingertips against both eyelids in a quick, angry gesture. "That's why I'm fixin' to get outta this damn town. Get my children where they be safe." He leans back in the chair, relaxing slightly. Rider's emotions are under control again; what has surprised me is that he did not seem to be embarrassed by them.

Now he gives a little shake of head, accompanying it with a narrow smile. "Can't do nothin' about gettin' my grandma to move. She old, and she kinda feisty." Rider's pride in his grandmother is evident. "She been through a lot, and don't nothin' scare her no more."

B-Dog has been listening to Rider with silent attention. Now he speaks up again. "Ain't nothin' scare me no more, either. But if they do somethin' to my family, then it's gonna be *on*. For real." The level of intensity in his voice has gone from zero to sixty in those two sentences. "I look at it this way: if somebody snatch my mama, then I'm gonna go take *they* mama."

Rider leans across the table to look at me; his gaze is as insistent as the buzz of a fly trapped against a window.

"These are untold stories here. There's been over ten kidnap-murders in the last six months. And the police don't give a damn about it. They pulled me in after Erik died, and this cop said to me, 'They fucked your homeboy up.' And I said, 'Yeah, I know. And I heard how scared you guys were to pursue the case.' Cop said, 'Knock off that "scared" shit—we just don't give a fuck about y'all.' " Rider shrugs; it's a small, careless gesture. "And I said, 'Yeah, I know.' " He leans back in the chair again, looking at me with that joyless smile playing around his mouth.

"And then he said, 'Next time it's gonna be you.' " The smile widens slightly. "And I said, 'Tell me somethin' I *don't* know.' "

It is late afternoon now, and Rider and B-Dog are getting ready to make the drive back to the Jungle. I walk with them as Rider guides B-Dog's chair down the driveway to where Rider's car is parked. He's driving a new Land Rover today. He helps B-Dog into the passenger seat, then folds the wheelchair and stashes it in the back. But before he swings up into the driver's seat, he turns to look at me again. There's something else he wants to say.

"I'll tell you this now—one day a revolution's gonna sweep down. And it's gonna move straight across. And we ain't gonna be thinkin' in terms of Bloods and Crips when it happens; there's gonna be a whole new enemy for us. Maybe it won't happen in my generation, but it's comin'."

His eyes scan the street, moving toward one corner, traveling back in the other direction. "Gangbangers don't have any kinda platform or media. So, right now, all we can do is reach out and touch the next man. If I can stop my little homies from goin' out and killin' in the neighborhoods, then that's a beginning. I can't go in the Crip neighborhoods and talk peace to them. Not yet. But I can tell my own little homies to stop worryin' about these streets and these parks that don't have nothin' to do with us. And I might not be able to touch 'em all, maybe just one kid gettin' ready to go on a potential drive-by. Maybe I can touch just one potential ghetto star and start him thinkin'."

11 Soledad

I f I had been born in '53 instead of '63, I would have been a Black Panther. If I had been born in Germany in the early thirties, I would probably have joined the National Socialist Party. If I had been born Jewish, I would have joined the Jewish Defense League. Because I have the energy, the vitality to be a part of something with 'power.' Either constructive or destructive. And because there was a destructive element around me when I was growing up, I went into the Crips."

I first met Monster Kody at Soledad Prison, located in the Salinas Valley, the rich, loamy farmland that is known as the Salad Bowl of California. Driving through one sees endless rows of lettuce, tomatoes, cabbage, strawberries, artichokes; jade-green legions parading in formation between the ranges of the Gabilan and Santa Lucia Mountains.

The prison is at the end of a forty-minute drive out of the city of Salinas. It sits alone, a pale hulk of sand-colored buildings with an unseen current, a river of wind, flowing through and around it at all times.

I have arrived early enough to secure a chair in the waiting room. About eight other women are there already, and in an hour or so there will be a line of people stretching out from the doorway to snake back toward the parking lot. I sit next to Debbie, who is here to see her boyfriend. She met him through an ad he placed in the Pen Pals Wanted section of a singles' newspaper, and they wrote letters for six months before Debbie came up from Long Beach to meet him. They are engaged now, and they will marry when he is released next year. Debbie is twenty-four years old, slightly overweight. She makes the trip here once a month, staying overnight at an inexpensive motel, taking time off from her job with a cable-TV company. She is vaguely pretty, with a mane of taffy-colored hair and carefully applied makeup. She pays special attention to her eyes—they are thickly layered with two shades of irides-cent lilac shadow.

There is a glass-topped counter across one end of the waiting room. Under the glass are shelves that contain items made by the inmates, all for sale at surprisingly reasonable prices. Wallets with designs burned into the leather, key-chains, elaborate silver crosses inlaid with mother-of-pearl, ear-rings, rings. A trusted inmate tends the counter, making change out of a large, old-fashioned register, writing up the sales slips. Cash only.

You wait to hear the name of the prisoner you are here to see. When it is called, you are given a locker in which you stash your handbag, and then you move through a metal detector and on into the main body of the prison. As you walk past buildings, heading toward the visiting room, disembodied voices and whistles waft randomly from behind the barred and heavily screened windows. You are watched by guards in gun turrets over your head.

The visiting room is a barn-like area that reverberates with the voices of men, women, and children. People sit in groups at plastic tables and chairs; collapsible playpens and battered highchairs are provided for babies. Vending machines against the walls dispense packages of cookies, chips, candy bars, and soft drinks.

Monster Kody is without such visiting privileges. He can be seen and talked to only when his visitor is protected by a thick glass shield. Monster Kody was removed from the general population after a prisoners' show in the yard in which he performed a Public Enemy rap song about a prison break, "Black Steel in the Hour of Chaos." The crowd of inmates loved it, wanted more, and the guards tried to put a stop to the show. They grabbed for Monster, but he ducked under the flailing arms and segued into an N.W.A. rap about "those who have the authority to kill a minority." His arms were pinned then, but when the black prisoners began to surge forward angrily, the guards lost focus and Monster Kody managed to slip away. He melted back into the general population, and for the next few days he "agitated," moving from group to group in the yard. The following week he was taken to the Security Housing Unit—solitary confinement—for an indefinite stay.

It was not his first time in Solitary. Or at Soledad. He was sent here for a seven-year sentence in 1984, convicted of mayhem. He shot a rival gang member who had come into Eight-Tray territory gunning for him. Monster used a hollow-point bullet in a .380 Browning, and the would-be assassin's right buttock was blown completely away. In that first year at Soledad he ran into trouble with a guard who was known to have racist views; the guard got Monster's knife in his side, and Monster got twenty-eight months in solitary confinement at San Quentin. He was then transferred to Folsom Prison until he gained his parole.

But it was during the time he spent in Solitary that Monster Kody began the process of conversion from gang member to revolutionary. He read everything he could get his hands on—politics, philosophy, history. Black history in particular. He stopped thinking of himself as a black American and began to think of himself as an "Afrikan." The narrow mindset of the gangbanger began to enlarge. It came to him, in that security cell in San Quentin, that he had spent most of his life defending a street he didn't own. And didn't live on. He thought about the lives wasted "like a spill of beer." He reflected upon what seemed to him to be his insignificance to this country, and the changes he could make in a system he hated. He made the decision to align himself with revolutionary, not gang, causes upon his release from prison. To that end he became a part of the Republic of New Afrika, an organization that advocates the seizure and restructuring of the five "slave states"— South Carolina, Mississippi, Alabama, Georgia, and Louisiana. As a revolutionary Monster Kody leans strongly toward a socialist government, with food, clothing, shelter, and education as priorities. He has not foresworn his pledge to weapons.

"Where the change comes in it's about 'armed against who?' now."

He was paroled from Folsom at the beginning of 1989. In June of that same year he was arrested for possession of an AK-47 with three clips of ammunition and sent back to Soledad.

A guard escorts me through the visiting room to an area in the back composed of a row of reinforced glass windows. Each window faces in on a tiny, densely barred cage. There are telephone receivers on either side of the glass, and molded, bright orange plastic chairs.

I am shown to one of the windows and told that the

prisoner will be brought in shortly. When I tell the guard, who is black, who it is I have come to see, he nods his head in a thoughtful gesture.

"Yeah, Monster Kody. He's a pretty cool guy."

He is led into the cage in chains, his hands cuffed behind his back. His head is shaven, he has on the same faded dungarees and neatly pressed work shirt with stenciled numbers on the pocket the other prisoners are wearing, but the words that pop into my mind when I see him are "movie star." It is the term I have heard applied to him for months by other gang members. It refers to his exploits and his legend, but this guy actually looks like a movie star, he is that handsome—too good-looking to get the part if they were making a movie about his life.

There is an armed guard on either side of him. He turns his back to one of them, offering his cuffed wrists to be freed, smiling polite thanks when one of the guards produces a key and unshackles him. Then he steps into the cage and the door is bolted behind him.

We look at each other for a long moment. We have been exchanging letters for a few months, and we spoke on the telephone once after he had read one of my articles, but this is our first face-to-face encounter. He smiles—a real smile this time—and places his right hand, palm toward me, on the glass. I put my hand over it, in lieu of a handshake. Then we pick up the receivers.

It's all small talk at first: the train trip up here from L.A.; the inconvenience of talking through glass. His mother, Birdie; his brother, Li'l Monster. My daughter, Lisa. His wife and three children. The book. And all the time we're checking each other out, making those small litmus tests of personality that tell you when you can get down to the business of real conversation.

I ask him about the gang hierarchy in prison. How it differs from what it is on the streets. Monster Kody settles himself against the unyielding backrest of the chair.

"There's a who's who of the gang world—an A-list, if you will—and there are maybe five or six cats in each neighborhood whose names are constantly in the news—on the wire, the grapevine. And these stars, these warriors, respect each other. Maybe it's not quite a détente, it's more like a standoff. 'You brake for me, I'll brake for you.'"

He leans forward a little in his chair, hunching one shoulder up against the receiver. "There are two categories of gang member, see—hustlers and warriors. The warrior is satisfied by wielding weapons within his own, or somebody else's neighborhood. He is propelled from here"—Monster taps the area over his heart. "He acts and reacts. The thing foremost in his mind is to put work in." He takes a beat before he continues. "The hustlers are thinkers. Constantly expanding their horizons through revenue. A hustler will look outside his own neighborhood at another state, say Hawaii, not as a place to conquer, but as another place to go to make money. Or to seek refuge, possibly.

"But taking the picture overall, you have to understand that out of all this seeming gang chaos whether you're a warrior or a hustler, there *is* an organized line, an unspoken constitution that runs through the communities, with laws and respect that we adhere to. There *is* a code of ethics, an etiquette." He leans forward, looking into my face searchingly, reading for signs of comprehension.

"Respect is not negotiable. You get and you give, but you don't get respect unless you give it. In prison you learn one of the virtues of life, and that's reciprocity. You learn to give and you learn to take. It's nothin' one-way about it, it's nothin' about lookin' out for number one. That's individualism, and that mentality disappears in prison, because prison's not about *you*. It's about survival of your unit, your people. There's no star system in prison, but the hierarchy exists. It's just not as apparent as it is on the street. The leader inside may be the humblest cat you'll ever see, whereas the leader out in the street has to be the one who is continually aggressive. Hyper. He can't be somebody who's just laid back and doin' his thing.

"Now, dreadfully so, even prison settings are being overturned by rambunctious gang members. The same erratic behavior you see in the streets is beginning to be the norm inside. Flaggin'. Saggin'. Braggin'.[1] Lettin' people know you're part of something that is powerful. Is mysterious. Is deadly."

He is quiet for a moment. The receiver hums with his silence.

"Understand, to you, yourself"—he taps his chest lightly again—"it's none of those things. Those words don't apply to you, because to you, it's just a bunch of cats who you love and who you dig, gettin' together. But to people who look upon you, people from the outside, you're this frightening mob who has the potential—at any time—to get loose and wreak havoc on their world. So you have to be contained. And you resist, and you have friction."

I ask if it isn't something that goes beyond friction. You hear the stories about stabbings and torchings in prisons.

"No doubt. But when things elevate to that level, it's usually racial." He pauses again. "Sure, Crips stab Crips in jail, and Bloods stab Crips, and vice-versa. And they rape each other." His face is a perfect blank, his voice is without rise or fall, without emotion.

"You know, they had to close 3800 down—that's the Crip

---

[1] throwing signs; wearing your pants hanging low; boasting about exploits

module in County Jail—because Crips were rapin' Crips and tyin' Crips up . . ."

I went through County Jail last year. I saw tier upon tier of single cells facing each other in huge, cat-walked blocks. Command pods slung between them with rows of computers and racks of riot guns. It was like being inside a submarine; even the air had a greenish, underwater cast. I heard about the rapes and the beatings then, from one of the deputies. He called the beatings "getting touched on," and he told me about warring factions slicing the initials of their sets into an enemy's skin with razor blades that had been smuggled inside.

Monster Kody goes on. "See, 'Crip' doesn't mean *nothin'* to a membership. Like"—in spite of the telephone receiver, he gestures broadly, putting both shoulders into it—" 'I'm a Crip, you're a Crip—so what? What set are you from? What neighborhood are you from? What street do you live on?' I may live on Sixty-ninth, he may live on Seventieth, and if Sixty-ninth don't get along with Seventieth Street . . ." He shrugs eloquently. "Then, what it is, you assassinate this cat's character. See, in County Jail, the war is goin', but it's a slow-motion war. More physical. More deadly weapons."

His eyes seem to turn inward. He is looking at something that only he can see, and whatever it is, it nearly makes him shudder. There is a tattoo on the left side of his throat— beautifully scripted dark blue letters with graceful serifs spelling out "Eight-Tray Gangsters." His brother, Li'l Monster, has the same tattoo on his forearm.

His eyes focus on mine again.

"I'd rather get shot than get stabbed. That's a dirty way to get wounded. In jail it's all about looking someone in the eye, and most people can't do that. Lotta people cowards. Lotta people only in the gang life because they have the advantage of drivin' by in a car and shootin' and not seein' the result. But if you in it, and you're serious, you *want* to see your enemy's eyes and deal with him straightforward. And let *other* people see you deal with him. Without faltering. 'Cause if someone sees you falter, they'll move in."

I check the time. We have about two more hours left in the visiting period. In one of his letters Monster Kody had written about "being on both sides of the gun." I ask him about that now.

"At any time you can be on either side of the gun. It's as simple as carrying one. And drawing first." He mimes the action of drawing and pointing a weapon; it is a short, deadly move, nothing flashy about it. "Speed, agility, experience determine who is going to be the victim and who will be the assailant. And, of course, luck enters into it." He smiles.

"It's a dashing, exciting game of cat and mouse with your own life. Only it doesn't seem like your own life when you're caught up in it. You do things you've seen other people do. You try to get out the car like Warren Beatty did in *Bonnie and Clyde.* You try to do things you saw other people do when they did it to you. The way you walk up to someone and shoot 'em; the way you run when somebody tries to shoot you. It all becomes scenes from movies—you're doin' James Cagney and Edward G. Robinson, or any of the people you grew up watchin' as gangsters." The smile intensifies. "I know people who will hum music under their breath . . ." He hums a brief snatch of sound, recognizable as the kind of music you hear during a movie chase scene. "It's a psych-up to put you in that ultimate moment, that climax of gunplay."

And afterward? How about the feeling you get when you have shot another person?

"You seldom see the end result of what you do after you shoot. You go, you leave the scene. No one ever sees the man—or woman—after they've fallen. It becomes almost un-real—because you don't see it—but, at the same time, very real, *because you did it.*"

I knew, because Li'l Monster had already told me that Monster Kody had been ambushed and shot six times at close range on New Year's Eve of 1980. He was seventeen years old, and he had an awesome reputation as an O.G. He was, as he puts it, a "hot topic." He was the star of the community, the one who was putting in more work than anyone else in Eight-Tray at that time, doing the dirty work that no one else would do.

Monster Kody describes "dirty work" as going into a house where no one else will go, to shoot people; walking down a street where no one else will walk, to shoot people. In other words, suicide missions. Now, ten years later, he will tell you that stupidity was often mistaken for courage. And he admits that he didn't correct people's misperceptions, even though he knew he was doing some mindless things.

"I wanted that star position."

On the afternoon of December 31 the seventeen-year-old Monster Kody got rid of a nine-millimeter Browning auto-matic pistol and a double-barreled shotgun just before the police stopped him for some random questioning. He knew he could handle the questions, but the weapons would have been a straight ticket to County Jail. So, he was unarmed that eve-ning when three young women—sisters, as it happened—asked him to ride up to the surplus store with them. The girls were new to the neighborhood, and Monster Kody didn't really know them that well, only that they had last lived in rival territory. But they made it clear that they knew all about him and his reputation. And they were good-looking women. He noticed—and wondered why—they kept asking about his best friend, Crazy Dee. Crazy Dee was known to be Monster Kody's "tight," his "road dog,"[2] but he wasn't around, so even though Monster's instincts were telling him not to get in to the car, he did, along with another one of his homies, Li'l Hunchie.

The first alarm went off in Monster's head when they hit the parking lot of the surplus store. The girl who was driving the car parked in the darkest corner of the lot. Monster got out of the passenger seat fast, followed by Li'l Hunchie, but the three girls dawdled, taking their time. Monster turned to hurry them along, and when he turned back around again, he saw "three Afrikan males comin' toward me. Older brothers, they didn't look like gang members. One guy had a beard, one had a moustache."

"You Monster Kody?" The one with the beard is talking.

Even now, ten years later, Monster Kody still rankles at the question, at the obviousness of it.

"I had a blue flag tied around my head, I had my hair corn-rowed to the back, I had on a Pendleton shirt over a T-shirt, a sweatshirt, and a County Jail shirt. I had on some Levis, some white Converses with black and white strings. And they come toward me askin' was I Monster Kody." His voice is sodden with contempt. "Yeah. I'm-Monster-Kody—Eight-Tray-Gangsters-what's-up?" An unmistakable challenge.

The guy with the beard reaches to unbutton his pea-coat. Only he has some trouble with the buttons, and he fumbles a little bit. Monster looks quickly to his left for Li'l Hunchie. Li'l Hunchie has vanished.

The guy with the beard pulls out a .38 and shoots Monster Kody in the stomach. The impact of the bullet knocks him back against the wall and the guy moves in closer to shoot

---

[2]Both terms are gang and prison slang for "best friend," "best buddy."

Monster in the chest. But Monster manages to make a grab at the gun and takes a bullet through his hand.

Now, somehow, from some wellspring of seventeen-year-old strength, Monster begins to run. The guy with the beard shoots him in the back. Monster falls to the ground, face down. The guy walks up to him, kicks him over on his side, and shoots him three more times. Then all three men run out of the parking lot. The car with the girls in it is long gone.

Monster Kody remembers the attack. "Vividly. The thought that came into my mind at that first shot was, 'These guys just killed me.'" And he says that he was scared.

"I was afraid they were gonna shoot me in the face, and I'd have to have a closed casket. I thought about my mom seein' me that way. And my homies."

He pulls in a deep breath. "And . . . I was afraid I was gonna look bad—scream, or do somethin' unmanly. I was afraid I wasn't going to die like a gangster. I thought about the reputation of this cat I had created—and that the public created—called Monster." He smiles sardonically. "That image had to be retained. Upheld."

The pain hadn't kicked in yet, even though he had been shot first in the stomach. (Earlier in the day he had been smoking pot and drinking Night Train, "a cheap wine distributed by the liquor manufacturers in low-income communities. It's ninety-nine-cent wine that gets you drunk fast. Gangbangers drank it because it gave us that 'we don't give an eff attitude,' and it also provided a slow-motion sense of things. It changed reality for us"). So Monster Kody remained calm. He lay on the pavement, and he waited to die. He remembers looking out across the parking lot and seeing the faces of every person he had known for seventeen years. And he saw faces of people he didn't know: people he had walked past at Magic

Mountain, people with whom he had stood in line at the movies. He saw those faces, too.

"All those people were retained in my memory bank, and in those few seconds they came up, just like they were on a computer screen." He holds his hand up between us and snaps his fingers. "I saw every face clearly."

And then he felt someone coming up on him, and it's Li'l Hunchie. He grabs Monster under the arms and drags him into the surplus store, where they call for an ambulance.

Two hospitals rejected Monster Kody. The first, Daniel Freeman, had no trauma center. Kaiser did, but they had made a policy decision not to treat gunshot wounds that night. The ambulance raced through the streets like a confused bee lost after sunset. Monster was finally taken in at Harbor General in downtown Los Angeles. He was rushed to surgery where twelve feet of his intestines were removed. He also had a broken left hand, three bullets in his left leg, and one in his back. All of them were hollow points, made to spread out on contact.

The whole thing surprised the hell out of him. He knew that gang life carried with it an occupational hazard, but he had successfully dodged bullets for years. Even at parties.

They came to finish him off at the hospital. But first, upon getting out of Intensive Care, he got a phone call. The voice on the other end of the line said, "Are you dead yet, tramp?"

Monster hung up the phone and called his fifteen-year-old brother, Kershaun—Li'l Monster. No answer.

"Within one hour the same three cats were at the door of my room. There I was, with two tubes in my nose runnin' down into my stomach, an I.V. in my arm, a tube in my penis, stitches all across my stomach, and a cast on one arm."

He smiles again. "A nurse shooed 'em off before they could do anything. I'll never forget her—name was Eloise.

When I called my brother 'Shaun again, he was home and I told him to bring me a weapon. He brought me a .25 automatic and a box of bullets. I tucked 'em under my pillow, and I was strapped. Ready."

He grins again, and shakes his head in that slow back and forth movement.

"I felt like Don Corleone in *The Godfather*. I know it sounds dramatic, but . . ." He shrugs.

The two guards are at the door of the cage to take Monster Kody back to his cell. One of them raps on the steel mesh with the tip of what looks like a heavy flashlight. He didn't need to bother; Monster Kody heard them coming.

■　　■　　■

"In 1980 there wasn't nothin' to do but just 'bang. We were bored, same then as now. Just no drugs and no AK-47s, no Uzis. Shotguns were the choice of weapons then. Not now."

When I met Li'l Monster he was the only one of Birdie's sons still at home. He came back here after having served a seven-year sentence at the California Youth Authority for one count of first-degree murder and four counts of attempted murder. Half of his teens and a chunk of his young manhood were spent in maximum-security confinement, and it has not left him unmarked. He smiles rarely now, and when he does his face changes very little. It still looks tough, and sad.

He was fifteen years old in 1980, and in the early evening of New Year's Eve he was over at a girlfriend's house, making plans to celebrate. For some reason he still cannot explain, he called home, and as he was talking to his sister a collect call came through from Kody. Li'l Monster hung up, waited a few minutes, and called back again. His brother's call had him scared; Kody never called collect. His sister told him, with a

flurry of tears, that Kody had been shot, and that it was someone else who had called collect with the news.

Li'l Monster went home immediately. He wanted to find
the weapons he knew his brother kept in the house, the double-
barreled shotgun and the nine-millimeter handgun. He wanted
to be ready to do what he had to do. When he couldn't find
the guns, he got back on his bicycle and pedaled over to
another homeboy's house. It was a long trip because as he rode
through the neighborhood, every person he passed waved him
down to talk about the shooting, and with each conversation
the reports got worse. By the time Li'l Monster got to Li'l
Hunchie's house he was afraid that his brother was dead. But
Li'l Hunchie actually laughed. He told Li'l Monster that Monster Kody was just fine.

"He only got shot in the leg, man. Take it easy."

Li'l Hunchie's attitude angered Li'l Monster. Monster
Kody wasn't just his big brother, he was his hero, the closest
person in the world to him.

"I left from Li'l Hunchie's 'cause he thought the whole
thing was a joke. So I passed by Li'l Spike's and put him up on
my handlebars to ride over to another homeboy's house. By
the time we got over there they were sayin' that Kody got shot
five times. So, basically, that night nothin' was done. We just
kinda kicked it around. We knew who had done it, right down
to the actual name of the triggerman, 'cause Li'l Hunchie was
there with Kody when it went down. And we knew he had been
framed, that some 'friends' took him up to that store and set
him up. We didn't have to talk about what was to be done. In
my mind there wasn't any doubt about what we were gonna do.
There was nothin' to talk about."

The next day, New Year's Day 1981, there was a meeting
at the neighborhood park and Li'l Monster rounded up every-

251

body who was going to be involved in the payback. Then they went back to his house.

"We just kicked it for the rest of the afternoon. Seven of us, I was the youngest. The oldest was eighteen."

The rest of the family was at the hospital. The report had come in that Kody was stable, although critical, but Li'l Monster couldn't yet bring himself to go and see his brother like that—helpless, wounded. So he and the homies watched the football game at the Rose Bowl on TV, ate some junk food, listened to a little music. Then two of the guys went out to find a car to steal. They got a TransVan out of a supermarket parking lot. By the time they got back to Li'l Monster's house he had rounded up two shotguns, and the other homeboys had found two .375 Pythons, another shotgun, and an eight-millimeter Mauser rifle. They were ready to go.

The seven homies got in the van and began the drive over to their enemies' neighborhood. It was a clear night, and you could still see football games being played on television screens through the windows of people's houses. Li'l Monster remembers every detail.

"I can still hear the music we had on the box—it was Heat Wave, and the song we kept playin' over and over was 'Groove Line.' We drove from Second Avenue to Eleventh Avenue— most of the enemy was inside they houses. They knew there was gonna be a retaliation, but, like idiots, some of 'em were out that night and we caught 'em. And we murdered 'em."

As Li'l Monster speaks his voice is as gentle as if he were telling a bedtime story to a child. "There was a party goin' on. We pulled the van up to the end of the street, got out real slow, careful not to talk or make a sound, and we slipped up on 'em. Then we started shooting. Everybody who was standin' in front of the house got hit. I remember there was one girl, she had on a black bomber jacket with white fur on the collar. She was the first to get hit, and I remember that fur just goin' red—bam—just like that. Looked like red flowers comin' out all over the white."

It took Li'l Monster five days to go to the hospital to see Monster Kody in the intensive care unit. When he walked into the room where his brother lay, they both began to cry.

"I idolized my brother, and until this happened I thought that nobody could ever hurt him, that he could never get shot. I thought he was infallible." Even now, when he talks about it, Li'l Monster's voice is clogged with emotion.

He knew he was going to be arrested. The way things were mishandled after the payback, there was no way he could get away. The stolen van was kept within the neighborhood instead of being driven somewhere out of town and dumped. That and the fact that it was his brother who had been shot added up to a simple solution. So he told his mother the police were probably going to come for him, and he stayed at home and waited for them. There was, after all, no place to run to.

Each morning Li'l Monster would find himself waking up at five, six o'clock—not scared, just watchful. He knew, somehow, that when they came it would be early. When he finally did hear the pounding on the front door, he glanced at the digital clock next to his bed—6:45 A.M. Only the night before he had gotten all the weapons out of the house. He knew it was that close.

He got out of bed and went into his mother's room. She had been awakened by the noise and was sitting up in bed, her eyes wide with fear. She reached out her arms to hug him, and he went to her, whispering, in his calmest voice, that the police were here for him.

His oldest brother, Kerwin, opened the front door. Kerwin was already in his early twenties and was working at a straight job in a market; he had never been involved with gang life. As Li'l Monster came down the hall from his mother's room, the police were moving up the hall toward him. Four cops, weapons drawn.

"They asked me if I was Kershaun and I told 'em 'yeah.' They told me I was under arrest for murder. And that was that."

They handcuffed him and took him to the Southwest Police Station. One of the homies who had been with him on the night of the payback, Killer Rob, was there before him. The police stuck them in different cells and left them there. At about three o'clock that afternoon they brought in another one of the homies. They had flown him in from Nevada, where he had been sent, unknowingly, by the Job Corps. The other four guys had already been taken into custody. Seven homeboys in all, but only six were ultimately convicted; one kid turned state's evidence.

Li'l Monster's face closes up as he talks about it.

"Turning state's evidence is like signing your own death warrant. But it's stacked up against time. Somebody says, 'You're getting twenty-seven years to life,' and a lotta people will say, 'Look, I didn't do it—such and such did it.' Even if it means stopping your own clock. Because your clock is stopped either way. Twenty-seven to life means *life*—you're not going home. Stopped clock. You're being told what to do, when to do it, and how to do it. And that is not living at all. Bein' told when you gotta get up, when you gotta go to bed, when you gotta eat—that's not living. I'd rather die than be told what to do for the rest of my life. To be in a cell with the door closed on you? Always having to watch your back?"

Li'l Monster was taken to Juvenile Hall. He saw his mother there, and they were allowed to visit for a short time.

And he made the usual promises, "Mom, if I beat this one, I won't do this no more." He meant gangbanging, of course.

"In a way I was scared, and in a way I wasn't. I knew they couldn't give me the death penalty, or lock me up for the rest of my life, because I was a juvenile. But"—his expression is coldly serious as he talks about it now—"I think I *was* afraid of what I might have to face down the line. Looking back now, that's what I would say I was afraid of. Fear of the unknown. Different jails, you know. I had already done nine months in camp for armed robbery in Redondo Beach. Just jacked some guy up on the street for about a hundred and fifty bucks." He grimaces, thinking about it. "Which is like doin' it for fifty cents, you know?"

By the time Li'l Monster got to Juvenile Hall, he was expected by the other kids. What he had done, the payback, wasn't looked on as that big a deal in and of itself; it was just accepted as putting in work for the set. All the same, the word was out. Li'l Monster from Eight-Tray Gangsters was coming in.

He was placed in R Unit, which is a kind of clearinghouse where kids are held until they are transferred. And he wasn't there twenty minutes when he had his fight with a member of the set he had gone out against. The other kid came over and sat down opposite Li'l Monster, asked where he was from. Li'l Monster told him. The kid announced *his* allegiance. And Li'l Monster went off on him.

The fight was broken up and Li'l Monster was sent to the box. He would have been put there anyway, even if he had not gotten into the beef. The box is where every youngster brought in for the crime of murder is put, for seven days. Li'l Monster still has vivid memories of being in there.

"The box—whew . . ." He snaps his head to one side and back again. "It's a dark room, no doubt. Fucked-up room. Get an hour out once a day, nothin' to read, nothin' to do. Fucked-up place. I guess they do it for psychological reasons, that's what I believe." He ticks off on his fingers. "One—in the event the murder just happened and you were just arrested for it, they give you time to cool off. Two—you got seven days in there, by yourself; you can think about what you done." Li'l Monster smiles. The smile doesn't change his face.

"I didn't stay in there for the full seven. I stayed for three days and what *I* thought about was how I could get *out*. That's what I really thought about—'Who do I know, what counselor have I ever met in here who can get me out of this box?' "

His face is solemn once again. He looks older than Monster Kody, and even though it is not necessarily the case, more lethal. It isn't that he's not good-looking—he is, but in a more sullen, a more threatening way.

"I went back over my arrest. I made no statements whatsoever to the police. I just kept tellin' them to take me to Juvenile Hall, that I didn't know what the hell they were talkin' about." His voice lifts as he acts out what it was he said at the time of his arrest. " 'If you gonna book me for murder, book me. Take me to the Hall! 'Cause I don't know what you talkin' about!'

"I really didn't think I'd be there for longer than three days—*common sense* told me I'd be gettin' out, 'cause if there's nobody to actually say 'I saw him do it,' then there's no evidence on you. Only what *you* yourself tell them. Even with that homie turnin', there's six other people's word sayin', 'We didn't do *that!*' But there were some people with us chose to make statements. All those questions, 'What happened January first? What did we do? Who was I with? What happened to my brother?' All that type stuff. I didn't answer one question."

Li'l Monster went away for five and a half years. He still

believes that if he had been tried as an adult and been given a jury trial that he would have beaten the case. He feels that if his court-appointed attorney had given a damn one way or the other, he would have gotten off.

I asked him how he feels now, ten years later—five and a half of them spent behind bars in a juvenile prison. He doesn't have to think long to come up with his reply.

"I feel that what we did that night wasn't enough. Justice, to me, would have been killing seven or eight of them. Not because I think Kody was worth seven or eight—I think he's worth more than their whole sorry-ass set—but I would have liked to have killed more than I actually did. Even though only one guy shot my brother, there were three guys there.

"It's like this: If you slap me, I'm gonna hit you with my closed fist. If you stab me, I'm gonna shoot you. An eye for an eye doesn't exist—it's one-up. One-up is what it is in gang life. You beat our homeboys, we kill yours. One to nothing.

"It's more tense now than ever before. Because back then, if you saw somebody from an enemy set, chances are you'd just fight with 'em. You know, you'd come at them from the shoulder. Whereas now—it's gunplay. Back then not as many sets were fightin' with each other. It was much simpler: Crips versus Bloods. Now, it seems as if every other Crip set is fightin' with each other, killin' each other. And everything is high-tech now. Weapons, surveillance, communications, everything. Makes you wonder what would happen if some 'banger with a hate on got his hands on a nuclear device, doesn't it?"

I ask if any of the people Li'l Monster shot were the ones who shot Monster Kody. He shakes his head.

"None of those people were the ones who actually shot my brother. But they were affiliated with the set who did. The triggerman who shot him went to jail for it. But by that time Kody was in jail on six counts of attempted murder. Somebody said he shot 'em—two weeks after *he* got shot. He beat the case, but he was six months in County Jail during the trial."

What about Li'l Hunchie? What happened to him?

Li'l Monster's upper lip curls with contempt. "It was all over for him. He was branded a coward the minute he panicked and ran outta that parkin' lot. He was marked from that time on, with the Eight-Tray Gangster Crips." Li'l Monster takes a beat. "That's the least should've happened to that buster."

■　　■　　■

Shortly after my visit to Soledad Prison, Monster Kody was transferred to the newly constructed Pelican Bay State Prison in Crescent City, near the Oregon border. He would finish his term here, in grindingly high-tech solitary confinement. And it was to prove a much more devastating isolation than Soledad's, where there was at least a sense of other people nearby. Even if you were completely alone at all times, you could still hear other voices. When your meals were brought in you could exchange a few words with the guard. At showertime, when they cuffed you and escorted you to the lavatory, you were able to see the other inmates in their cells, maybe say "what's up."

In Pelican Bay you heard no other voices, you saw no other person. Unseen hands pushed your meals in to you through a slot in the quarter-inch thick reinforced steel door that separated your seventy-square-foot cell from the corridor. This door slid back when the guard pressed a button at the same time every day, and a shower cubicle was locked on in its place for five minutes. You got your exercise when another steel door at the other end of your cell slid back to allow you to walk around a twelve-by-twenty-seven-foot patch of cement enclosed by a twenty-five-foot wall. There was a screen over your head out there, with a bubble in the center that held a video camera.

Upon arrival at Pelican Bay Monster Kody, according to the rules, surrendered all his personal possessions—books, toiletries (with the exception of his toothbrush), and most of his personal articles. He was allowed to keep two magazines, from which the staples were removed, and his paperback dictionary. He read the dictionary like a novel, from cover to cover, rationing himself to a set number of pages each day. He wrote letters and waited for the incoming mail. To relieve the tedium he counted the tiny holes drilled into the steel door that opened into the corridor. Eight thousand two hundred.

He could, he was told, get an early release date if he chose to plea-bargain and give out a few names. He declined the offer.

The next time I saw Monster Kody was shortly after his release from Pelican Bay. He and his wife, Tamu, came over to my house with their three kids. Tamu is the Swahili word for "sweet"; Monster Kody calls her that, and she uses it in preference to her given name. He has taken a Swahili name as well. Tamu is a striking woman, slightly taller than her husband, with an air of unyielding strength and quiet intelligence. She and Monster have been together for twelve years; their children, a girl and two boys, range in age from just over a year to eleven years. Tamu has never been involved in gang activity—her only association with gang life has been as Monster's girlfriend and, later, as his wife.

Out of prison Monster still wears what he calls his "uniform": black sweatpants, a black or white T-shirt, black L.A. Raiders cap, black and white Reebok running shoes. No watch, no jewelry except for his wedding ring and a medallion in the shape of the African continent enameled in red, white, and black. It is a uniform that attracts some attention in South Central Los Angeles. On the way over to my house, before they got on the freeway, Monster and his family were pulled over by a black and white. Both patrolmen got out of the squad car and approached Monster Kody for a field check. He was handed an interrogation form, known as a white card, to fill out—name, address, date of birth, gang name, and gang affiliation. As Monster began to write out the information, the senior of the two officers, a two-striper, leaned in to take a closer look. Then he grinned and turned to his partner.

"Hey, you know who this is? This is Monster Kody—I arrested him once!" Then he leaned into the window again. Still grinning.

"Don't you remember me, Monster?"

In spite of this somewhat jovial exchange, Monster Kody feels nothing but animosity toward the police as a whole. He tells of instances when he was picked up and told, "We'll give you fifteen minutes to go on up to Fifty-ninth Street [or Sixty-third, or wherever the gang wars were raging hottest at that moment], and then we're coming in."

"And then we'd go and shoot 'em up. I've never been caught for murder, and I've never been chased for assault. The police have always come to my house a month after the incident and captured me."

His biggest fear is not of death, but of the police. "It's not that they're the law. We don't give a damn about the law. That's why we do what we do—we don't even think about the law. We think about getting murdered, or getting captured. And we don't get captured because we broke the law—we get captured because we got *caught,* we did something wrong. We didn't put the pedal to the metal fast enough. Or we didn't run the right way.

"We will defend our neighborhood against another set to the death. They can come in a car with every conceivable kind of weapon, and we will fight to the death without fear. But let one black and white with two officers, two weapons—a standard .38 and one shotgun—roll in and we will run like dogs. And discard our own weapons. The psychological trip, the fear, is that *their* gang is more together, more organized, more powerful than ours."

A little later Monster Kody takes the two older kids, and they make a market run for some juice for the baby. Tamu and I sit facing each other across the table, and I ask how she feels about her husband's extremist attitudes.

"I feel like he does—he's what he is because it's what it's gonna take to deal with extreme problems. Extreme measures."

We both know there is more to her answer.

"Okay, I'm scared. And I'm not scared. Selfishly, for the family, I sometimes wish he'd just be content to get a job and live his life." The baby fusses a little in her arms, and she moves him up to lean against her shoulder, patting him gently on the back. "But that's not Kody. Never will be. So I just take every day as it comes along, and I pray that he'll be with us a little bit longer."

I ask what it's like since he came home from prison. She smiles.

"Well, you know—it's Monster Kody. Everywhere we go they come crowdin' around him like he was a real movie star, which, to a lotta people, he is. The young guys just about ask him for his autograph, and the girls flirt with him right in front of me. He gets offered everything from dope to weapons to sex. And you know something? None of it goes to his head. He just gets kinda embarrassed, blushes a little, and goes on his way."

The baby is sleeping now. Tamu takes him into my bedroom and sets him down on the bed, pillows on either side of him. Then she comes back and sits down at the table again.

"I'll tell you this, and I've thought about it every night for years, when I'm layin' alone in bed because he got sent away. I want Kody to always believe what he needs to believe. Because he's fighting for a chance for *us*. Our people. He wants to make it better for our children and their children. Me, I'm selfish—I just want him to be around to see it."

Months earlier, when Monster Kody was still at Soledad, I asked him to write a letter to Hart at Camp Kilpatrick. He did, and in it he urged this kid, whom he knew only through the letters of a stranger, to take advantage of the class time provided at camp. He wrote, "There is no shame in not knowing how to read. The shame is in not learning how when you have the chance."

Now I ask him what he thinks the future holds for Hart and other kids like him. Monster shakes his head.

"The Harts will waste away in the communities. I was a Hart until I decided to get out of that narrow, gangbanger mindset. To take a look at, and a listen to, global issues."

I ask Monster what he sees for his own future. He looks at me for a long moment before he answers.

"I want to say I see success. But what I see is death. Because I know what they do to people who are poor. Who are active. Who don't relent or recant."

They?

"My real enemy—the United States Government. That's who controls the Crips, the Bloods, and me."

It's time to take the kids home. They have watched TV, played with the dog, colored in their book. They're ready to go now. Before Monster leaves, I ask if he has a message for the young gang members out there. He looks sharply at me. Surprised, pleased.

"Yeah, I do. And I been waiting years to say it. What I ask of the Harts, and the Li'l Monsters, and all the young gang members, Crips and Bloods alike, is to look at me as a success story comin' out of a hellhole. Not to put too much on it, I was one of those considered a real lost cause. One who would continuously be in prison, which I have been. One who would get shot, which I was. And killed. But as of today, this minute, I have circumvented statistics and made them, in a strange sense, lie. Because I'm out of prison, I'm still healthy, and I am not caught up in the vicious cycle of gang activity, even though I exist inside that realm. Look at this person who was once Monster Kody, who has transformed himself into a . . ." He hesitates over the words, "a ghetto intellectual. So I could come back to the community and teach you that you can get out without going into the army, without joining the police force, without being co-opted. You can be you and still make it without being criminals.

"You do it by education. Defend whatever street you live on—Piru Street, Sixty-ninth Street, whatever—but also pick up a book. Not a mainstream, Book-of-the-Month Club book, either. Pick up something about *you*. Because if you don't know where you come from, you sure as hell don't know where you're goin'. I did twelve years in the L.A. Unified School System, but I didn't begin to get an education until I picked up that book in San Quentin. And learned that I am a descendant from Africa.

"Be your own selves. Don't bend or break under peer pressure. It's individuals who make up a gang, and it's you as individuals, who will get captured, get shot, do the time, get killed. It's you, as individuals, who have to make the decision to educate yourselves. Or not. It's you who keep yourselves down if you choose not to get educated. Or to be misinformed.

"Anyone can make money, and almost anyone can count it. Two and two make four all over the world, but it takes knowledge to make that money grow. And it takes education to keep it."

Monster Kody looks at me now, as if he expects me to tell him to stop talking. He looks at Tamu and, by the smallest gesture of her head, she encourages him to finish his statement. The baby is sleeping in her arms again; the two older children are standing, one on either side of their father's chair, listening to him as he speaks. He looks at each of them in turn.

"The system we live in is oppressive, no doubt. But there is always going to be individual will. Now, that will alone may not be able to turn the tide, but if one person, one youngster decides to stop the cycle of wanton killing, that's a success. And that individual success will be a beacon to others."

It is dark as I walk with Monster Kody and his family to their car. He carries the sleeping baby in one arm. His daughter's Cabbage Patch doll dangles from his free hand. Tamu is just ahead of him, with the other two children, holding one by each hand. As we come abreast of the car Monster passes the baby to Tamu and unlocks the doors. The car is a sensible gray Honda Civic with a baby seat up front and a spray of comic books across the ledge under the back window.

Monster helps Tamu and the kids into the car, and then he stands looking up and down the street. The small park across the way is quiet; swings and sandbox are deserted for the night. A plot of blooming roses glows under the lights. At the corner two dogwalkers stand talking as their respective dogs sniff warily at each other. The occasional car glides slowly past us on its way toward the main thoroughfare a few blocks away.

Monster Kody stands quietly, watching this panorama for a moment. Then he turns to me and he smiles.

"It's sure a nice thing to be able to stand and watch the cars go past and not worry about who might be behind the windows."

Afterword

It was the closed windows of an '81 Coupe de Ville that snapped Monster Kody back into combat awareness three weeks after our last conversation. He had pulled up to a stop sign when the other car eased in next to his left rear bumper. Kody glanced back out of habit and thanked God that Tamu and the kids were safe at home. Just as he began his slide down in the driver's seat, he saw the windows of the Cadillac inch down to allow space for the muzzles of three automatic rifles.

The body of the Honda took seventeen bullets; all the windows (except the windshield) were blown away; one bullet went straight through the driver's neckrest. Amazingly, Kody was not hit.

This assault did not take place in the war zone of South Central. Kody was some sixty miles away from there when he was attacked; he had gone to visit his wife and children in the small community she moved to a couple of years ago. He lives in Los Angeles, according to the terms of his parole. The local police arrived on the scene shortly after the shooting occurred, but by that time the blue Coupe de Ville was long gone. The cops questioned Kody at length, readily accepting his theory that the shooters were probably three kids who had spotted him in L.A. and followed him out of town, figuring they could make their reputations by killing Monster Kody of the Eight-Tray Gangster Crips. The police were much more interested in the terms of Kody's parole than in the occupants of the Cadillac. They wanted to make sure that everyone involved in the shooting came out of L.A. They didn't want to think about the possibility of any permanent gang activity in their backyard. They didn't want to know about it.

Nobody does, really. The overriding attitude from most people is that as long as the gangs stay in their own territory, as long as they war only with each other, they can be pretty much ignored. Most people see them as frightening stereotypes: lethal, faceless, and vaguely nonhuman. These imprecise and distanced images—which don't include the idea that every gang member is an individual—seem to come out of a necessity to erect a protective screen between us and the threatening entity of the gangs. In other words, if we don't find out too much about the people who make up the gangs, we can keep them at a safe distance.

We are apparently unable to directly confront an entire generation of young Americans who are subliterate and without marketable skills. Who have virtually no options except the gangs. With an average life expectancy of nineteen years.

When I first began interviews with gang members in the streets, the question I heard most often from friends and acquaintances—even from some of the homeboys themselves—was, "Aren't you afraid?" My answer was always the same: I wasn't. Not because I am so courageous a person; I'm afraid of nearly everything—illness, pain, the loss of loved ones, strange sounds outside my door, heights. But with the exception of the random creep, I felt no fear toward the youngsters

I interviewed. What I did feel was surprise at the discoveries I made about myself.

I found that I could like people and recoil from them at the same time, at some of the acts they were capable of, and at the ruthlessness of purpose with which some of those acts were carried out. And I uncovered, in the course of some fifteen months, a small corner of something hidden away in myself that understood very well the emotions that could trigger episodes of throat-clenching violence.

When Nancy Reagan made her foray into South Central for a photo-op at an alleged crack house, she waited in a trailer hauled in for the occasion. Then, wearing a stiffly lacquered coiffure and an L.A.P.D. field jacket with her given name scripted coyly above the breast pocket, she chicken-stepped her way to the rammed-in front door. The television and still cameras recorded a cavalcade of manufactured expressions as they lumbered, trunk to tail, across her face: shock, disgust, horror, concern. Honed to perfection, it was a performance straight out of an old-time B-movie.

The next day I asked one of the neighborhood homeboys what he thought about the display. The corners of his mouth turned down, his head moved back and forth in a slow gesture.

"Good thing I wasn't around last night to see that shit. I woulda shot her right in the face."

As chilling a statement as that was, I knew just how he felt.

I first saw Herb Giron on a Tom Brokaw special about the L.A. gangs. Giron has lived and worked in the gang world for eighteen years. As a detective with the Lennox Sheriff's Station he rides the streets of Inglewood daily, and he knows the name of every 'banger in every set who claims them, block by block. He likes most of these kids and, in turn, they like and respect him. To Herb Giron, respect is what it's all about.

"What a lot of people don't realize is—hey—your interpretation of respect and theirs might be a whole different thing. You got to remember what it means to them and deal with it from there. Don't try to tell them how they shouldn't believe their homeboys love them more than their mothers do; try to see things from *their* angle. And treat 'em like human beings, show 'em a little something."

I saw Giron "show 'em a little something" the day I rode with him in his black and white. There had been a murder the night before; a kid from one set walked up to a kid from a rival set and blew him away on a street corner. Giron slowed down to talk to people. He got out from behind the wheel for low-pitched conversations, and what I noticed was the complete absence of fear or resentment in any of the faces on the other side of his badge. When I asked one youngster how he felt about Detective Giron, the kid looked over to where Giron was talking to a young woman holding a baby balanced on one hip. The kid watched them for a moment, then he turned to face me again.

"Dude's straight ahead. If y'all gotta talk to a pig, he's the one you wanna deal with. He don't make no threats, he don't make no promises. And he don't dis' you. Giron's okay."

Later in the day I asked Giron if he had any answers to the seemingly insoluble problems concerning the gangs.

He smiled politely. "It's awfully vast at this point. I'm hoping there's some intellectuals somewhere out there thinking about this every day, working their way to some real answers that require more than some little six-month program that just brings us back here next year talking about the same damn thing. We need some expenditures of resources, some ongoing programs that will make a difference."

Whatever intellectuals are out there, you can bet the ranch they're not pondering the gang problem. And maybe there aren't any answers. Building more jails isn't an answer, or mobilizing the National Guard. Underfunded community projects that nobody pays much attention to aren't an answer, either. And as long as African-American gang members kill each other in African-American neighborhoods, the gang problem will continue to be a twenty-second shudder on the eleven o'clock news.

It's not so hard to understand those feelings. I'd go down to South Central and talk to those youngsters, conduct my little interviews, step into their chaos, and then I'd go home to my well-ordered bookcases and my hardwood floors and my clean windows that overlook an enclosed courtyard. I'd sit at my typewriter, and the only sounds I'd hear from outside would be the plash of the fountain and the sounds of birds in the trees. I didn't have to worry about a bullet coming in my window, or a sixteen-year-old son going out into the street to kill some other kid before they killed him.

Norman Rockwell would have loved Los Angeles County Sheriff Sherman Block. His face is all elliptic curves and arcs; his lips seem ready to curl into a smile. The eyes are a dead giveaway, though. Too austere for Rockwell. It is very hard to imagine a twinkle forming in those eyes.

"My feeling is that where we have failed—the collective 'we,' society, government in particular—is that we have not provided enough meaningful options and opportunities for young people in too many of these communities where gangs flourish. Things that youngsters could get involved in that will provide the same things the gang provide. The sense of self-esteem, the feeling of belonging. An athletic program, like the one we have in East Los Angeles, or in Lynwood. A boxing program. Whatever. But we have become a crisis-oriented society. We rally to raise funds for flood or earthquake victims, we rally to fight disease, but only at the crisis point. There just doesn't seem to be the energy or the enthusiasm to do that before the crisis develops. Beef up the levees, and maybe we

271

wouldn't have to worry about flood relief, you know?"

Sherman Block's office overlooks downtown Los Angeles from windows that form a right angle behind his desk. The wall space there is covered with framed certificates, awards, and photographs of Block standing with three or four American presidents, members of the military and law enforcement, the odd celebrity.

"We have to do something to keep these kids from becoming criminals, and that's where we're failing." He gestures back toward the windows and the city outside. "We have under construction or approved for construction in Los Angeles County, about seven hundred million dollars' worth of jail facilities. That will give us another five thousand beds, approximately. Well, we are currently nine thousand inmates over our capacity. The point I'm making is that people approve those kinds of things. They approve jail bonds, they approve prison bonds. Somehow they think we are going to build our way out of this dilemma. Well, we'll go bankrupt. Because they are losing sight of the fact that while we're finding housing for this current crop of criminals, a new crop is coming along that we're not going to have any place for."

I have a question to ask Sheriff Block about the Job Corps. I had heard a rumor that gang members—mostly Crips, mostly wannabes—were joining up with that program in order to get themselves a ticket out of L.A. so that they could be big shots in new territories. Salt Lake City had been mentioned in particular.

Block shakes his head; he has heard nothing about anything like that in connection with the Job Corps.

"But you have just hit on a very significant point. We have areas like the Antelope Valley, Palmdale, Lancaster, where the gang problem is in its infancy. And we have families with children in South Central and other parts of this community where there are full-blown gang problems—and when they saw signs of their kids starting to turn in that direction, they physically moved and went to those outlying areas. And those kids who were hang-arounds and fringe gang members in South Central suddenly take on leadership roles. They try to organize the locals, and they begin to take on a kind of hero's status—because they come from South Central Los Angeles."

He goes on to illustrate his point with an example. Just after the Attica State Prison riot in 1971, one of the Attica inmates came out to the L.A. County Jail. And when the buzz traveled through the jail that this guy, this star from Attica, was in their midst, the word was passed on to him that if he wanted to get something going, he would be backed up. The guy's reply was, "You kidding? You call this a jail? Don't bother me, I'm just gonna do my time peacefully." But to the County inmates, he was big-time, he was the real thing. He was from Attica.

"And that's what's happening now in places like Salt Lake, in places like Seattle, places like Portland and Omaha. The kids in those communities are vying for a piece of the action. They want some of that public recognition, some of that identity that comes with being in a gang. We have kids here, you know, individual gang members who can take a pocketful of rock cocaine and get on a Greyhound bus and head for Omaha or St. Louis, or somewhere, and make themselves a few thousand dollars."

The way Sherman Block sees it, what originally happened was that Crips and Bloods from L.A. went into those areas to try to deal drugs. And there were some conflicts with the local people. So the L.A. gangsters got into the entrepreneurial system and became brokers and jobbers by supplying local dealers and recruiting local kids to go out and sell the dope.

"It's like they're saying, 'Hey, I can provide . . . and you know your community, you know your neighborhood, so you guys go out and deal the dope and we'll all make money.'"

Block says that he gets calls from chiefs of police all over the country.

"They say, 'What are you guys doing out there? You're driving all the Bloods and Crips into our community.' I tell them I'd like to believe that. But their motive for leaving is not law enforcement. It's purely profit and greed."

We speak for a moment about the glut of drugs in Los Angeles and who it is that makes up the market. Block leans forward slightly in his chair.

"Let me tell you something. The people who used to do the lines of coke in the back seats of limousines are now driving down to South Central L.A. in their Jaguars, their Mercedes, their B.M.W.'s and they're buying crack cocaine. We're scooping them up all the time."

I start to say something, but Block holds up one hand; he's not through talking.

"Let me say one more thing I want to make clear. The use of crack in gang communities is high, but what has been overstated is this thing about gang members killing each other over drug dealing territories and turf. These are not drug wars. The gun battles aren't about profit; the battles are because gangs fight each other and kill each other over an address or a color.

"All they do is, you know, you're walking down the street and they say, 'Man, where're you from?' And if you ain't from the right place, that's enough to kill you. Or if you happen to be wearing a Dodger Blue baseball cap and you're in a Blood territory, sitting on the bus on your way home from school, somebody will shoot you." Block lifts both hands, palms facing up. "I mean it has nothing to do with anything. It's violence for the sake of violence. There's absolutely no . . ." His voice trails away for an instant. Then his eyes narrow just enough for it to be noticeable behind the lenses of his glasses.

"If there is such a thing as rational violence . . . I guess I could understand going in and committing a robbery and shooting somebody because they may be a witness against you. There is some"—he hesitates for a fraction of an instant—"relationship. But seeing somebody walking down the street who's wearing the wrong color, and you shoot and kill him—that's violence for the sake of violence. It has no logic, no rationale."

I ask him what he sees down the line, five years from now. His answer is quick in coming, as if he has been asked this before.

"If we don't make a dramatic change in our value system, in our cultural approach, in our return to a concept of individual accountability, then I really fear for the future. Because what I see happening, and what scares me more than anything else, is not merely the level of violence, but the level of *tolerance* for violence that is developing. We are beginning to accept violence as a normal consequence of our time and of our lifestyle. And to me that's the most frightening thing of all, because once you begin to accept something, then it continues to grow. And one morning you wake up and wonder what the hell happened.

"The stakes are very high here. Because what we are really gambling with is our survival as a nation. We have only one next generation at any one time."

That Sherman Block is a sincere man is evident. He believes that there is still some modicum of hope for some of the kids in South Central and other gang communities. He believes, and there's no way to argue with it, that the focus has to be on those youngsters who are pre-gang, pre-drug. That means those kids who are under nine or ten years of age. And no matter how difficult it is to agree, what he says makes sense. We have to accept the fact that the Harts and G-Rocs, the Faros, the Sidewinders, and Bopetes may be beyond reclamation.

Some of the kids I interviewed for this book have vanished

into the system; I don't know where they are now. In other instances I was able to make contact.

Bianca is still at home with her mother and grandmother. She continues to hang with the homies, but she has gone back to school and is making fair grades.

Baby Track remains at home, too. He still shows up for school, but his real interest is in putting in work for his set.

Tashay Roberts has, so far, fulfilled all of D.P.O. Jim Galipeau's requirements. She worked at her job in the community park, went to school, got her diploma. She is pregnant now, but, according to Galipeau, she maintains a realistic outlook. She expects no support from the baby's father, a seventeen-year-old homeboy; she'll work to support her child.

Hart is serving three years at California Youth Authority for drug sales.

G-Roc is serving six years at C.Y.A. for bank robbery.

Faro is in custody, awaiting trial as an adult for first degree murder.

It's easy to speculate about why young African-Americans kill each other with such enthusiasm. Easy to theorize that their acts of violence might be the only mechanism they know of that might put them in touch with any larger world. In every interview, with every youngster I talked to, the same theme ran through the conversation. They all said that if they didn't have an enemy to go after, they'd fight themselves, that, "you got to have somebody to fight with." Maybe, in some unconscious way, they are seeking the clarity of the warrior in battle. Maybe, through violence and death, they are seeking to feel alive. Certainly we, as a society, have let them know how worthless we think they are, and how unwelcome they are in their own country. We have given them our permission to kill themselves. There are so many casualties of gang warfare, so many lives fusing and sinking into the greedy sand of blind hatred. You ask questions and you look for information, and the only words that keep coming at you are the ones spoken by A. C. Jones in Gang Class, when he told those nineteen kids that however down they were for their sets, whoever they killed or however they died, nothing really changes. The beat goes on.